EARLY ASCOT

ROYAL ASCOT

By the same author

HOW THE QUEEN REIGNS

PADDY HENDERSON

QUEEN ELIZABETH THE QUEEN MOTHER

DOROTHY LAIRD

Royal Ascot

HODDER AND STOUGHTON
LONDON SYDNEY AUCKLAND TORONTO

All quoted material is taken from The Times unless otherwise stated.

Contents

Illustrations

ACKNOWLEDGMENTS

[1] Hulton Picture Library
[2] Windsor Royal Library. Reproduced by gracious permission of Her Majesty Queen Elizabeth II
[3] Author
[4] W. W. Rouch and Co. Ltd.
[5] Press Association
[6] Bernard Parkin
[7] *Daily Mail*
[8] Ron Hammond
[9] Racing Information Bureau
[10] De Beers Diamonds Ltd.
[11] Central Press

Foreword

I am grateful to the Ascot Authority for allowing me to write this book, to consult the Minutes of the Ascot Grandstand Company, and for much valuable help, and am particularly indebted for numerous acts of kindness to the late Sir David Dawnay; the Hon Nicholas Beaumont; Mr Douglas Butt; Mr Hugh Mounsey; the late Mr Metcalfe; the late Mr Mabey, and Mrs Mabey; Mr J. Bowyer for the loan of an interesting early history of Ascot; Mr Harry Jaggard and many others at Ascot; as well as to Mr Nick Gaselee and Mr Tim Thompson.

Brigadier Henry Green made it possible to take photographs inside the racecourse stables. Miss Anne Ainscough not only gave information about the Ascot Office, but kindly read part of the MS and made valuable suggestions. Miss Margot Burbage gave of her knowledge of Ascot through many years.

Mr Martin Eversfield, author of the section on English racing in *Thoroughbred Breeding of the World*, most generously read the MS and eliminated errors in the accounts of eighteenth- and nineteenth-century thoroughbreds; and Miss Vivian Pratt of the Thoroughbred Breeders Association and Mr Martin Pickering of the *Stud Book* also gave generously of their knowledge.

Mr Geoffrey Hamlyn, for so long senior Starting Price reporter for *The Sporting Life*, most kindly wrote an account of Ascot betting for the book; and information about betting also came from Mr Stanley Longstaff of Ladbrokes and Mr Pat Reekie of The Tote.

On the catering side I was helped by Colonel Lennox Livingstone-Learmonth and Mr J. P. N. Lowe. Thanks for help are also due to many at Weatherbys; Mr E. V. Collins, chief architect for George Wimpey and Co, who built the new stands; Mr Richard Dickson of De Beers Consolidated Mines; Miss Hilda Marshall; Mr Bill Garland; Miss Louise Gold and Mr Geoffrey Webster of the Racing Information Bureau;

Mr Bryan Robinson for information about his great-grandfather, John Clark, judge and racecourse architect; and Mr John Wrottesley and my husband John Carr for information about the railways, especially the projected line from Windsor to Ascot.

If it had not been for the time-consuming success of the International Racing Bureau, and the packed work-schedule of its director David Hedges, he would have been co-author of this book, and I am deeply grateful to him for advice and encouragement. Thanks also to Robert Carter, who read the proofs and gave much valued advice.

Much new ground has been broken on the photographic front, where Mr Bernard Parkin and Mr Ron Hammond were cheerful and indefatigable colleagues, while Mr Guy Wilmot allowed me to browse through the fascinating Rouch photographs of old Ascot.

Hodder and Stoughton are forebearing and helpful publishers, and I am particularly grateful to Mr Jonathan Loake for all his help and advice.

DOROTHY LAIRD
Hampstead: 1975

CHAPTER ONE

It all began with Queen Anne

SINCE THE FIRST RACE WAS RUN AT ASCOT IN BERKSHIRE ON SATURDAY, August 11th, 1711, Royal Ascot has become a world symbol for all that is best in horseracing and elegant in fashion. Yet Ascot very nearly did not have a racecourse at all.

If Sarah, Duchess of Marlborough had not been toppled from favour a few months earlier by her despised kinswoman Abigail Hill, afterwards Lady Masham . . . if Abigail Masham had not been pregnant and forced by ill health to withdraw temporarily from Court . . . if she had not been succeeded as favourite by the sporting Duchess of Somerset . . . or if Queen Anne, whose health was so uncertain, had died three years earlier, then there would have been no Royal Ascot.

Queen Anne, daughter of James, Duke of York (later James II), by his first wife Anne Hyde, has often been dismissed as a nonentity, but she was, in fact, a complex and unappreciated woman. She was tall, fair, comely when young, with a particularly musical speaking voice.

Anna, as she called herself as a little girl, was the darling of her father, who took her riding every day, whatever the weather and taught her to love outdoor sports.

She married the dull, but courageous Prince George of Denmark. She was happy in her marriage, but the tragedy of her life was her inability to bear a healthy child. The exact number of her pregnancies, miscarriages and stillbirths is not known, but has been put as high as twelve miscarriages and six children alive at birth, of whom only one, her fourth child created Duke of Gloucester, lived more than a few days. And that pitiful little boy lived only until he was eleven years old. The strain of continual unsuccessful pregnancies was a significant cause of Queen Anne's poor health.

She became estranged from her father because of religion. James II was an unacknowledged Roman Catholic, her husband a staunch

Protestant. Princess Anne deserted James II to support her sister Mary II and her husband William of Orange (William III) in their successful bid for the throne. In spite of this, she was ignored during their joint reign.

She succeeded her brother-in-law as sovereign in 1702, and was widowed in 1708. Even as Queen she had minimal independence. For years she had been dominated by the vitriolic Duchess of Marlborough, from whom she had just struggled free. It would have been unthinkable for the Duchess to allow the Queen to spend money on a *racecourse*. (She had successfully prevented Queen Anne from giving a £5 per annum rise to the laundrymaid, and sometimes even refused to allow the Queen to buy a new gown.)

Abigail Hill, installed as the Queen's Dresser by the Duchess to keep an eye on her, had helped herself to power and influence instead. Although she was genuinely kindly and affectionate towards the Queen, she would hardly have encouraged her royal mistress to squander even the smallest sum on the construction of a racecourse. But Abigail Hill had secretly married a courtier, Mr Masham, and during the summer of 1711 was pregnant and unwell.

Like all the Stuarts Queen Anne was passionately addicted to hunting, and nothing could make her give this up, neither ill health nor her enormous weight. Queen Anne was self-indulgent at the table to the point of gluttony, and she suffered from gout. Even at her coronation she had to be carried in a sedan chair, her long train spread out over the chairback, because of an attack of gout, and gout continued to plague her during the summer of 1711, when the racecourse at Ascot was opened. Now forty-six years old, she was said to weigh upwards of twenty stone. (After her death three years later Coke commented '. . . she died monstrously fat, so much so that her coffin was almost square'.)

Despite this, Queen Anne continued to follow hounds, and it was said that hunting could do what the affairs of state could not—cause her to put back the time of dinner.

No horse could carry her, but Queen Anne hunted in a specially-built, light, two-wheeled vehicle, said 'to be something like a chaise'. With a strong hackney in the shafts, Queen Anne drove herself at a furious pace for very long distances. Once she is said to have covered sixty miles in one day.

The chaise was a dangerous, easily overturned contraption, but Queen Anne must have been a good whip, as there is no record of her ever having overturned herself. But her ladies-in-waiting, whose duty it was to follow their sovereign, as best they might, in a similar vehicle, dreaded the experience. The Duchess of Somerset, the Mistress of the Robes, had the misfortune to have a crashing fall when following Queen Anne out hunting. '... Everybody thought I had broken all my bones', she wrote to another lady-in-waiting, 'but thank God, I had as little hurt as was possible.'

Queen Anne established the Buckhounds, with which she had hunted even before her accession, on a permanent basis, and she had new kennels built for them near Swinley Bottom, not far from the site of the water-jump at Ascot. She also had many rides cut through Windsor Forest, so that she could keep close to hounds in her chaise during the hunt.

It was after Queen Anne had enjoyed a gallop in her light chaise that she decided to have a racecourse built on Ascot Heath. In this she was aided and abetted by her Master of the Horse, the Duke of Somerset and his wife, her Mistress of the Robes.

During Mrs Masham's temporary eclipse the Duchess of Somerset — the same who had been unceremoniously tipped from her chaise while following the Queen — had risen in favour and power. A woman of aristocratic background, unlike the Duchess of Marlborough, the Duchess of Somerset, then in her mid-forties, served the Queen with dignity. Yet her own life had been as sensational — as tragic — as that of any heroine of fiction.

By birth she was a Percy of Northumberland, and an heiress. She was married off as a girl of thirteen to Lord Ogle, the heir of the Duke of Newcastle, but her bridegroom died a year later. A plain girl with red hair, the child widow appeared in black at the court of Charles II, where, because she was so young, so heartbroken and so very rich she was nicknamed *la triste heritière*.

Her mother and her guardians, who were led by the formidable Dowager Countess of Northumberland, quarrelled and scrambled to find her a second husband. Her grandmother, quicker off the mark, engaged her to a man of immense wealth, Thomas Thynne of Longleat Hall in Wiltshire, who was many years her senior. The marriage took place in London, but before it could be consumated Elizabeth Thynne escaped to the Continent with her mother. There the mother fell under the influence of an unscrupulous German adventurer, Count Charles John Königsmark. Königsmark cold-bloodedly decided to improve his chances and had Thynne murdered by assassins as he drove in his coach in Pall Mall in February 1682 — a crime commemorated by a vivid tablet in Westminster Abbey.

It is not known whether Elizabeth's mother had any inkling of this assassination, but Elizabeth herself was considered completely innocent. She returned to England and eventually married Charles Seymour,

sixth Duke of Somerset, who was Master of the Horse, and so she came
to the Court of Queen Anne.

The Somersets were, in general, well-liked but Dean Swift, who was at
Court at Windsor Castle in the summer of 1711, was a bitter enemy.
When he became aware of the Duchess of Somerset's growing influence
over Queen Anne he wrote a vindictive poem, of which one verse read:

England, dear England! if I understand
Beware of *carrots* from Northumberland.   (a reference to the colour of the
                                                                    Duchess's hair and origin)

Carrots sown *thin* a deeper root may get   (Thynne)
    If so be they are in *summer set*.   (Somerset)
Their *cunning's mark* though, for I have been told,   (Königsmark)
They *assasine* when young, and poison when old.   (assassinate)
Root out those carrots, O thou whose name,
Wich, spelled backwards and forewards, is *almost* the same.   (Anne)
And England, wouldst thou be happy still,
Bury those *carrots* under a *Hill*.   (Abigail Hill, Lady Masham.)

Jonathan Swift showed his verses to Lady Masham, but she took fright
and begged him to destroy them. The author's pride was too strong;
he kept the poem and a copy fell into the hands of the Duchess of Somerset,
who bided her time. Then, just as Dean Swift was about to be appointed
Bishop of Hereford, she showed them to the Queen—and Dean Swift
never gained a bishopric.

So during the short summer months of 1711 Queen Anne had for the
first time the opportunity and the means to indulge her fancy for a
racecourse at Ascot, six miles from Windsor Castle. The Duke of
Somerset, owner of a famous stud and one of the greatest supporters of
racing in England, had already tried to interest William III in racing. In
his capacity of Master of the Buckhounds he was put in charge of the
actual construction of the racecourse, and thereafter the Master of the
Buckhounds—whether or no the incumbent knew anything about racing
—was responsible for the running of Ascot racecourse for 190 years.

The making of the course was very simple and very cheap. Accounts
for the construction of 'the round Heat on Ascott Common in July and
August 1711' are lodged at the Public Record Office. These show the
racecourse itself cost £558 19s 5d, which was paid to William Lowen.
The carpenter, William Erlybrown, received £15 2s 8d for making and
fixing the posts, which were painted by Benjamin Culchott for £2 15s.
It cost a further £1 1s 6d to engross (that is to express in legal form) the
articles for the Queen's Plate.

In the early eighteenth century English racing consisted of matches, and Plates which were run in heats. Horseracing had not disappeared entirely when it was suppressed during the Commonwealth, but it became an organised sport only with the Restoration of Charles II, Queen Anne's uncle, in 1660. Now it was prospering, and the basis of Rules was forming, with Newmarket always to the fore. Numerous racemeetings were held all over the country. In the south Newmarket led. Salisbury was an enterprising meeting, Epsom was a comparative new-comer, and there were meetings at Kenilworth, Newport Pagnall, Burford, soon to be linked with the famous Bibury meeting, Woodstock and many other places. Yorkshire was the most important centre of racing in the north with its greatest meetings at Black Hambleton, York and Doncaster.

The breeding of racehorses was all the rage. The Royal Stud had been re-established at Hampton Court, and the great noblemen vied with each other in mating the best imported Arabs and Barbs with English mares. Queen Anne used to go to Newmarket for the spring and autumn meetings, staying there up to a month at a time. She is also said to have attended a race meeting at York. The Queen's racing horses were kept at Newmarket, and there is no record that she ever ran a horse at Ascot. On her accession the unattractive but methodical Tregonwell Frampton 'Father of English Racing', was re-appointed as Keeper of the Running Horses. Frampton was a misogynist, but he acknowledged respect for Queen Anne, whom he called 'the Governor'.

The construction of Ascot racecourse was one of Queen Anne's last pleasures and her best memorial. Dean Swift sketches in the Queen's pursuits at that time in his letters to Stella. On July 31st, 1711, he wrote: '. . . the Queen was abroad today to hunt, but finding it disposed to rain she kept to her coach, she hunts in a chaise with one horse, which she drives like Jehu, and is a mighty hunter like Nimrod.' On August 7th, 1711, Swift noted: '. . . the Queen hunted the stag until four in the after-noon, and drove forty miles that day, beyond the usual hour of her dinner, which was not served until five o'clock that evening.'

The racecourse was the great excitement of the Court at Windsor Castle. Even Swift, who detested riding and was indifferent to horseracing was persuaded to inspect the course. He wrote to Stella on Friday, August 10th, 1711, the day before the first race was run at Ascot: 'Dr Arbuthnot, the Queen's favourite physician, went out with me to see a place they have made for a famous horserace tomorrow, where the Queen will come.'

On his way to Ascot: 'We overtook Miss Forester, one of Her Majesty's

maids-of-honour, on her palfrey, taking the air; we made her go along
with us. The Queen passed us coming back, and Miss Forester stood
by the roadside like us, with her hat in her hand as Her Majesty went by.'
It was fashionable for women to ride in mannish clothes, but Miss
Forester carried the mode to extremes by bowing instead of curtseying.
Swift describes the clothes she wore at one Ascot racemeeting that year
—a long white riding coat over a full-flapped waistcoat and a habit skirt.
On her head, over a long, white-powdered periwig, she wore a small
three-cornered cocked hat, bound with gold lace, the point placed
exactly in front. Dean Swift made no secret of his opinion of her: he
remarked drily, 'I do not like her, though she be a toast, and was dressed
like a man.'

It was indulgent of Queen Anne, who was a stickler for correct dress,
precise in enforcement of the correct colour and width of a riband, to
allow Miss Forester her eccentricities of dress and behaviour. Indeed Miss
Forester's presence at Court was in itself a sign of Queen Anne's kindness.
Like the Duchess of Somerset, Miss Forester had been a child bride,
married at the age of ten to a son of Sir George Downing, the speculative
builder of Downing Street. The marriage, bitterly unhappy, had been
dissolved. But a divorced woman, however innocent, however beautiful,
was then something of an outcast, and Queen Anne, in appointing Miss
Forester a maid-of-honour, had re-established her socially.

The first day's racing at Ascot took place on Saturday, 11th August,
1711, in the presence of the Queen and Court, but not, alas, of Dean
Swift who was entertaining a visitor at Windsor Castle. He missed the
coach on the second day, and 'not wishing to ride', stayed behind. So
there is no account of the atmosphere or of the results of the first Ascot
meeting. We do know that the race on Saturday was for a £50 Plate
and that seven horses started—the Duke of St Albans' chestnut horse
Doctor, Mr Erwell's grey horse Have-at-all, Mr Smith's grey gelding
Teauge, Mr William Hall's bay stone horse Dimple, Mr John Biddolph's
brown bay horse Flint, Mr Charles May's grey gelding Grey Jack and
Mr Merrit's iron-grey horse Grim.

The Queen's Plate of £100 was run on the Monday, again in the
presence of the Queen. Four horses, Mr Raylton's brown horse, Lord
Craven's grey horse, Sir William Gorry's brown horse and Mrs (surely
it should be Mr) Orme's bay horse, were entered.

There are brief records of the racing at the second Ascot meeting of
1711, held on Monday, 17th and Tuesday, 18th September. On each
day there was only one race, which was run in heats. The Monday race
was a Plate of fifty guineas for any horse carrying ten stone 'that never

won in money or Plate the value of £20'. The three entries consisted of the Duke of Somerset's grey horse Crofts, Mr Barber's chestnut gelding Speed Cut and Mr Edmund's dark brown gelding Hoboy.

On the Tuesday four horses ran for a £20 Plate, being Sir W. Wyndham's grey gelding Cricket, Lord Lifford's nutmeg gelding Shares, Sir Thomas Palmer's bay gelding Lumber and Mr Newman's grey gelding Have-a-care.

In the following year The Queen's Plate was run for at Ascot on August 25th, 1712, in the presence of Queen Anne and a brilliant company. There were six runners, four of them being distanced in the first heat, and the Plate was won by 'Robert Fagg, Esq, son of Sir Robert Fagg, Baronet of Sussex'.

Another meeting was advertised in *The London Gazette* for Monday September 1st, 1712, when a subscription race for a £50 Plate was to be run.

The meeting was again held in August 1713. The Queen's Plate was run in the presence of the Queen on August 12th, 1713, and on the following day there was a £50 Plate for horses 'that had never won £100 since they were six years old'. A second race, the Windsor Town Plate of 20 guineas, open to any horse carrying ten stone, was also advertised.

The names of the stewards to officiate were advertised at this meeting, a further sign of the increasing organisation of racing. They were to be 'the Hon Conyers Darcey, Esquire or the Hon Colonel George Fielding Esquire, Commissioners to execute the office of Master of the Horse, or in their absence Richard Marshall Esquire, Master of Her Majesty's Stud at Hampton Court.'

In 1714 Queen Anne intimated her intention of giving her usual Queen's Plate to be raced for at Ascot, and this was advertised for August 13th, 1714. But the Queen's health had been failing fast, and she did not live till the proposed date of the race.

Queen Anne, like other owners, was delighted when her horses won. On July 31st, 1714, she had a winner named Star in a £40 Plate at York, but she never knew of this win, for she lay dying in Kensington Palace. The faithful Lady Masham wrote: '. . . her pain deprives her of all sense, and in the intervals she does [nothing] and speaks to nobody.'

Between seven and eight on the following morning Queen Anne died, in her fiftieth year and the thirteenth year of her reign. When the news reached York, there was a great bustle as the noblemen and gentlemen had their horses put to, and set out in their coaches for London.

The Ascot racemeeting, fixed for less than two weeks later was at first postponed and later cancelled.

Today the opening race of the royal meeting, the Queen Anne Stakes, remembers Ascot's founder.

After the death of Queen Anne, Ascot fell into a period of decline. King George I, who had difficulty with the English language let alone the English way of life, was not interested in sporting activities. He did once attend a racemeeting at Newmarket, but he took no interest in Ascot, and racing there lapsed.

It was not until August 15th and 16th, 1720, that racing was revived at Ascot, and then on a very limited scale, with races only for horses that had been hunted with the Royal Buckhounds. On each day the customary single race, run in heats, took place. Each race was a thirty-guinea Plate for hunters 'which had never run for money or Plate, and which had been used in hunting twelve months last past'. For horses entered 'with Barlow at Hatchet Lane' a week before the meeting the entry money was two guineas, which was doubled if the horse were entered at the post.

The next Ascot meeting was in 1722, when a single race was run for forty guineas, open to 'horses that have stag-hunted in Epping or Windsor Forest with the King's hounds', and the entries were taken by John Tempiro at Sunninghill Wells. In 1727 John Cheny of Arundel published in his *Annual Racing Calendar* purses of thirty and forty guineas open to 'such Hunters as had been at the death of a Lesh of Staggs with His Majesty's Hounds in Windsor Forest between the first day of March last and the first day of running.' In 1728 there was only one day's racing for a purse of forty guineas, and in 1729 there was no racing at all at Ascot.

There seems to have been an exciting day's sport in 1730 when the race—now worth £50—was won by the Duke of Newcastle's chestnut horse Fidler. The Duke gave the stakes to his groom 'for his care and diligence' and Frederick, Prince of Wales, elder son of King George II, (who died in 1751, nine years before his father), added a gift of a further thirty guineas.

In the 1730s there were three-day meetings in 1735 and 1736, and a meeting in 1739, but in the other years there was no racing at Ascot.

The 1740s opened with a body-blow for racing, and Ascot might have been eliminated for ever. As a result of a campaign against badly conducted small racemeetings, an Act of Parliament, instigated by the Duke of Bolton, was passed (the 13th George II Cap 19), of which the preamble read: 'An Act to restrain and prevent the excessive Increase of Horse Races; and for amending an Act made in the last Session of Parliament intituled "an Act for the more effectual preventing of excessive and deceitful gaming" ...' The preamble continued that horseracing for 'small prizes or sums of money had contributed very much to the encouragement of idleness, to the impoverishment of many of the meaner sort of the subjects of this kingdom and the breed of strong and useful horses hath been much prejudiced thereby.'

The Act made it illegal for horses to run for any prize of less value than £50, except at Newmarket and Black Hambleton in Yorkshire. Other clauses decreed that horses must be the *bona fide* property of their owner, and that no owner could run two horses in one race. To improve the size and weight-carrying capabilities of horses, then the vital form of transport, it was actually decreed by Act of Parliament what weights horses must carry in races—ten stone, at fourteen pounds the stone, for five years old, eleven stone for six years old, and twelve stone for seven years old.

Many little racemeetings all over the country perished as a result of this Act, and no meetings were held at Ascot until 1744, when the races included a Yeomen Prickers' Plate of £50. In an Act of 1745 (18th George II Cap 34) mostly devoted to the control of gaming at cards, the compulsory allocation of weights was revoked, with the explanation: 'Whereas the thirteen Royal Plates, of one hundred guineas each, annually run for, as also the high prices that are constantly given for horses of strength and size, are sufficient to encourage breeders to raise their cattle to the utmost size and strength possible . . .'

Ascot had found a new patron, in the unlikely shape of William Augustus, Duke of Cumberland, second son of George II, victor of the bloody battle of Culloden Moor, Ranger of Windsor Great Park, employer of the artist Thomas Sandby, and the breeder of Eclipse. There were to be three Dukes of Cumberland, all related yet all separate creations, and each concerned with the progress of Ascot.

The Duke had emerged as hero of the Hanoverians after Culloden, but had swiftly lost popularity through his defeats on the Continent. Too unpopular to pursue an army or a political career, he was free to apply his considerable abilities to horsebreeding, greatly to the advantage of the British thoroughbred.

This first Duke of Cumberland was hardly an attractive man. He was said to look 'like both the prodigal son and the fatted calf'. In character he was decisive and brave, although he was so shortsighted he was once nearly captured by the French, mistaking their troops for his own men. But he was haughty and harsh, sentencing malefactors among his *own* troops to 1,200 lashes.

The Duke of Cumberland was also a compulsive and heavy gambler. Horace Walpole recounts that in 1750, when out hunting 'As the Duke has taken a turn of gaming, Sandwich [The Earl of Sandwich, whose habit of clapping a piece of meat between two slices of bread in order to eat without leaving the gaming table has perpetuated his name] to make his court—and fortune—carries a box and dice in his pocket, and so they throw a main whenever the hounds are at fault, upon every green hill and under every green tree.'

The Duke of Cumberland was not fastidious about his gambling companions, and had much trouble with 'black-legs' (as swindlers on the turf were then known, either because they generally appeared in boots, or from game-cocks whose legs are always black). He was a keen racing man, and an early, probably a founder member of the Jockey Club, which came into being between 1750 and 1753, because the Jockey Club Plate, which Marske, the sire of Eclipse, won for him in 1754, was open only to horses owned by members of the Jockey Club. He has also been credited with winning the earliest Challenge Whip with Dunlin in 1764, but in fact several earlier winners of the Whip have been recorded.

However he indubitably headed the first official List of Colours allocated by the Jockey Club in 1762, when his colours were listed simply as *purple*. At that time all riders wore black caps, and these were not named in the colours.

His horses, which were only moderately successful, were trained at Kate's Gore, near Ilsley in Berkshire. The Duke was fond of making matches, but lost most of them.

It is for his stud rather than his racing stable that the Duke of Cumberland will always be famous. From 1748 until his death in 1765 he lived principally at Windsor, sometimes at Cumberland Lodge, where he stabled his coach and riding horses, sometimes at Cranbourne Lodge, where he kept his mares and young stock. With the help of his horsemaster Smith, after whom the Windsor polo ground of Smith's Lawn is named, the Duke built up one of the largest and best studs in England. His name is for ever linked with that of Eclipse, although the Duke was dead before the chestnut wonder horse was seen on a racecourse. He owned both Marske, the sire and Spiletta, the dam of Eclipse. Eclipse was foaled, almost certainly in a paddock at Cranbourne Lodge in 1764, during the Great Eclipse of that year, and was named by the Duke himself, who is said to have had great hopes for the foal.

Marske was bred in 1750 by John Hutton, a famous Yorkshire breeder, who sold him to the Duke. Marske was by Sir Harry Harper's Squirt (a chestnut by Bartlet's Childers), out of The Ruby Mare, who was by Hutton's Blacklegs out of Bay Bolton Mare. His mark on the following generation of racehorses is illustrated in this poem, published shortly after the death of Marske:

> Ye sportsmen, for awhile refrain your mirth;
> Old *Marsk* is dead! consigned to peaceful earth
> The King of horses now, alas! is gone,
> Sire of *Eclipse* who ne'er was beat by one ...
> His well-descended blood the sportsmen trace,
> And sound his fame in each contested race,
> The stock of *Marsk* we circumspectly view,
> Announce that they were runners swift and true.
> Say, shall I mention *Shark* and *Masquerade*
> Whose great preeminence was oft displayed?
> Or shall *Hephestion* crown my humble lays?
> Or shall I of *Sphynx* or *Pontac's* praise?
> *Salopian* and *Pretender* shall I name?
> Or speak of *Honest Kitt* and *Transit's* fame?
> Shall brave *Leviathan* adorn my theme
> For which he was justly held in high esteem?
> *Revenge* and *Caesar* both occur to mind
> And *Flying Jib* went briskly as the wind;
> There's *Jack of Hilton* too, and *John-a-Nokes*
> Have often pleased and seldom grieved the folks,
> Let me not pass *Young Marsk* in silence O'er,
> Though once he started only and no more;
> Misfortune checked him in his swift career
> Or from competitors he had naught to fear.
> Fain would I now attempt the whole detail,
> But well I know my numbers soon would fail;
> With *Temperance* therefore I shall pass the rest
> And briefly say that *Stripling* stood the test ...

What can possibly be said that is new about Eclipse? He did not run until he was five, and he was never beaten. He won eighteen recorded races, including eleven King's Plates. Eclipse came back once to race at Ascot, so near to his birthplace, when, on May 29th, 1769, he won a fifty-guinea Plate from Mr Fettyplace's bay horse Cream de Barbade by Snap. The race, run in two heats each of two miles, went easily to Eclipse, who won both heats without the slightest difficulty.

The Duke also bred Herod—or King Herod, as he was originally called—who was foaled in 1758, and, like Marske, was a better stallion than a racehorse. Herod was descended from the Byerley Turk and among his many famous descendants is his son Highflyer. Herod's dam Cypron was also the dam of Senlis, by Bajazet, who was purchased after the Duke's death by Lord Barrymore, and of Dorimond, a good-looking bay son of Dormouse, with whom the Duke, unusually enough, won three matches at Newmarket in 1761. Dorimond afterwards won a Jockey Club Plate when owned by the Hon Fulke Greville.

Towards the end of his life the Duke of Cumberland was a somewhat pathetic figure. After the Duke had attended his father's funeral, five years before his death, Horace Walpole wrote in a letter to George Montagu:

> The real serious part was the figure of the Duke of Cumberland . . . He had a dark brown adonis and a cloak of black cloth with a train of five yards. Attending the funeral of a father could not be pleasant; his leg was extremely bad, yet forced to stand upon it near two hours; his face was bloated and distorted with his late paralytic stroke which has affected, too, one of his eyes; and placed over the mouth of the vault into which in all probability he must himself soon descend; think how unpleasant the situation! He bore it all with a firm and unaffected countenance . . . sinking with the heat, he felt himself weighed down, and turning round found it was the Duke of Newcastle, standing on his train to avoid the chill of the marble.

The Duke of Cumberland's interest in racing continued right to the end of his life. In the week before he died he went racing at Newmarket, where he won his last race, a 500-guinea match against the Duke of Bridgwater. Walpole wrote of the Duke: 'His profound understanding had taught him to profit of his mortifications; and though he never condescended to make himself amiable but to the very few, he became as much respected, though deprived of power, as if his heroism had been victorious . . . In London his death was deeply felt . . . the middling and lower people almost universally went into the closest mourning with weepers.'

We know more about the Duke of Cumberland and the contemporary scene at Windsor and Ascot because he employed the artist Thomas Sandby as Deputy Ranger of Windsor Great Park. There is a fine picture of *Ascot Heath Races* in the royal collection. It is believed that Thomas Sandby was responsible for the topographical details, and that his better-known brother Paul, a Royal Acadamecian whose *Cries of London* are still popular, drew the figures. Thomas Sandby, who had accompanied the Duke of Cumberland on his Highland campaign as a topographical artist and surveyor, lived in a strawberry-pink villa, the Ranger's Cottage, in Windsor Great Park, afterwards the site of the Royal Lodge. At the 1959 Christie sale of Paul Sandby's paintings the Queen bought a Paul

Sandby painting of this lodge as a present for her mother, who has such a deep affection for the Royal Lodge and who restored its original pink colour.

The Sandby watercolour of Ascot was bought by the Prince of Wales, afterwards George IV, from Colnaghi in 1799 for five guineas. It shows that there were rough posts and rails on the inner side of the course from the distance to the winning-post. Behind this carriages were drawn up as temporary grandstands, with spectators on foot ranging in front of them. There were no rails on the outer side of the track, and racewatchers crowded forward on to the track itself during the progress of the race. Horsemen mingled with the crowd, but it was not the custom at Ascot, as it was at Newmarket, for the spectators to gallop in with the racing horses, although they did so occasionally.

Also on the outside of the course there stood one great tree, and beside it a somewhat ramshackle stand, with room for about a score of men abreast to stand in each of five or six rows, partially protected from the weather by a flimsy roof, sloping backwards. These early stands were movable, mere wooden stagings or galleries, sometimes, as in this case, topped with a rough roof. A notice in 1777 announced that 'those having booths not to begin building until the horses are entered, except the booth for the Grand Stand, which is not to be appropriated to the benefit of the places, and is to be built a fortnight before the races'. Each private speculator who built a viewing gallery paid two guineas to the racefund.

Behind the grandstand one can see a line of covered wagons and booths, separated from the racecourse spectators by another post-and-rails. Here were many booths and tents devoted to gambling and drinking, for which the owners paid one guinea apiece into the prize fund. The supervision of these booths was in the 1770s under the control of two officers named Spencer and Nunn.

After the death of the Duke of Cumberland on October 21st, 1765 racing at Ascot was sufficiently re-established to survive, but it took on a new pattern. The main – often the only – meeting of the year, which had been held in July or August, shifted to June, and became linked with various entertainments held in the neighbourhood. For example the following advertisement appeared in 1767 and 1768.

... Their most obedient, humble servant R. Hodges would open the Assembly Room in Sunninghill, Windsor Forest, Berks, with a public breakfast on June 13th [when the races would be held] and would continue to do so every Monday throughout the season, for the reception of ladies and gentlemen who would be pleased to honour the place with their company. The balls taking place in Hodges' Long Room on Monday and Wednesday, and at the Town Hall, Windsor, on Tuesday and Thursday ... Great sport is expected at the races and a full season at Sunninghill.

In 1768 there were five days of racing at this June meeting, which opened with 'The Noblemen's and Gentlemen's Plate of £50 for four and five year old horses', which was run in the usual heats and was won by the stalwart five-years-old Bison owned by Mr Fettyplace (whose horse was beaten by Eclipse at Ascot in the following year). Bison came in fourth in the first heat, but won the second and third two-mile heats.

That year, according to Cawthorne and Herod's *Royal Ascot*: 'During the meeting a contemporary records that one of the leading ladies of fashion undertook, for a wager of £5,000, to ride a hundred miles in ten hours. The bet appears to have been made by her husband, who offered to hold £5,000 more that she would eat a leg of lamb and drink two bottles of claret into the bargain.' Alas, I have not been able to discover more about this tough lady, but possibly there is a confusion with the feat of Miss Pond, daughter of the publisher of a well-known early *Racing Calendar*, who had won a bet of 200 guineas to ride one thousand miles in one thousand hours on May 3rd, 1758, but at Newmarket.

The first Gold Cup race at Ascot was inaugurated in 1772, although the conditions were different from those of the Ascot Gold Cup established some thirty-five years later. The new cup was for five-years-old horses, the property of the subscribers, and was run over a four-mile course. The subscribers were the Duke of Cumberland (the second creation), the Dukes of Northumberland and Ancaster, the Earls of Orrery, Oxford and March, Viscount Bolingbroke, Sir Charles Bunbury and Messrs Blake, Ogilvie and Vernon. But the race itself was a non-event; a walk-over for the Duke of Cumberland's Maria, by Snap out of the Tartar mare.

This second Duke of Cumberland in a new creation was Henry Frederick, born in 1744, and the brother of George III and nephew of the first Duke of Cumberland. With purple waistband and black cap, he virtually adopted his uncle's racing colours. Although he interested himself in racing and in Ascot it was his brother William Henry, Duke of Gloucester, who was made Ranger of Windsor Great Park, and who had nominal charge of the races, which were still run by the Master of the Buckhounds. The Duke of Gloucester twice changed the title of the races, known in 1772 as the Windsor and Ascot Heath Races, and in the following year as Windsor Races, Ascot Heath, when he also changed the time of the first heat from one to five p.m. — Ascot's first evening racing.

The racing was by no means the only recreation offered at the time of the races. Apart from the breakfasts and 'ordinaries' at local halls, on the racecourse itself cockfighting, prizefighting, wrestling and gaming took place. On the last day of the 1777 races, for example, there was a bloody prizefight for the large purse of 500 guineas between a boxer named Selway, noted for a victory over a well-known boxer called Cochran, and Woods, a weaver. Eventually Selway lost an eye, and Woods won.

In the same year a cockfight was put on at the Old Cock Pit at the Marquis of Granby's Head at Windsor, which was advertised as 'a main of cocks between the gentlemen of Oxfordshire and the gentlemen of Berkshire, to show thirty-one cocks on each side in the main for five guineas a battle and 100 guineas the odd battle, and to show twenty cocks each in the byes for two guineas a battle. To weigh on Monday June 2nd, 1777, and to fight the four following days.'

The racing crowds attracted sharks and pickpockets who, when caught, had rough justice meted out to them. On July 6th, 1791, *The Morning Chronicle* reported 'that the light-fingered *gentleman* who experienced the democratic treatment of *ducking* and *docking* at Ascot races on Tuesday, had the audacity of visiting Windsor on Thursday and was present at that day's Friday's and Saturday's sport with a piece of crape and a handkerchief round his head to conceal his *amputated tail*; and by the deception of his story of his having been robbed and ill-treated secured to himself kindly treatment, and actually left Windsor without discovery'. But the tale had a sad ending. *The Public Advertiser* of July 9th, 1791, followed up '. . . that the same poor wretch is since dead from the severe whipping the jockey boys gave him. He put up at Brentford in a small ale house, and was found dead in his bed.'

Disorder on the course had already reached a tragic climax in 1784, when a Mr Rose, a brewer from Kingston, believed he had been cheated by a notorious gambler Dick England to whom he had lost £200 in play. Rose refused to pay and a duel resulted, which took place on the following day at Cranford Bridge. The first pistols were discharged without either man being hit, but they would not be reconciled. At the fourth shot Mr Rose fell with a bullet in his side, and, despite medical aid, he died a few hours later.

Stricter controls were attempted. The positioning of the booths was regulated, and stalls and gaming tables were forbidden between the betting stand and the winning post, where the Royal Enclosure is now situated. Racing was also more strictly ordered. Riders had to wear colours from 1783, and five years later the steward, Lord Hinchinbrook, ordered, 'No person do bring dogs on the course, as there will be proper persons appointed to destroy them.' In 1790 the first of many vain efforts was made to clear the course of spectators before the start of the races. Racegoers continually walked to and fro across the track, until it was as hard as an earth road, and it was many years before they were effectively excluded.

The races gradually became more valuable, and were more fully reported. 1777 was a particularly good year for racing at Ascot, when a 500-guinea match between the Duke of Cumberland's Caesar and Mr Jennings' Count, run over four miles, resulted in 'a smart win for the Duke's horse'.

In 1789 there was a disqualification in a race for a sixty-guinea cup – another sign of the increased discipline exercised over the races – when Count Melfort's grey gelding Magog finished first, but was placed second on an objection for crossing being sustained, to Lord Barrymore's Tongs.

All this was insignificant compared with the Oatlands Stakes, Ascot's first really big race, which was run on June 28th, 1791. The Oatlands moved Ascot from semi-obscurity to the forefront of the racing scene. The stakes were prodigious. In a year in which the Derby was worth only £1,079 5s to the winner, the Oatlands was worth 2,950 guineas to the winning owner. There were forty-one subscribers of 100 guineas each, half forfeit if the horse did not run.

Even this prize-money was small compared with the enormous sums that were bet upon the race, and which were estimated at the time at almost one million pounds!

The race took its name from Oatlands Park, the newly acquired residence of the Duke of York, second son of George III, who had just married Princess Frederique, the Princess Royal of Prussia. This is the Duke, the not-very-successful commander-in-chief of the British forces, who 'marched his troops to the top of the hill, and marched them down again'.

The Duke of York was an enthusiastic, knowledgeable patron of the turf and also a heavy gambler, who ran up enormous debts, but he had no runner in the Oatlands.

At this time, King George III was enjoying an interval of health and sanity, which lasted from 1788 to 1811, between his two bouts of terrible mental illness. The King, his wife Queen Charlotte and their six daughters spent the early part of the summer as usual at Kew Palace, returning to St James's Palace for the King's Levée and Birthday Court.

It was the custom for noblemen to come to these Court occasions in new coaches and carriages, and these carriages afterwards appeared at Ascot. At the Courts dress was formal, not to say magnificent, with the men as brilliantly garbed as the women. Even on such an occasion, however, King George III dressed soberly in a plain cloth suit.

Not so his eldest son, afterwards the Prince Regent and King George IV. He was always 'the best dressed Gentleman at Court', wearing such a concoction as (in 1792) 'a carmelite (fine woollen cloth or it may be a slip for carmenite or scarlet) and pale blue striped silk coat and breeches, the whole very richly embroidered in silver and gold stones and very curious flowers of different colours. The seams were all covered with an *appliqué* to correspond with the coat border; and the body of the coat was covered with silver spangles, which gave the dress a very splendid light appearance, notwithstanding it was so richly embroidered. His Royal Highness wore diamond shoe and knee buckles, George and Garter, and the diamond sword and epaulettes which had been so much admired on former birthdays.'

The life-styles of father and son, King George III and the Prince of Wales, were as dissimilar as their dress.

A fortnight before the big race the King, his wife and daughters moved to Frogmore House, Windsor, for the summer. The Prince of Wales was meantime travelling restlessly between Carlton House in the Mall, Bagshot and his apartments at Windsor Castle. He was already estranged from his father, and having a worrying time. In the newspapers it was said he would close down his Newmarket stables — and this was *before* the Escape scandal, always said to be the cause of the Prince of Wales's withdrawal from Newmarket. He was selling nine of his horses. The Prince had embarked on ownership immediately upon reaching the age of twenty-one in 1784, but with such ill-judgment and abandon that only two years later he had to be redeemed from his racing debts by a reluctant Parliament. Undaunted, he had returned to large-scale ownership and in the previous year ran no fewer than thirty-nine horses. A correspondent wrote in *The Times* shortly before the Oatlands Stakes in 1791, 'The Prince of Wales is acknowledged to be in possession of the finest racing stud in the kingdom, and yet how seldom it is that his Royal Highness wins a match,' continuing smoothly, 'This circumstance serves but to prove what has so often been said, that a man of generous mind and noble conduct, whatever advantages he may possess in the mere way of business, can never be successful on the *Turf*.'

To cap the Prince of Wales's misfortunes, on Friday June 17th, 1791, a mad dog got into his kennel at Kempton in Hampshire, and bit eighteen couple of his hounds, which had to be destroyed.

Moreover the Prince had bet heavily on the result of the Oatlands Stakes. By a piece of serendipity we know a great deal about the pre- liminaries to the Oatlands, and the running of the race. It comes about as a result of the Escape scandal, which took place at Newmarket on October 21st of the same year, 1791. The story has often been told, but briefly Escape, ridden by Sam Chifney, the Prince's jockey and said by him to need the race, finished last on that day in a field of four. He ran again on the following day and won. Chifney was brought before the stewards, his betting-book examined, and the Prince of Wales was told that if he put Chifney up again no gentleman would put a horse against him. The Prince of Wales was not short of faults, but he stood by Chifney, who seems to have been innocent on this occasion, withdrew his horses from Newmarket, and temporarily left the turf. For several years the Prince gave Chifney a handsome pension of £200 a year, and if Sam Chifney had difficulty later in collecting the money, he was not the only man that the Prince of Wales was slow to pay.

The bonus is that Sam Chifney gives in his autobiography not only his version of the Escape affair, but a detailed account of the training of the Prince of Wales's horses for the Oatlands Stakes at Ascot. The dapper Sam Chifney, a Norfolk man, was the outstanding jockey of his time, an opinion he wholeheartedly endorsed. His autobiography bore the imposing title:

'Genius Genuine,' by Samuel Chifney of Newmarket: A FINE PART IN RIDING A RACE, KNOWN ONLY TO THE AUTHOR. WHY THERE ARE SO FEW GOOD RUNNERS, or WHY THE TURF HORSES DEGENERATE. A GUIDE TO RECOVER THEM TO THEIR STRENGTH AND SPEED: as well as TO TRAIN HORSES FOR RUNNING, and Hunters and Hacks for Hard Riding TO PRESERVE THEIR STRENGTH, and their sinews from being so often destroyed; with Reasons for Horses Changing in their running. Likewise A FULL ACCOUNT OF THE PRINCE'S HORSE ESCAPE RUNNING AT NEWMARKET ON THE 20TH and 21ST DAYS OF OCTOBER 1791 with other interesting particulars. Sold for the Author, 232 Piccadilly and nowhere else. January 9th, 1804.

Sam Chifney begins with an account of arranging for a trial at Epsom of the Prince's horses which were to run in the Oatlands, June 21st, 1791, with Mr Warwick Lake, the Prince of Wales's manager and an old enemy of Chifney's.

Early on that morning I came from Mickleham, and met Mr W. Lake at the stable gate on Epsom Downs, before day-light. I observed that I had made myself nine stone ten lbs, thinking he would have me ride Escape.

'No!' said he in a sharp tone, 'I meant you to ride Pegasus; but I don't care what you ride.' . . . I then made myself ready to ride Pegasus . . .

As soon as it was light enough, the horses ran two miles, at the same weights they were to run for at the Oatlands, on the Tuesday following, at Ascot Heath. Escape won this trial; he beat Baronet about a neck; Pegasus was beaten a great way, and I think Smoker was beaten more than a hundred yards from Pegasus.

When Escape and Baronet had about three hundred yards to run, they were going by themselves in a very severe manner, and very fast, and Baronet was then running at his utmost, and he could not lay nearer than within about two lengths of Escape; but from Escape's making so very free with himself in most parts of the race, it made him come back to Baronet. I think Escape would have beaten Baronet three lengths or more if Escape had waited.

Escape, then a six-years-old, carried nine stone ten pounds, Baronet, also six, carried eight stone four pounds, Pegasus, who was seven, carried nine stone and the four-years-old Smoker carried seven stone.

After the trial, in spite of the bad blood between them, Chifney asked Warwick Lake to place a fifty-guinea bet on Escape for him, at Tattersalls.

. . . On the next day the horses set out for Ascot, and on Sunday afternoon Gaskein, His Royal Highness's groom at Carlton House, went with me to see them . . . I [went] into Escape's loose stable. I found him stripped, and the lad brushing him over. I instantly saw Escape was not well to run, and I was very certain that his chances for the Oatlands Stakes were all done away, and entirely so from mismanagement. I then went up to Escape, I coaxed him, kissed him, then left him.

. . . I then proceeded to Baronet's loose stable, and I also found him stripped, and brushing over. I saw him very well, and I thought he was likely to run for the race as he had done for his trial; and I immediately made up my mind to ride him for the Oatlands . . .

Chifney also backed Baronet, which, of course, was then permitted. On the day of the race the Prince of Wales arrived early on the course in his phaeton, drawn by six black horses, and then mounted a hack and rode about the course for the whole day. Chifney was determined to have a word with the Prince, who had, he knew, wagered more on the result of the Oatlands than on any other previous race.

I was the next morning on the race ground to wait for His Royal Highness, who came on it with Mr W. Lake on horseback. I immediately placed myself in sight, and His Royal Highness called to me, saying, 'Sam Chifney,

come this way.' I immediately got to the side of His Royal Highness and
Mr W. Lake, and His Royal Highness said, 'Sam Chifney, I shall run Escape
and Baronet only, which do you ride? Ride which you please—say which
you ride—I am in a hurry.

Chifney immediately chose Baronet, telling the Prince he did not think
Escape (whom he considered the best horse in England when he was
right) was well in himself, an opinion with which Warwick Lake and
Bill Price, the Prince's groom (who got the ride on Escape), did not agree.
The Prince of Wales told Chifney that he would run Escape, notwithstanding, as he would make a great deal of money if he won, but gave
him to understand that he would also win £17,000 if Baronet won.

Meanwhile an immense and somewhat unruly crowd, estimated at
40,000, was assembling on the racecourse. *The Times* reported: 'At one
o'clock their Majesties and all the Princesses arrived upon the Heath, and
quitting their carriages, entered the Royal Stand . . . the Duke of Clarence
joined the Princesses immediately on their arrival, and accompanied them
both upon the stand and in their carriages around the Heath.'

There was extremely heavy betting, even on the opening race, which
was a conventional King's Plate of 100 guineas for hunters carrying
twelve stone, which was run in two four-mile heats. The Duke of Bedford
was said to have bet £15,000 that his horse would win this race. Both
heats were won by Mr Wyndham's grey gelding by Bourdeaux, and the
Duke of Bedford's name does not appear among the owners of the starters,
although he may well have run a horse under a cover name, according to
the common practice of the time.

The next race was the Oatlands Stakes, and the Prince of Wales came
to see Chifney mount, and to wish him good luck. A huge field for those
days of nineteen horses went to the post amid the press and jostling of
the crowd. Many could not get their bets on, several people were injured
in the mêlée near the ropes.

The favourite, at three to one, was Vermin, a three-years-old by
Highflyer, owned by Lord Foley (who had started favourite for the
Derby, in which he had finished second to Eager), and who was set to
carry only five stone three pounds. (Little lads not yet into their teens
were found to ride at these very light weights.) Second favourite was
Precipitate, from the enormous racing stable of Lord Egremont, a
four-years-old carrying eight stone eight pounds. Lord Barrymore's
four-years-old Chanticleer started at nine to one, and the Prince of
Wales's Baronet was priced at twenty to one. Baronet ran in the name of
Colonel Lade.

Chifney's own account of the race ran:

... This was a very hard race with Baronet and Express till within a few yards of the end. My very favourite horse Escape was beaten a great way; for when these horses had near half a mile to run, Baronet at that time was about four lengths behind the front horse. Baronet was there by choice. Escape was at that time about two lengths behind Baronet; but I saw him clearly beaten, and the man getting very severe upon him. I was about to call to the rider to pull Escape up but thought better of it, because Escape was not only behind me, but wide from me, and there were horses between us, and I was fearful of keeping my head turned till the rider should hear me, lest my horse's fore legs should get entangled with the other horse's hind legs. I very much wished Escape to be pulled up, that he might not be abused after being so much beaten. I saw no more of him in this race, but from the situation I left him in, and the front horses renewing their pace, he must have been beaten a very great way. It is to be remarked, that the same person that trained Escape for the trial and race rode Escape for trial and race.

... a short distance before coming to the winning-post Express' and Baronet's heads were even with each other and both horses at their utmost. Express tired first in this severe run, which flung Baronet clear before him just before getting to the winning-post ...

The victory of Baronet in the Oatlands Stakes was generally attributed to Chifney's riding. *The Times'* reporter commented:—'There were five horses of the eighteen [sic] which ran, that were almost equal in coming in, but by the superior skill of the rider, Baronet outstripped the others just half a length.' Another account, apparently written by a reporter with little knowledge of racing as he did not recognise the best jockey of the day, reported, 'The Oatlands Stakes was won chiefly by the stratagem and ability of a boy, whose name is Cheffney. He rode Baronet. Vermin, who was the favourite in the field, was ridden by another boy, but so badly, that the race was evidently lost by his management.'

The Royal Family was delighted. Family feuds were forgotten as the King, elated with his son's success, remarked to him, 'Your Baronets are more productive than mine. I made fourteen last week, but I get nothing by them. Your single Baronet is worth all mine put together.' On the next evening the Prince of Wales celebrated his victory with 'a grand dinner to several gentlemen', held appropriately at his brother, the Duke of York's seat of Oatlands Park. *The Times*, often a critic of the Prince of Wales, commented drily: 'The Prince won everything at Ascot on Tuesday—and we are happy to add, that on that day at least "The Baronet had NOT a bloody tumble!" '

3

The Oatlands Stakes, although by far the most important race run at Ascot—or indeed in England—that year, was only the centrepiece of five-days' racing from Tuesday to Saturday inclusive. There were two further races and a match on the Tuesday. The second year of the Prince's Stakes for three-years-old fillies over the New Mile provided a double for the Prince of Wales when it was won by his filly Amelia by Highflyer.

Immediately after the Oatlands Stakes had been run the restless King, attended by the Duke of Montrose, got into his phaeton. The Queen, who was attended by Lady Holderness, entered her own phaeton, which was drawn by Highland ponies, and the Princesses packed into a landau. They then drove to the side of the course, where they watched the win of the Prince of Wales's filly. 'The Royal party then drove round the Heath to view the company, and again entered the stand, to view the conclusion of the day's sport, after which they returned to Windsor.'

On the Wednesday five races were planned, but two degenerated into walk-overs. The principal race was the Prince of Wales's (Handicap) Plate of £50 for all ages run over four miles and won by the favourite, Sir C. Turner's chestnut horse Gunpowder by Eclipse.

On Thursday the Royal party returned, but they cannot have been greatly pleased with their view of the Oatlands Stakes from the Royal Box, as it had been moved 'to a more eligible situation, near the centre of the New Mile'.

The Thursday card consisted of four races. The most important, a fifty-guinea sweepstake for three-years-old fillies over the New Mile, was won by 'Mr Lade's' brown filly by Highflyer out of his Greyling mare, possibly again owned by the Prince of Wales. Three-years-old colts and fillies were then subjected to a race in three heats run over the Old Mile, which was won by Mr Brand's bay colt by Challenger, who was wisely given an easy first race in which he finished only fifth, before going on to win the last two heats. A fifty-guinea match and a £50 race 'for horses belonging to Huntsmen, Yeomen Prickers and Keepers of Windsor Forest carrying twelve stone', run in two heats of four miles each, completed the programme.

On the Friday a tough bay horse, Mount Pleasant by Javelin, owned by Mr Wilson, won both two-mile heats of a £50 race, and was brought out later in the afternoon to win a twenty-five guinea match over the New Mile! a total of five miles and three wins in the same afternoon. The Saturday card consisted of five matches and only one race—but what a race! It consisted of *four* three-mile heats. Only three of the seven original starters completed all the legs, and it was won by Sir F. Poole's brown horse Mentor by Justice, who finished 2−1−2−1 over the twelve-mile total distance.

Although the Oatlands Stakes was over and done with, its effects were long felt. Rice, whose book was published in 1879, quoted from an unknown source of the suffering which followed among the losing punters, who had bet much more than they could afford. 'Horses are daily thrown out of training, jockeys are going into mourning, grooms are becoming E.O. merchants, and strappers are going on the highway.'

The confusion and lack of crowd-control at Ascot resulted in the removal of the Oatlands Stakes to Newmarket in the following year, where it was run in April for the even greater prize of 3,275 guineas in stake money. The Oatlands Stakes continued to be run as a minor race at Ascot until the end of George IV's reign, when it had declined to a thirty-guinea sweepstake run over two and a half miles. There is now no Oatlands Stakes among the Ascot races.

As for Baronet, who had been purchased for the Prince of Wales from Sir W. Vavasour, the Oatlands Stakes initiated a splendid season for him, in which he was never beaten on the racecourse. He went on to walk-over in the King's Plate at Winchester, to win a race of two four-mile heats at Lewes and to walk-over for a King's Plate at Canterbury, before winning the King's Plate over the Rowley Mile course at Newmarket in October. By Vertumnus and one of the fourteen foals out of a prolific winning mare Penultima, he was later exported to America.

Sam Chifney himself died in a debtor's prison.

Thus ended the romantic, chaotic early years of Ascot Racecourse.

CHAPTER TWO

Regency Ascot

I<small>T IS REMARKABLE HOW EARLY IN THE HISTORY OF</small> A<small>SCOT THE PRESENT</small>
pattern of days and even of races became established. From the 1790s
until today the principal and often the only racemeeting of the year at
Ascot has been held in June.

The individual quality of each day was early established. By the end of
the eighteenth century Tuesday was already always the opening day,
and was generally attended by the sovereign or his deputy the Prince
Regent. Wednesday was quiet, at least until the establishment of the Royal
Hunt Cup in 1843, which immediately became a big betting medium.
Thursday became the principal day from the first running of the Ascot
Gold Cup in 1807: it attracted the greatest crowds, the most fashionably
dressed ladies, and it was early and often referred to as 'Ladies Day'.
Friday was for long a rag-bag affair, far below the standard of the other
days in the quality of the racing, the prize-money and the attendance. It
was occasionally called 'Grooms Day'. Even today, although Friday
provides some of the best racing of Royal Ascot, attendances are usually
lower than during the rest of the week.

Ascot history runs in unbroken continuity from the eighteenth century
to today. The actors on the well-known turf overlap each other, generation after generation, as each racegoer changes imperceptibly from a
stripling to an old man, from a debutante to a dowager.

The period of prominence of each individual averages about fifteen
years. Owners were the first upon whom the limelight shone, then
jockeys and only much later did trainers become household names.

The Ascot picture may seem unchanging from year to year, but old
customs are continually eroded by new habits in the march of evolution.
Most are almost imperceptible but the death of one individual, the
sovereign, is always marked by change. Ascot was the sovereign's playground, and his personality set its mark upon the racecourse. There is

therefore reason, as well as convenience, in cutting the continual ribbon of Ascot history into chapters corresponding with the reigns, although the division between the period when the Prince Regent was deputising for his father, and his reign as King George IV is naturally less marked than most. This chapter covers a period which can roughly be described as Regency, and which runs from the Oatlands Stakes, Ascot's first great race, of 1791 up to the death of King George III in 1820. It also contains a pastiche of Ascot in the days when the horse was the only form of transport, a period which only came to an end with the age of the railways in the 1830s.

The Regency was in force in 1788, and then again from 1811 until the death of King George III at Windsor on January 28th, 1820. When the King was well, he lived a quiet and orderly life, which Greville described when the King was seventy-one years old and living at Windsor Castle: 'The King is still undertaking duties, and enjoys the most perfect health ... notwithstanding his sight not being good ... He in general rides daily on horseback at a slow pace, for two hours in Windsor Park except on Sundays.'

The King rose early, saw the despatches brought overnight, and rode from six to eight a.m. before attending chapel. He breakfasted at nine, dined at one, and joined the Queen and Princesses for dessert, after they had dined at four. In the evening he sometimes played chess, sometimes listened to the music of Handel, supped about ten and retired to rest about eleven p.m. It was a decent, dull life which did not appeal to the dissolute Prince of Wales, who had his own suite of rooms at Windsor Castle, but did not fully identify himself with the Ascot scene until he built for himself the Royal Lodge in Windsor Great Park.

The Duke of York, second son of George III, was the member of the Royal Family most closely associated with Ascot. He had withdrawn from the army in some disgrace, following exposure of his habit of selling commissions through his mistress, Mrs Mary Anne Clarke. He devoted much thought and time to his racing stable and Charles Greville, the diarist and Clerk to the Privy Council was his Master of the Horse.

The quality of the Duke's horses varied with his fluctuating fortunes. In 1789 'the four hacks in his post chaise' were described as 'poor and lean ... and like to cost their master more in whips than hay', while in the 1820s his favourite grey hack, which he always rode at Ascot, was enviously called 'one of the most powerful in England'.

Greville wrote of him:

... The Duke of York is not clever, but he has a justness of understanding which enables him to avoid the errors into which most of his brothers have fallen and which have made them contemptible and unpopular. Although his talents are not rated high, and in public life he has never been honourably distinguished, the Duke of York is loved and respected. He is the only one of the Princes who has the feelings of an English gentleman; his amiable disposition and excellent temper endeared himself to his friends by the warmth and steadiness of his attachments, and from the implicit confidence they all have in his truth, straightforwardness and sincerity ... He delights in the society of men of the world, and in a life of gaiety and pleasure. He is very easily amused, and particularly with jokes full of coarseness and indelicacy ...

The Duke of York won the Derby in 1816 with Prince Leopold, which ran in the name of Warwick Lake, and in 1821 with Moses. The Duke of York twice won the Ascot Gold Cup, with Aladdin in 1815 and in 1821, when Banker walked over. The Duke had an unusual quirk for changing his racing colours: eight different sets of colours were allocated to him, all, except one, permutations on the royal purple.

If the Duke of York were the most popular of the royal dukes, then the most unpopular undoubtedly was the Duke of Cumberland, fifth son of George III. Ernest August was created Duke of Cumberland (the third creation) in 1799, and eventually succeeded to the title of King of Hanover, which could only be inherited by a male, on the death of William IV in 1837. Gross in his habits, loathed by almost all who knew him, the Duke of Cumberland was generally believed to have murdered his valet.

From the time of the Oatlands in 1791, Ascot remained a great annual festival. It had a quite different atmosphere from Epsom Downs on Derby Day. The Derby was a vast folk-festival crammed into one day from dawn to midnight. But Epsom could be easily reached in a day from London, for the racecourse was only sixteen miles from the centre of London. Ascot racecourse lay nearly thirty miles from London. Only a few 'bloods' drove out daily, for most Ascot races were a four-day safari, whether you were a guest at Windsor Castle, or luxuriating in one of the country houses expensively rented for the week, or crammed uncomfortably into a local inn, or even roosting illegally in an outhouse in the neighbourhood.

Preparations for Ascot began well in advance of the meeting. The racehorses to take part converged slowly under their own power or in wagons, and were installed in various stables around the course. Visitors from the provinces set out on their journey days before the meeting.

Even in London many people began to migrate to the neighbourhood in the week before the races.

> For a week before the Ascot Heath races there was not a jobbing horse to hire at the post-masters in London, or even at Newman's, the biggest livery stables . . . As early as Monday a multitude of persons began to flood from London and the vicinity towards Ascot . . . it was curious to see the London coaches roll along crowded with dead and living lumber . . . Huge hampers of venison, fish and confectionery were piled upon roofs, in many instances far beyond the legal standard, to the imminent danger of those dainties and His Majesty's loco-motive lieges, who accompany them . . .
>
> All was life, bustle, motion, from Hyde Park corner to Windsor Castle. [At a great posting establishment at Hounslow] upwards of twenty carriages were seen waiting at the same time, the traffic was not confined to posting, as gigs, taxed carts etc were *en route* till three in the morning.

Even at Belfont, the little green in the centre of the village was 'covered with post-horses'.

Charles Apperley, born in 1779, who wrote under the pseudonym of Nimrod, described in an autobiographical sketch a visit as a young man with 'Sir John Inkleton', to Ascot, calling himself Frank Raby. The party travelled each day from Stevens' Hotel in Bind Street and 'Sir John' explained:

> The nags are all in town—two rare teams and two rest-horses, ten in all; they will be quite ready for Ascot on Tuesday, when you shall have a seat on the box . . . I shall send one team to Staines, where it will remain during the meeting; so that we shall go and return on each day, which will add much to our amusement; and I . . . have given orders that a good dinner, for eight, shall await us every day, at the 'Bush', so that we shall have the road clear for us on our return to town, and travel in the cool of the evening, when the crowd of cockneys will be dispersed.
>
> On the first morning of the meeting—a beautiful one in June and at the hour of ten o'clock, Sir John's team was at the door of Stevens' Hotel and nothing could be more correct than its appointments. The coach was a bright yellow, neatly picked out in black, and a plain crest on the upper door-panel. The mountings were, of course, of brass, to suit the furniture of the horses; there were roof-irons to the front roof, which held three persons, and a comfortable dickey behind, to carry the two servants. The box was likewise of the true coaching principle, made to sail forward towards the wheel-horses, with a good roomy footboard and well-cushioned seat allowing plenty of elbow-room for two. The horses were dappled greys, which did credit to all parties; first to their owner, for the selection of them;

next, to the men who had care of them; for the white hairs on their bodies were as white as the driven snow, and their harness equally well polished. But Sir John's order for *soap* was unlimited, one severe tax on the use of grey coach horses; and it is said he never grumbled if the year's bill for that purifying article did not exceed £100.

... inside were two friends of the Baronet's, non-coaching men, and an old and warm relation, who promised to pay for the champagne, both on the course and at dinner, for the four days of the meeting, on condition that he was not upset, either in going or in returning.

After the party passed through Hyde Park turnpike ... The first stop was at Hounslow, there, according to the usage of those days—slow compared with the present—the bearing reins were let down, and the noses of the horses plunged into a bucket of cold water, with a swallow or two each, and most refreshing it must have been to them, after toiling through ten miles of dirt, for there were no watered roads in those days. A glass of sherry and a biscuit were also partaken of by the party, and onward they proceeded towards the course.

The team 'threw themselves into their collars, in ascending the hill out of Egham, and on the flat between the towns, it was as much as Sir John could do to restrain their ardour ... "Those leaders cost me two hundred guineas apiece, and the wheelers more than two-thirds of that sum".'

After racing and dining, 'the party arrived each night at Stevens' Hotel as the clock struck eleven, so exactly did the Baronet keep his time; and both men and horses appeared the better for their four days of clear country air.'

Thus did young bloods travel to Ascot at the beginning of the nineteenth century. The operation required ten horses, an unstated number of servants in addition to the two who travelled on the coach, and the most careful advance planning, involving a thirteen-hour day, for a round journey of some sixty miles. But what attention to detail, what style!

This was the Rolls-Royce end of the business: lesser mortals had to contend with greater discomfort. All sorts of vehicles poured down the road to Windsor, providing a free show for the towns and villages through which they passed. Even Eton 'poured forth its numerous scholars to gaze upon the passing show'. Windsor was reached late on Monday evening; the travellers dined and sallied forth to view the castle by moonlight or, less innocently, to patronise the various gaming-halls which opened for raceweek. There was a poorish theatre in Windsor, sometimes patronised by George III and his family. In 1802 there was an unseemly fracas during their race-week visit to see *Wives Astray* and

Lover's Quarrels, in which Quick doubled the parts of Lord Priory and
Sancho. 'In the course of the evening, the performance was interrupted
by the indecorous behaviour of some inebriated Etonians, who "Valiant
in their Cups", considerably over-stretched the bounds of decorum, by
quarrelling in various parts of the house, to the great annoyance of the
Royal Family and the Audience; at length they were driven out of the
house by the Police officers in attendance.'

Later, the Windsor Theatre fell upon hard times and a racegoer in 1820
said that at one performance in Ascot week 'some wretched actors
performed before an audience scarcely more numerous than the company
itself'.

Windsor's worst fracas during raceweek took place in 1833, and was
reported in *The Times* by two reporters taking very different views. It
seems that officers of the Household Brigade stationed at Windsor,
dined well and sallied forth into the town in search of amusement. They
lost their money in a gaming establishment, believed they had been
cheated, and broke the place up, afterwards proceeding to Eton to take
revenge on an unpopular man named Solomons.

The first reporter sided with the officers, who had, he declared, been
cheated and when they tried to retrieve their losses, were refused credit.
So — naturally — 'they kicked the house and its inmates out of the window'.

The second reporter was less indulgent. He spoke of 'a party of officers
of the regiments stationed in the town, elevated by the indulgencies of
the mess table', went forth 'on the spree' — a gaming-house was naturally
looked upon as fair game — they broke the tables to pieces, threw the
material into the street, smashed the windows, maltreated the unfortunate
gamblers — the row lasted a considerable time and ended in favour of the
'gentlemen'. 'Hot with the Tuscan grape and high in blood,' the officers,
after being dislodged by Windsor police, went on to Eton 'to give old
Solomons a turn'. They forced their way into his house, threw his clothes
about and burnt his wig. Eventually the police got together a punitive
force, and there ensued a considerable fight after which four army
officers were arrested. 'Four were lodged in *the cage* for the whole of the
next day, and four others got away, but were much marked.' In the
following year the magistrates of Windsor banned all gaming establishments from the town during raceweek, but the displaced gamesters
only invaded Ascot racecourse in greater numbers than before.

Even for those who stayed clear of trouble, the stay in Windsor could
be less than comfortable. 'In Windsor there was, in innkeeper's phrase-
ology, "a vast deal of sleeping company". Happy the wight who obtained
the felicity of a bed! A doze upon a sofa, a roll upon a hearth-rug — the

nightmare on a table—a cold caught lying on the boards, a cramp catching you lying upon chairs—an apoplectic slumber in a post-chaise—such are a few of the amenities of the night before a Cup race in the neighbourhood of Ascot.'

Moreover prices for such accommodation were astronomic. Indignantly it was reported in 1828: '... one instance of the system of extortion practised on these occasions. A gentleman stopped (on Tuesday) at the inn at Englefield, where he slept. The charge for the bed was sufficiently large, but it will hardly be believed that, besides 1s 6d for a feed of corn and 2s 6d for hay, there was an item of 10s for the *horse's bed*.'

After their night's rest the travellers set off for the course in the morning. The road from Windsor and Ascot lay between 'elder bushes in full blossom, which gave out their odour; the beautiful china-rose bushes, by which many of the houses about Windsor are covered to the very eaves, to a height of twenty feet or upwards, burst upon the eye in masses of delicately fragrant bloom, and the magnificent forest scenery completed a picture of rural beauty such as no country outside England can exhibit'.

The road was crowded with coaches, tilburies, carts, gigs, chaises, 'cruelty vans' and plodding among them slow-moving wagons with oak branches in full leaf arched over them to protect their load of country-folk from the heat of the sun. The humbler vehicles were crowded, 'an average of nine persons to one horse ... without much regard to the capabilities of the wretched animals that drew them, we observed one vehicle of capacious dimensions in which thirty-six passengers were dragged painfully and slowly along by three horses harnessed unicorn-fashion ... The people whose horses were not their own as usual carried everything on the road before them; in fact the vigour of one man's beast under another man's discipline is proverbial.' Threading their swift superior way among these slower vehicles were 'the splendid barouches with its brilliant company and rich appointments drawn by blood cattle'. In 1829 the first *omnibus* was reported, 'a huge machine, carrying a multitude of people, who were ever and anon amused with the notes of a keyed bugle, played by a guard stationed in the forepart of the carriage'.

But surely the most unusual vehicle ever to be seen on the road to Ascot races was the Kite Coach, reported in *The Times* in 1828:

The amusements of the afternoon were not confined to racing, for ... the attention of all present was attracted by a novel exhibition, which was none other than the famous Kite Coach, which, drawn by two kites, travelled at a rapid pace, at the back of the Royal Stand. His Majesty left the front of the Stand in order to have a full view of it.

On our return from the races, we had a better opportunity of witnessing the power of this extraordinary machine; an immense number of carriages were assembled about half a mile this side of Staines, and the Kite Coach starting with them, not only left them all in the lurch, passing every thing on the road, but actually beat Mr Shearman's Bull-and-Mouth coach, a quick one, by half an hour in the short distance between Staines and Smallberry-green, eight miles. It was managed by the inventors, Mr Pocock and sons.

One marvels at the ability of Mr Pocock and his sons to manoeuvre the Kite Coach, which must have required a stiff breeze, among heavy horse-drawn traffic.

The roads of the period were very bad, and it is not surprising to find that the country roads round Ascot failed to stand up to the heavy traffic. In dry weather dust rose in choking clouds, covering horses, vehicles and travellers. In 1827 when the weather was particularly dry, bright young men provided themselves with green veils 'being tied round their hats after the manner of the ladies' as a protection. Wet weather churned the roads to mud and during particularly bad weather in 1824 'many of the vehicles were lighted of their passengers at least a mile from the scene of action—a walk through the mud being thought preferable to the risk of broken bones'. In both extremes of climate, the horses suffered great distress, and every raceday some dropped dead in their traces.

Accidents on the road were commonplace. Death on the road in the eighteenth and early nineteenth centuries seems to have constituted 'the acceptable death', as psychologists declare death by motor-car remains in the twentieth century. Even Princess Elizabeth, daughter of George III, had to jump from her carriage which was overturning, when the shaft horses were frightened and plunging as the coach was driven down the course before racing in 1794. In 1825 'a boy who was driving a cart used the whip and handled the reins with so little judgment that the horse took fright, overturned the cart and broke from it. Two ladies and the driver escaped unhurt, but an elderly man was thrown out with such violence that it is feared he has suffered a concussion of the brain. We left him bleeding and insensible.' In the following year 'one equestrian, whose name we don't mention, but who was said to be "first thimble" at a very consequential establishment not far from Conduit Street, coming suddenly into contact with a pair of return post-horses, he was projected from the back of his own into the air, like a Congreve rocket or a meteor.'

Twice the royal carriages returning to Windsor after racing, were involved in fatal accidents: in one case a postillion was unseated and the carriage ran over and killed him; in the other one of the Household in attendance knocked over and killed a pedestrian. Ascot in fact had fewer accidents than other racecourses at the time, 'a circumstance principally to be attributed to the scarcity of horsemen. There being no view of the races from on horseback, this course has no attraction for equestrians.'

As the weary traveller at last came into sight of Ascot, the racecourse resembled a vast encampment. On the outside of the course, from distance to winning-post, rose a serried row of temporary stands. Biggest was the betting stand erected by a Mr Slingsby, a Windsor builder, while towards the winning-post rose the Royal Stand, and the stands of the Jockey Club and the Master of the Buckhounds. Below the betting stand there was a diminishing line of minor stands.

All along the rails on the inside of the track, sometimes for nearly a mile, were ranged lines of carriages, with space in front of them to accommodate, during the races, the spectators who had been temporarily driven from the track, which was used as a promenade between races. In bumper years, when the weather was fine, the carriages were in some places ten and on an average five deep for nearly a mile. On the other hand, on a really bad day, such as a rain-soaked Friday, there might only be eighteen carriages on the ground. Only those in carriages in the front couple of rows had much hope of seeing the racing. 'Those in the back rows of the carriages have as much chance of seeing the race as if they had been in Oxford.'

In the centre and along the edges of the course was a vast concourse of tents and booths. There were vendors of every kind of refreshment, especially spruce beer. In 1826 there were even purveyors of that new luxury-food, ice cream. 'However difficult any commodity is of production, it would seem that a demand is all that is necessary in this country — there was absolutely "ice-cream" to be had on the course. The amount of "cream" (or ice) was perhaps not very considerable in their composition; but they were cooler than any other material at hand.'

There were entertainers in plenty, jugglers, ballad singers, glee-singers, 'A company of ladies, dancing on stilts eight feet high . . . not only made money, but saw the race admirable (over other people's heads).' There were show-booths, where for a penny a wide variety of freaks could be seen. 'There was one [caravan] just below the betting stand . . . which offered a "Sussex Giantess", a "Dwarf from the Low Countries", a "Bohemian" who balanced coach-wheels on his chin; and a "Black sleight-of-hand player, equal to the celebrated Ramo Sameej", all besides several dogs, and a lady who "took money" dwelling in a covered cart not twelve feet square.'

'Upon the whole, the people least exalted in rank seemed ... to be the most perfectly delighted and free from care' (1826).

A less innocent form of pleasure was offered by the profusion of gaming-tents. E O was the backbone of Ascot gambling. This was an early form of roulette (which came in as early as 1794) with forty-two compartments on the wheel, twenty marked E and twenty O, with two bar-holes for the benefit of the operator. James Rice in his *History of the British Turf*, after saying how often the E O tables were rigged, commented: 'The booths on Ascot Heath and the taverns of Windsor were at race-time great haunts for the keepers of the E O tables, some of whom were respectable men in their calling, and might be trusted to give twenty, or even more, shillings for a guinea; but the majority, gambling for two-penny-pieces and sixpences, were little if anything better than the thimble-rig and prick-the-garter gentry.'

The E O tables were licensed, and the money went to the racefund. In 1796 it cost twelve guineas to have an E O table, with the gold table let out at forty guineas. In bad weather, especially, the gaming tents were well patronised. 'The deluge out of doors caused an overflow in some of the "hells", where many flocked for warmth and shelter, purchasing the blessing of dry garments at the expense of light pockets.' They were the source of much trouble throughout the years. For example, in 1799 a gentleman's servant was fleeced, denounced the gaming table proprietor, bystanders joined in and fighting became widespread; and in 1844 it was complained, 'There was ... no paucity of the *sable-skinned fraternity*. Immediately about the stand there is the usual number of *rouge et noir, une, deux, cinque, E O,* and other *attractive* sports at which the uninitiated are permitted to lose their time and their money for the profit of a few of the low *blacks*, who have journeyed from their dens about St James's to make their annual harvest.'

Thimble-rig men were particularly numerous on the Heath, working in the open on a table formed from a board propped up on bricks. 'Nimrod' described the operation from the mug's angle.

Can that simple-looking country bumpkin, in a smock frock, find out the pea, and neither you nor I be able to do the same? Why, he has won seven guineas already from the rascals, and how I should like to break them, for they look very much like thieves.

'There will be no difficulty in it,' observed the other; 'I can see the pea every time, and I am quite sure I can always tell the thimble it is under. We will risk five guineas apiece ...'

There was much theft also. In addition to money and watches, on one hot day in 1817 a gang of thieves made off with over seventy great-coats, stolen from different carriages and stands. 'One fellow, who was driving a cart with two sacks, was stopped at the turnpike gate, and the sacks were found to be full of box-coats, some worth as much as £9.' But the prize for audacity must surely go to the man who had been given two of the Duke of York's horses to hold, and who simply rode away with them and was never seen again.

The constables of Bow Street were on the ground, together with 'a strong force of mounted and dismounted patrol' and the local constabulary, who received nothing but criticism from the press and public. Even the Bow Street patrol was far from universally praised, and a typical comment was that of a *Times* reporter in 1826 who, after faithfully listing by name the considerable number of senior officers on duty, continued 'which does make it a little extraordinary that gangs of thieves — whose persons are known to every officer — should be allowed to show themselves with very little reserve as to their calling — upon the ground. We overheard (personally) a most instructive dialogue carried on, at the door of a booth, by a party of *seven* gentlemen to the effect that "seven were too many, properly to *work* together, but that, as they had come down in company, they would nevertheless make one party and divide".'

The royal party drove over from Windsor Castle for the Tuesday and Thursday races, arriving about one o'clock. It is always said that the royal drive, that unique feature of Royal Ascot, was initiated with the first state drive of George IV in 1825. Yet there were many earlier royal drives down the course, although they were not quite so formal in pattern. In 1797, for example, 'After the first heat, the Royal Family rode in procession up and down the course, His Majesty (George III) and his suite were on horseback, the Queen and the Princesses and female attendants were in sociables.'

When the King was safely ensconced in the Royal Stand a bell was rung, and the course, which was used as a promenade, was slowly cleared of the press of people. Originally Yeomen Prickers cleared the course, but they were succeeded by mounted patrols of police.

As a result of all the traffic upon it the state of the track would give any modern clerk of the course apoplexy. In dry weather the constant tramping of pedestrians removed almost every blade of grass from the hard-baked ground, while in wet weather the straight turned into a quagmire.

Nor did the runners always have the course to themselves. In 1823 the Duke of York, who had cut it a bit fine, arrived on the course literally during the running of the first race, which incidentally was the Duke of

York's Plate. 'The Duke of York, who is stopping at Frogmore, where His Royal Highness entertains a party during the races, did not arrive until after the horses had started in the first race: his Royal Highness then made his appearance galloping up the course, accompanied by some of his party, and followed by a brace of outriders, and had scarcely time to alight from his horse and ascend the Royal Stand, before the racers reached the winning-post.'

Once Sam Arnull, the great jockey who won the Derby four times and who also trained, galloped on his hack beside one of his racing fillies, turning off the course as the horses entered the straight. The filly then followed him out, and of course lost the race.

Spectators crowding back on to the track caused recurrent accidents. In the Oatlands in 1827 Barnard, riding an unnamed colt brother to Barefoot 'some distance behind all the other horses at the turn, was entirely forgotten by the mob, who, thinking all of them had passed, closed in and eventually blocked up the course, insomuch that Barnard on coming up with his horse, was knocked down'. Barnard was at first reported killed, but proved to be not too seriously injured. Two years later Dockeray, riding a filly Ada in the Royal Stakes, suddenly found a man on horseback in his path: 'he pulled out of the way, but the fellow at the same time backing his horse and Ada went right against him, falling down and rolling over Dockeray, who providentially missed the man by about six inches.'

Racing was interrupted by a one-hour luncheon interval, originally between the first and second races, which persisted until the 1930s. Magnificent picnics took place on or beside the carriages, with 'a boundless profusion of cold viands, with hock or champagne to keep up the ladies' delicate frames'. This contributed to the poor timekeeping, which was the greatest defect of the well-conducted Ascot races. The races were supposed to take place at half-hourly intervals, but the last race often lagged until half past six or seven p.m.

After racing came the slow dispersal, and partly owing to the high consumption of alcohol, accidents were more frequent after racing. *The Times'* sporting correspondent of 1826, a self-satisfied man, wrote: 'The dispersal of an immense heap of vehicles, mixed with persons on foot and on horseback, is an intricate affair, especially when some of the latter are of the unskilful. And happy is he at such a juncture—though seen in a rusty coat—who has ridden at Albuera or Waterloo! for a man should be able to manage a horse a little, and to fight upon occasion a little, to do the thing pleasantly in coming away from a race.'

A great revolution in the form of racing was taking place: races run in heats were being replaced by races run once only over shorter distances and at a much faster pace. The King's Plate continued: at Ascot the certificate which was awarded to the winning owner was not, as on other courses, signed by the Lord Lieutenant of the County, but by the Master of Buckhounds. A popular early race which was dropped in 1792 was the Bagshot Stakes, a two-mile race for maidens at starting 'rode by Members of the Bagshot Club' for a prize of £50. The Prince of Wales's Stakes was introduced in 1789 as a four-mile race for all ages, and after one or two runs in the nineties was dropped until 1806, when it reappeared with the same distance and conditions. The first race for two-years-old horses was run at Ascot in 1796. The Swinley Stakes was first run in 1806 as a twenty-five guinea sweepstake for three- and four-years-olds, run over the last mile and a half of the Swinley course, and was a regular race with the same conditions throughout the period.

Ascot's greatest race, the Ascot Gold Cup, was introduced in 1807. The first race was over two miles, increased to the present distance of two and a half miles in the following year. The race created interest second only to that generated by the Oatlands. The Queen and the Princesses watched the race from a special pavilion erected at the turn of the course, and another special box was built opposite the judge's box for the Prince of Wales. The Queen and the Princesses were wearing 'mantles in the Spanish-style with gypsy hats' — the Queen was all in white. They were received on the course by the Prince of Wales, dressed in 'bottle-blue', and his younger brothers the Duke of York, the Duke of Kent and the Duke of Cumberland, all wearing the Windsor uniform. The Gold Cup was won for Mr Durand by Master Jackey, by Johnny out of Seedling, a three-years-old carrying six stone twelve pounds. Details of the history of the Gold Cup may be found in the appendices.

The Duke of York's Stakes was introduced in the following year, a £50 Plate for all ages 'once round and in', which continued with one or two short breaks, until the Duke's death in 1825. The Albany Stakes which carried his second title, which he gave to his still-famous residence in Piccadilly, was a popular Ascot race for three-years-old fillies, originally run over the Old but later over the New Mile, until it was discontinued in 1830.

A race of remarkable longevity and consistency was introduced in 1813, the Wokingham Handicap, now the Wokingham Stakes. It is generally called Ascot's first handicap, although horses were handicapped in some earlier races. It has always been run over the last six furlongs of the straight mile. The Wokingham was popular from the outset, and in early years was always run in two divisions. The first running was won by the Duke of York's Pointers, after a start at a walk, a somewhat surprising feature of a sprint!

The best-known jockeys of the period were Sam Chifney senior and John Arnull, who both rode for the Prince of Wales, Tom Goodison, also from Newmarket, and Billy Pierce, the famous Yorkshire jockey, who rode for Lord Darlington, afterwards the Duke of Cleveland. A jockey of great promise was Dennis Fitzpatrick, who had been brought over from Ireland by Lord Clermont, but who died from a chill caught when he was weak from wasting.

Among owners prominent at Ascot during the Regency period were the Duke of York, Lord Grosvenor, Lord Egremont, the dissolute Lord Barrymore, Charles Fox the politician and Charles Greville. Mr J. Clark was a lucky winning owner, especially with his grey horse Merry Andrew. Sir John Lade, coaching friend of the Prince of Wales, often appears among the winning owners, but the horses were probably owned by the Prince. Captain Durand was a prolific winner of the races for amateur riders which were featured, particularly at any secondary meeting held at Ascot from time to time.

Charles Fox, politician and inveterate gambler, was a remarkable man. He was born in 1749, the younger son of Henry Fox, the first Lord Holland. He had great black eyebrows and 'big, wicked, good-natured eyes', and held tremendous charm both for men and for women. He was a reformer who thought the American colonies should be allowed to secede, he wanted the slaves to be liberated and Roman Catholics to be allowed to worship freely. He was also a revolutionary, the only Whig in Parliament actively supporting the French Revolution, at the very time that Vermin, owned jointly by him and Lord Foley, started favourite in the Oatlands Stakes. Yet he remained 'the best loved Englishman of his day', 'Charles to all the world'. He had many women friends, but his boast was 'I never broke up a home or ruined a woman'.

Before the Oatlands, Charles Fox had thirty horses in training. Prince was his training groom, and Sam Chifney senior or South generally rode for him. Vermin, who had won a 500-guinea match at Ascot in the previous year, started favourite for the Oatlands Stakes and Fox, who bet like a madman, had gambled heavily on him, but he was a good loser then as always.

No one could say that Charles Fox took his racing phlegmatically.

When his horse ran he was all eagerness and anxiety. He placed himself where the animal was to make a push, or where the race was to be most strongly contested. From this spot he eyed the horses advancing with the

most immovable looks; he breathed quicker as they accelerated their pace;
and when they came opposite to him he rode in with them at full speed,
whipping, spurring, and blowing, as if he would have infused his whole
soul into his favourite racer ... But when the race was over, whether he
won or lost seemed to be a matter of perfect indifference to him, and he
immediately directed his conversation to the next race, whether he had a
horse to run or not.

Charles Fox had one of the earliest plans to correlate form. In those days,
when travel was difficult and records scanty, little was known about the
form of horses in other parts of the country. Fox planned out 'a kind of
itinerant trade which was going from horserace to horserace, and so by
knowing the value and speed of all the horses in England to acquire a
certain fortune'. The ebullient Fox continued racing, gambling and
burning the candle at both ends until his death in 1806. Robert Burns the
poet, who greatly admired him, wrote of Fox:

> Thou first of our orators, first of our wits,
> Yet whose parts and acquirements seem mere lucky hits,
> With knowledge so vast and with judgment so strong
> No man with the half of them e'er went far wrong,
> With passions so potent and fancies so bright
> No man with the half of 'em e'er went quite right.

But there was little that was endearing about the faults of some contemporaries on the turf. A very different owner, and one extremely
successful at Ascot, was the seventh Earl of Barrymore, nicknamed in no
kindly spirit 'Hellgate'. He had equally unpopular brothers nicknamed
'Cripplegate' and 'Newgate', a clergyman called after the notorious prison.
His sister, Lady Melford, was, on account of her lurid language, called
'Billingsgate' by the Prince of Wales, in a rare stroke of wit. 'Hellgate'
was said to be the best of an unsavoury bunch. In his younger days he was
a good amateur rider, and in 1789 won a ten-guinea sweep in a two-mile
race 'rode by gentlemen' on his grey horse Magog. That same year, when
he was joint leading owner at Ascot with the Prince of Wales, *The Times*
commented slily: 'Lord BARRYMORE, with the true spirit of turf *mania*,
comes express from Paris to be present at Ascot Races. His Lordship
could even leave Gallic Beauty for equestrian delight.'

He was the centre of much gossip at Ascot in 1792, in an age when
having a mistress was far less reprehensible than making a mesalliance.
The newspapers reported: 'It is generally believed that the Earl of Barry-

more was last week married in Scotland to a Miss Golding, a niece of LADY LADE's!!!'

The Lades were among the least respected of all the dubious friends the Prince of Wales gathered round them. Sir John Lade was the posthumous son of a baronet. Of portly figure, and admiringly nicknamed 'Sir John Jehu' he was a magnificent whip who won a bet that he could drive both off-wheels of his coach over a sixpenny bit, but his wife Letty was truly notorious—although she too was a very fair whip and a magnificent horsewoman. Born in the slums of St Giles, she had been the mistress of a highwayman 'Sixteen-stringed Jack', who had been hanged at Tyburn, but only after he had taught her language of unparalleled foulness, even for an unfastidious period.

On the Thursday of the Ascot meeting

Lord and Lady BARRYMORE, accompanied by Lady LADE, appeared on the raceground in Sir John's pheaton [sic] and four. Everyone stared at this newly-created Peeress, and well might they talk of Lord BARRYMORE's romantic expedition to the Gretna Green blacksmith and his love epistles to his new inamorata who is the daughter of one of those HUMAN BURTHEN CARRIERS well known under the Piazza of Covent Garden by the just appel-lation of *Christian Ponies*, we may justly say, with one alteration:
'Speed the soft intercourse from soul to soul
And waft a sigh from PEERAGE to the POLE.'

Another sally read: 'Lord BARRYMORE took care not to be much encum-bered in his late trip to *Gretna Green*, for he took with him only "a *very* little baggage".'

Sir John Lade was a terrible gambler, and later ran through his entire fortune. The Prince of Wales then took him into his service, some say as his coachman, but it would be fairer to say as his adviser on coaches and carriage horses. Sir John was said to be particularly astute in picking the black-pointed bay carriage horses preferred by royalty. The carriage horses, selected by Sir John Lade, were more generally admired than the Prince's racehorses. In *Royal Ascot* there is a quotation from a contem-porary account: 'The different sets of coach horses were an honour to the country that bred them, and the uniform cleanliness of the servants and their appointments did infinite credit to the person who was at the head of the establishment.' Great changes of design in the liveries, such as 'new suits of liveries in a different style of embroidery have been made up (for the Prince Regent), and the edges of the hats bound with an em-broidery to correspond with the cloaths.' Incidentally he was the first man to wear trousers in public.

Although scandals proliferated it was still possible to shock in Regency times. Society was shocked when the Duke of Grafton brought his mistress to Ascot. This was not because she was his mistress, which was a commonplace, but because he was said to have picked her up off the streets. And Queen Charlotte refused to meet Lady Hamilton when she married Sir William Hamilton after being under the protection of several well-known men, including the father of Charles Greville, the diarist. Her subsequent liaison with Horatio Nelson has earned her an enduring place in folk lore.

'Old Q', 'The Rake of Piccadilly' as he was known, was probably the most notorious of all the Regency bucks. Born in 1724 he succeeded his father as Earl of March in 1731 and became Duke of Queensberry in 1779. Although Lord of the Bedchamber to George III for nearly thirty years, he was dismissed in 1789 for his support of the Prince of Wales, whom he had led into many escapades. The Duke of Queensberry did have runners at Ascot from time to time, and even an occasional winner, but he was better known as a racegoer in the Prince's entourage than as a winning owner at Ascot.

Lord Egremont, on the other hand, was a benevolent owner of an enormous and casually managed stud at Petworth in Sussex. He was a racehorse owner on the grandest scale. His stable produced no fewer than five Derby winners and five Oaks winners, some of whom may have been four-years-old. For all the casual lavishness with which his racing affairs were managed, Lord Egremont was a shrewd betting man, who was said to have doubled his very large income by his speculation on the turf. Lord Egremont won many races at Ascot. His Colonel won a 200-guinea match over the New Mile in 1789 and in 1794 he won two successive races, the King's Plate with Stag-Hunter by Trentham, following it up by the second year of a biennial stakes with his bay colt later named Ragged Jack, by Highflyer out of Camilla on the following day. His Olive won the King's Plate in 1798 on very heavy ground. Lord Egremont's fourth Derby winner Election, which remained in training till eight years old, won the Swinley Stakes for him at Ascot as a four-years-old.

Sir Richard Grosvenor, born in 1731 and created Earl Grosvenor in 1784, the head of an ancient Cheshire family and owner of one of the principal studs in England, was a sufferer from 'seconditis', owning the second in the Derby for four consecutive years before he sent out the winner in Rhadamanthus in 1790. At Ascot he was more fortunate with his racewinning, making rather a speciality of winning one-mile races with his three-years-old. Even at Ascot his bad luck did not entirely desert him. In 1792 the newspapers reported: 'At the Ascot Heath races on

Thursday Lord GROSVENOR lost his watch by one of the light-fingered gentry, who practised the mode of kicking his Lordship's shins, while he eased his pocket of his time-piece.'

The observant diarist Charles Greville, Clerk of the Privy Council, owner and bloodstock expert, graphically described the personalities of the period — though we could wish he had written more about racing and rather less about contemporary politics. As to the man himself, Charles Greville was described in his obituary in *Bailey's Magazine*: 'His is a nature that shrinks from having his good seeds brought before the glare of public eye. No man, ever so high or low ever sought his advice and assistance in vain; and to no one individual, probably, have so many and such various difficulties been submitted. Neither can we remember a new trial or even an appeal demanded by those who sought his counsel. Beloved by his friends and feared by his opponents, Mr Greville will ever be considered one of the most remarkable men that have lent lustre to the English turf.'

In 1813 Ascot Heath, which had been common ground, was specially assigned to the Crown in the Enclosure Act, with the important proviso that it 'should be kept and continued as a Race Course for the public use at all times as it has usually been'. The change was effected without public comment.

This was not the case, however with regard to the Prince Regent, who was engaged in building himself a residence in Windsor Great Park. During June 1813 questions had been asked in Parliament regarding rumours that the Prince Regent was indulging his passion for building grandiose establishments. He had decided to have his own residence in the grounds of the Great Park, and had chosen the modest Ranger's Lodge for the site of his operations. Up till now he had stayed, when at Windsor, either in his own suite of rooms in the Castle, where his sick father the King was incarcerated, or at Bagshot or at Frogmore House. What the Prince Regent's plans were, in reality, is not known but it is a fact that the saloon of his new residence is on a very grand scale indeed.

Then questions were asked in the House. Mr Whitbread, a Member who was often on his feet, spoke of the inhabitants of Windsor being alarmed by a report 'that the timber that decorated these fine grounds was to be cut down and a palace built with the proceeds of the sale'. It was said that the doomed trees had already been marked out with paint.

Mr Wharton, for the Government, replied soothingly that it was true that many trees had been cut down in Windsor Great Park — these had been stolen for firewood. 'The depredations of this kind lately committed were really daring.' The trees in question had been marked so that their value could be ascertained. The residence the Prince Regent had in mind was *not* a palace—certainly not—it was merely a lodge.

Thereafter the reconstruction of the Ranger's Lodge—now known as the Royal Lodge and the present Windsor home of Queen Elizabeth the Queen Mother—proceeded in a more modest manner, but the difference in scale between the Regent's Saloon and the other rooms at the Royal Lodge is quite noticeable.

The Ascot Meeting took on the appearance of an international occasion for the first time in 1814, when it appeared as if the Napoleonic Wars were over. Napoleon had abdicated on April 11th, 1814, and been exiled to Elba. Who was to know that he would return in March 1815 at the head of an army and that the 'demn'd close-run battle' of Waterloo was to come?

Europe had been dominated by the fear of Napoleon for seventeen years. No wonder this meeting in England of the Allies who had defeated the 'invincible' Napoleon and forced him into exile only two months earlier should be greeted with almost hysterical jubilation. The Allied guests were Alexander I, Emperor of Russia, and the King of Prussia. Alexander I, who had succeeded to the throne on the murder of his father Paul I in 1801, believed in the divine right of kings, but was nevertheless a monarch of remarkably liberal views for a czar. He had prevented the dismemberment of Prussia, and in 1813 had taken a leading part in the uprising of Europe which had resulted in the fall of Napoleon. He was always friendlily disposed towards Britain.

There is a long account of the visit in *The Chronicle and Whitehall Evening Post* of June 11th–14th, 1814. The royal visitors left London very early, breaking their journey at the Star and Garter Tavern on Richmond Hill, where they arrived at nine a.m. 'The party consisted of the Emperor of Russia, his sister, the Duchess of Oldenburg, and several foreign ladies, the King of Prussia, the Prince Royal and other Prussian Princes, Marshal Blucher, General Platoff and many distinguished foreigners. Lord Yarmouth, Lord Cathcart and Lord Charles Bentinck filled a cortège of eight or nine open carriages, attended by the Prince Regent's servants in dress liveries.'

After a rest of an hour and a half and admiring the view ('The Emperor of Russia . . . observed to some of his illustrious companions, that it was the most beautiful situation he had ever seen'), they set off again for Ascot.

Alas, the Prince Regent's servants might have been wearing their dress livery, but they had failed to check their route. The parties separated, the Emperor being driven by way of Kingston and the King of Prussia over Richmond Bridge and through Twickenham and Bushy Park. *The Times* reporter remarked . . . 'the neighbourhood being unappraised of their coming, they were relieved, if one may say so, for one forenoon from the tumultuous, though grateful, expression of public feeling.' Security appears, to say the least, to have been somewhat slack.

The Prince Regent was, meanwhile, proceeding independently in his travelling carriage to Ascot, accompanied by the Prince of Mecklenberg and his suite, but he did not arrive on the course until after his distinguished guests. An account quoted by Cawthorne and Herod in *Royal Ascot* describes the scene:

A thunder of British cheering announced the Arrival of the Emperor of all the Russias; he was soon followed by Her Majesty Queen Charlotte, and another burst of applause welcomed the King of Prussia. The cheering was renewed when the Prince Regent next arrived with his brother the Duke of York. The Royal Box was by this time full, and after the crowd had almost cheered itself hoarse, a universal call from the multitude was given for 'Blucher! Blucher! Platoff! Platoff!'

All thought of racing was banished, and the crowd was determined to give the heroes of the hour a genuine ovation. When the Prince Regent, therefore, stepped forward and informed them neither of the famous generals had yet arrived, calls were given for Alexander, and the Pacificator of Europe came forward and bowed his thanks to the shouts of applause which greeted him.

. . . Ere this was over, an attempt was made to start the first race, but it was found impossible to clear the course. Then a carriage eased its way through the crowd, and the gallant Blucher came in for his share of congratulation. Cheer after cheer greeted the grand old veteran as he made his way to the Royal Box, and he who was so cool midst the cannons' roar was fairly overwhelmed with the intensity of British cheers. . . . Anon the Prince Regent informed the onlookers that General Platoff was approaching on horseback, and asking that way might be made for him. This was like a match to a powder magazine; there was a movement through the crowd, and as the brave Platoff made his way with difficulty towards his august host, the people thronged round him, shouting compliments and cheering, ladies and gentlemen seizing him by the hands in their eagerness. After the Prince had placed the two generals in the front of the box, and three last cheers had been given, racing commenced.

The Gold Cup had been moved from the Thursday to the Friday to give a good centrepiece to the day's racing, and provided a fine race, which was won by Pranks, a five-years-old bay mare by Hyperion out of Frisky, owned by Mr Batson.

After this heady stuff, the following year's Ascot races were held in a very different atmosphere. On March 1st, 1815, Napoleon had escaped from Elba. Ascot races were held from 6th to 9th June: the Battle of Waterloo was fought on June 18th. In London there was much public anxiety and even agitation—indeed the Prince Regent broke his visit to Ascot to return to London after the races on Tuesday. In his absence Queen Charlotte 'had a select party to dinner at Frogmore; the Duke and Duchess of Orleans were of the party'.

But racing went on as usual. The Duke of York remained at Ascot throughout the week, which was one of his luckiest. His five-years-old Aladdin, a chestnut horse by Giles out of a Walnut mare, who had run unplaced in the Derby of 1813, performed a remarkable feat. Aladdin won the Gold Cup over two and a half miles on the Thursday (in which he started at five to two on), and was pulled out on the following day to win the Wokingham Stakes over six furlongs. This was a very fine race. He gave thirty-seven pounds to General Gower's three-years-old filly by Rubens and beat her by a head. The Rubens filly was brought out again immediately, to run in and win the very next race, a £50 Plate. Those were certainly the days of tough horses.

The Duke of York had two other winners at the meeting. His chestnut colt Scrapall by Granicus, a five-years-old, won the Swinley Stakes, and his colt by Zodiak won a twenty-guinea sweepstake, both on the Wednesday, and both from horses owned by the Duke of Rutland.

When the Prince of Wales had been appointed Prince Regent for the second time in February 1811, it at first appeared that this might, like his first Regency, last only a matter of months. So, to begin with, the Prince was in a delicate position, and dared not do too much. But with King George III's continuing illness the Regent gradually felt more secure, and this growing confidence showed at Ascot, as elsewhere. The King's Stand at Ascot became known briefly as the Queen's Stand, and then as the Prince Regent's Stand, to which the Queen came only as a guest.

George III's life was now entering upon its last stage. The Prince Regent was established with his mistress at the Royal Lodge, which he had begun to use as his Ascot headquarters in 1816. On June 5th, 1816, which was George III's seventy-eighth birthday, 'the Royal Family kept the day with the mournful privacy best suited to the melancholy condition of the Monarch'. With the death of the Prince Regent's only child Charlotte in 1817, succession to the Throne was thrown wide open. An unseemly struggle began among the Princes to arm themselves with wives and to produce legitimate heirs.

It was a farcical situation, and one which lent itself to the pen of the

The Oatlands Stakes, run over two miles on June 28th, 1791, was Ascot's first great race, and attracted enormous crowds, who proved so difficult to control that the race was afterwards moved to Newmarket. The Ascot race was won by Baronet, ridden by Sam Chifney. Baronet was owned by the Prince of Wales (afterwards George IV) who won £17,000 in bets.

Engraving by James Pollard of an Ascot race in 1820.

The Royal Box, with George IV and the Duke of York. The pictures on these pages show the alterations to the Royal Box, and the progressive changes in the nearby stands.

Queen Victoria's procession passes the Royal Box: 1840.

Czar Nicholas I presented the Emperor's Plate, which was run in place of the Gold Cup, after his visit to Ascot in 1844. Here The Emperor, named in his honour, wins the Plate for the second year running, from Faugh a Ballagh and Alice Hawthorn.

A rare glimpse of the interior of the Royal Box: the Royal party, 1868.

Ascot Heath Races: by Paul and Thomas Sandby, from the Windsor Royal Collection, reproduced by gracious permission of Her Majesty Queen Elizabeth II. Thomas Sandby was Deputy Ranger of Windsor Great Park.

The change from rakish Regency to staid Victorianism was strongly marked at Ascot. The Prince of Wales (afterwards George IV) going to Ascot Races with 'a lady of quality'.

The infinitely more respectable 'Royal Cortège' arrives on the course in 1847.

An elegant racecourse picnic: Ascot, 1844.

Carriage horses assembled on the course, requiring rest and water: Ascot, 1846.

Valentine at Ascot.

Saddling and mounting on the course for the Gold Cup of 1839, won by Caravan.

satirist of which Peter Pinder's book of verse was a typical example. Entitled:

HUNTING FOR THE HEIR
THE R---L H-MB-GS
or
LUMPS OF LOVE

it contained such passages as:

> Yoics! The R---l Sport's begun
> I'faith but it is glorious fun
> For hot and hard each R---l pair
> Are at it hunting for the Heir. . . .
> Who gets the Heir—a Cr--n shall win
> The Com--ns are the whippers-in.

The reign of George III ended and the Prince Regent became the actual as well as the acting sovereign in a hectic atmosphere of royal re-alignment.

King George III died on January 29th, 1820.

The newspapers appeared black-edged, to announce 'his most gracious Majesty King George III expired on Saturday evening at 35 minutes past eight o'clock'. His death was greeted with a genuine sense of loss by his people, who had always hoped that he might be restored to health. 'He has never until this melancholy moment been lost irrevocably to the grateful love, the sympathies and the prayers of his people.'

CHAPTER THREE

In the reign of George IV

THE FIRST ROYAL ASCOT IN THE REIGN OF GEORGE IV OPENED ON TUESDAY May 31st, 1820. The new king was installed at his cottage in Windsor Great Park with his mistress, Lady Conyngham, and a houseful of guests. At the royal cottage time passed quietly and agreeably, and Greville noted in his diary: 'Lady Conyngham looked remarkably well in the morning, her complexion being so fine.

'The king was at Ascot every day: he generally rode on the course, and the ladies came in carriages. One day they all rode . . . on Friday she [Lady Conyngham] said she was bored with the races and should not go; he accordingly would not go either, and sent word to say he would not be there.'

Meanwhile King George IV's estranged wife, now in title at least Queen Caroline, continued her eccentric tour of the Continent. Although Queen Caroline was far more popular with the people than King George IV, he was always well received at Ascot. '[The King] was always cheered by the mob as he went away,' commented Greville. 'One day only a man in the crowd called out, "Where's the Queen?"'

On the Monday after the races George IV and Lady Conyngham returned to London. That same day Queen Caroline impulsively returned from the Continent to claim her place as Consort. There was always an element of tragi-comedy about everything undertaken by poor Queen Caroline: she arrived at Dover unexpectedly, and had to come ashore in an open boat. But a large, cheering crowd, who quickly assembled to greet her, took the horses out of her carriage and she was drawn in triumph to an hotel hastily prepared to receive her.

King George IV was furious at the Queen's return and at her reception. Immediately he had a Bill introduced into Parliament, seeking to dissolve his marriage on the grounds of the Queen's alleged adultery. In Parliament she was so eloquently defended by Lord Brougham that the Bill had to be dropped. George IV became so unpopular that it was imprudent for him to appear on the streets without a guard, and when he travelled to Ascot for the 1821 meeting he was escorted by a party of light horse.

Yet the king was as well received as usual at Ascot, and the races were as successful. *The Times* reported: 'ASCOT: Tuesday June 19th, 1821. The above great races commenced this day. His Majesty arrived at the Royal Stand one o'clock. The course was thronged by a display of rank, beauty and fashion.'

The coronation of King George IV took place in the following month. No provision had been made for the Queen to play any part in the ceremony, but on the day Queen Caroline insisted on driving to Westminster Abbey to demand admission, which was refused. Less than three weeks later, on August 7th, 1821, Queen Caroline died, quite unexpectedly.

Relieved of the embarrassment of his eccentric, unwanted and misused wife, King George IV began to set his mark as sovereign upon his reign and its pleasures. Ascot received the royal attention, and the man whose taste was so splendidly elegant and whose morals were so gross, brought to Ascot the atmosphere which sets it apart from all other racecourses.

First of all he had constructed for himself a new Royal Box, designed by no less an architect than John Nash, who was responsible for Buckingham Palace, Regent Street and the Nash Terraces of Regent's Park. In May 1822 *The Times* reported: 'The new Royal Stand erecting at Ascot Heath racecourse, under the direction of Mr Nash, is in a very forward state, and is expected to be complete by the time of the ensuing races.' The new box was duly occupied at the meeting and described as: 'immediately opposite the winning-post, a light tasteful building, with fluted pilasters of composition supporting the roof, in imitation of a Greek portico'. The Royal Stand had two storeys, of which the upper part only was used by the King, and was divided into two rooms 'plainly fitted out with white muslin curtains, etc'.

Round this Royal Stand a very small enclosure was made, guarded by police officers and gatemen and only those invited by George IV were admitted. This was the beginning of the Royal Enclosure.

On either side of the Royal Box there were eight or nine other stands, of varying sizes. In 1826 the Duke of York had his stand moved next to the King's Stand. In the same year the betting stand, the first permanent stand at Ascot, which had been built by George Slingsby, master brick-layer from Windsor in the early part of the nineteenth century, was repaired and extended to hold around 1,650 people. The Slingsby Stand was said to be demolished in 1830, but it was, in fact, spared and survived until 1859.

There had been doubts whether George IV would appear at Ascot in 1822. He was said to be suffering from 'a severe and dangerous attack of gout'. However on the opening day 'at about one o'clock a cheer announced the arrival of the King. His Majesty did not drive along the course in front, as was the late King's custom, but proceeded along the rear of the booths . . . For some time after his arrival, he appeared a good deal at the windows where he was silently stared at by the crowd collected before them. During the remainder of the day he was less frequently seen. His Majesty was clad in the Windsor uniform with a single star on his breast.'

The royal party included the Duke of York in green, the Duke of Rutland, the Duke of Wellington, the Marquess of Conyngham, the accommodating husband of Lady Conyngham, who was also in the party, and four or five other ladies. Prince and Princess Esterhazy were in the stand opposite the Royal Stand. The weather was incredibly warm early that week, 'the intense heat of the weather rendered the amusement extremely tedious. Its effects have been particularly distressing to the post horses, four or five of which dropped dead on both days.'

In spite of the heat, the Duke of York enjoyed his best-ever Royal Ascot in 1822, when his horses won him 'something handsome' in the way of bets. On the Tuesday the Duke of York named Trance against the Duke, named by the Duke of Grafton in an all ages sweep, the winner to receive 300 guineas. 'This was a very pretty race, well contested by the winner and the second horse; the former apparently owing his success to the advantage which the whip hand gave him over his antagonist, the rider of the latter being obliged to shift his whip to his left hand.'

On the Wednesday, which was equally hot, the Duke of York won his own £50 Selling Plate, run over two and a half miles with a three-years-old bay colt by Election out of a Sorcerer mare, from Mr Braithwaite's Cardenio with Mr Green's Trance third.

As they turned the corner in sight of the winning-post Trance and Cardenio pushed forward in front, and maintained a hard and doubtful struggle for the foremost place until they came within a couple of hundred yards of the judge. Here, however, Boyce, the lad who rode the Duke of York's colt, after apparently trying to get the whip side in vain, brought his whip to bear in his left hand in a way which proved that he was nearly as much *au fait* with that as with his better hand, and very unexpectedly (by the spectators) passed the others by and won the race cleverly.

The Duke of York followed this up with winning the Albany Stakes with a more distinguished inmate of his stables, his Derby winner Moses, home-bred by the Duke, a bay by Whalebone or Seymour. 'The betting was not very spirited, particularly in the Albany Stakes,' it was reported, 'for, in consequence of Moses having won the Derby Stakes, the sporting gentry were rather shy of offering the odds against him, nor did the result cast any discredit upon their judgment ... He beat his two antagonists without being whipped, not, however, with a tight rein. He really is a very fine looking horse, and has now a high character on the turf.' The Duke of York completed his success when Electress ridden by Buckle, won the Windsor Forest Stakes on Gold Cup day.

In 1823 racing took place 'under all the advantages to be derived from the most favourable weather. The rain which fell on the preceding afternoon rendered the roads pleasant for travelling by laying the dust; and the heat of the sun, whose fierce rays last year rendered the Heath almost intolerable, was now agreeably tempered by the fleeces of light vapour by which it was veiled for the greater part of the day.'

Again there was speculation as to whether the King would be well enough to attend. Again he drove up the rear of the stands, and appeared at the window of the Royal Box. 'He appeared somewhat, but not much, lame, and walked about the room with a stick with a crutch-head, which His Majesty only used with his hand, not the arm. In face he was a little thinner than last year and quite colourless.' On the Wednesday, 'after remaining for a very short time at the window, His Majesty retired, and seated himself upon a chair, in doing which he appeared to have difficulty in stooping; his lameness too was more apparent to those outside than on the former day.'

The Duke of York's luck was out in 1823, but he owned the first and second in the Wokingham Stakes in 1824 when he also won a 200-guinea sweepstakes for fillies over the New Mile with Dahlia, a name to reappear in Ascot's history. 'Three to one on Dahlia, who took the lead, and kept it with such ease, that Goodison several times turned round as if to deride the useless efforts of the other two to reach him.' The Duke of York's last win was in 1825, when he won the Albany Stakes with another of Phantom's offspring, a colt out of a Rubens mare, again ridden by Goodison who 'made a rush, got in front and won by two lengths. His Majesty was heard to compliment the Duke upon his success.' The Duke of York was well enough to attend Ascot in 1826, when he went over Windsor Castle with the faithful Greville, although he had been ill ever since the Duke of Rutland had taken him for a lengthy sojourn in the family vault in the previous November.

We went to Frogmore two days before the party began, [wrote Greville] and for those two days he lived a quiet life. When the party assembled he lived as he had been used to do, going to the races, sitting at table, and playing for hours at whist. He slept wretchedly . . . passed the greater part of the night walking about the room or dosing in his chair . . . He showed me his legs, which were always swelled. Still he went on till the last day of the party, when he took ill on his return to town. From that moment his illness was established which ended in his death.

The Duke of York died on January 4th, 1827.

By this time jockeys were being named, although it was many years before trainers were identified. From the close of the Regency until the death of George IV in 1830 the jockeys who won most frequently at Ascot were Chifney, Goodison, Arnold, Shrog, Barnett, Edwards (G., C., and E.), Day and Sayer, while in 1822 Buckle won race after race. Other successful Ascot jockeys included Robinson, Macdonald, Robert Boyce, Dockeray, Arnull, Arthur, Davis and S. Mann.

In Brown's *Turf Expositor*, published in 1829, a contemporary view of jockeys is neatly tabulated in the index under the succinct notation 'Jockeys . . . northern, southern and dirty'.

Jockeys I regard, in the aggregate, as honester men than Trainers, unless indeed the two professions are united; and when I behold a man thus circumstanced, I cannot help viewing him in the light of a Janus of Mischief, calculated to put to practice every species of trickery, on both sides of the question.

Jockeys may be divided into two, if not three, classes: namely the Southern Jockeys, the Northern Jockeys, and the *Dirty* Jockeys. The first class are those which are seen at Newmarket, Ascot, Epsom, and indeed most of the races in the Southern Counties, and also at Doncaster.

. . . The second class attend the Yorkshire Meetings, and what, for the sake of distinction, I will call the Northern Circuit.

. . . The third or *Dirty* class, are met with still farther to the north, in Westmorland, Cumberland etc and are remarkable for their slovenly, dirty, and unworkmanlike appearance.

. . . it is no uncommon occurrence to see these wretched apologies for Jockeys (at Kendall for instance) ride in dirty jackets, dark greasy corduroys, and gaiters of a similar complexion. Mr Thomas Simpson's Jockey frequently appears thus, though Mr Simpson is wealthy and highly respectable; but evidently not very scrupulous on the score of cleanliness.

The Southern Jockeys, much to their credit, appear on horseback with a neatness and cleanliness bordering upon elegance; their performance is, for the most part, of a superior order—superior, in fact, to their rivals of the North; they are illiterate ignorant men, with little exception; though, in private, they affect a mysterious, but plebeian, importance, and would willingly be thought a sort of semi-gentleman, which, however, their very attempt to assume such a character renders impossible. There is much less of this ridiculous and ignorant affectation in the Northern Jockeys, who yet seem, it must be confessed, not nearly so anxious about their appearance (as far as it relates to the advantages of dress;) as their brethren of the South.

Sam Chifney senior was the first jockey to earn renown at Ascot. A Norfolk man, about five foot five inches tall and well proportioned, muscular and strong, he was undoubtedly the greatest racerider of his day, and his comments are therefore valuable. He was a great believer in shifting his weight to ease his horse.

The first fine point in riding a race is to command your horse so that he runs light on his mouth: it keeps him better together, his legs are more under him, his sinews are less extended, he has less exertion, and his wind is less locked. The horse running thus to order, his parts are more at ease, and he can run considerably faster when called upon, than one who has been running in fretting, sprawling attitudes, with part of the rider's weight on his mouth.

As he comes to the last extremity, the finish of the race, he is better forced, and kept straight with manner, on a fine touch to his mouth. In this situation his mouth should be eased of the rein; if not, it stops him a little or much. The phrase at Newmarket is that you should pull your horse to ease him, but when he is in his greatest distress in running, he cannot bear that *visible* manner of pulling. He should be enticed to ease himself an inch at a time, as his situation will allow: this should be done as if you had a silken rein as fine as a hair, and that you are afraid of breaking it.

Sam Chifney had a long-standing feud with Tom Goodison and said Goodison was 'the original cause of the Duke of Bedford and the Prince of Wales having been thus troubled and disturbed concerning me in my riding'. Goodison was a Yorkshireman, blunt and outspoken, a good sound rider and a powerful enemy. Born in 1782, he was the son of the jockey, Dick Goodison, known as 'Hell-fire Dick'. Tom, who was the favourite match rider of the Duke of Queensberry, often rode for the Duke of York, as we have seen, and four times rode the winner of the Derby. He died in 1840.

Frank Buckle, born in 1766, the son of a Newmarket saddler, was one of the greatest jockeys of his or any time. He weighed only four stone when he first rode in public at the age of seventeen, and fifty years later could ride at eight stone seven without wasting. It was said 'there is nothing big about Frank Buckle except his heart and his nose'. His integrity, as well as his late rush at the finish, were famous.

> A Buckle large was formerly the rage
> A Buckle small now fills the sporting page.

Buckle's best year at Ascot was 1822, when he won the Swinley Stakes and the Ascot Gold Cup on Mr Ramsbottom's Sir Huldibrand, the Windsor Forest Stakes on the Duke of York's Electress, and a 100-guinea sweep on a colt belonging to Lord Lowther. When Brown summed up his jockeys in 1829 he declared, 'Buckle is now grown old, and does not often appear otherwise, I place him at the head of the list'. He died, greatly lamented, in 1832. Although Frank Buckle's three sons went into professions and did not ride, 'a kinsman, young Buckle' won the Swinley Stakes on General Grosvenor's filly Tears in 1826 and—no longer distinguished as 'young'—won his last race at Ascot in 1841.

'Young' Sam Chifney was however the son of Sam Chifney senior. He was suspected of pulling horses, and he was certainly very lazy. '. . . When he had made an engagement to ride in Yorkshire, the carriage often waited for him in vain at the cross roads, for he was rarely on the coach when he was wanted.' As a little boy, when his father was in favour, the Prince Regent made a fuss of him, sitting him on his knee and giving him a guinea. Sam Chifney used to stay for weeks with the Duke of Cleveland at Raby Castle. '. . . They dined together alone nearly every night, after a day with the Raby Hounds, at which the Duke easily outstripped the jockey, for he was always timid across country.' Thanks to his nephew Frank Butler Sam Chifney junior did not die, like his father, in a debtors' prison, but lived out his last years on a pension in Brighton. His Ascot successes included the Gold Cup on Lord Darlington's Memnon in 1827. 'Very pretty running to the Windsor turn, about half the ground,' noted *The Times* (who proudly copied the result 'from the judge's book'). 'Mortgage (Robinson, named by Mr Delmé Redcliffe) came to the front until the home turn, where four horses were abreast. Opposite the betting stand Memnon and Mortgage let loose . . . and made a severe race till about fifty yards from home, when the crack Yorkshire horse came out and beat Newmarket in handsome style, by two lengths.'

Jem Robinson, like the Chifneys, liked to win with a short late burst, but his intentions were not so cleverly masked. Like them, an excellent judge of pace, undoubtedly Jem Robinson was more honest and more dependable than either Chifney. Jem Robinson, who rode the winner of the Derby on six occasions, rode many famous races at Ascot. In 1824 in the Windsor Forest Stakes, he rode Katharine, owned by the Duke of Rutland. 'Four horses started, but two only, namely Katharine and Hurly Burly were placed, and between these two a beautiful race took place. During the whole of the run the horses were nearly neck and neck; as they approached the winning-post Hurly Burly was a little ahead, but Katharine suddenly sprang forward and won by a neck only.'

The Gold Cup of 1825 was long remembered by all who saw it, although in this race Jem Robinson on Mr F. Craven's Longwaist finished second to Bizarre, ridden by Arnull. Six horses started, and Frank Boyce on Mr Cooper's Streatham occupied third place.

> This was one of the finest races ever seen at Ascot, nor do we recollect ever having beheld better jockeyship by all three riders. Longwaist, ridden by Robinson, made the first running at a brisk rate to the dog kennels, where Streatham, rode by Frank Boyce, came in front, and made the most severe running down the hill until the turn of the course, where Bizarre, rode by Arnull, came up, hard pushed by Longwaist, a tremendous, slashing struggle ensued between these famous horses which ended in favour of Bizarre, who won by a head.

Jem Robinson got something of a revenge by winning a race for two-years-old on the same afternoon, and the Wokingham on the following day.

Jem Robinson was said to be severe on his horses, and there is corroboration of this in the Ascot reports. In the Gold Cup of 1831 he won on Sir M. Wood's Cetus with a late run 'after a severe, punishing race'. (There was an early complaint from the owner that, as the cup was worth only £100, but he had to pay £40 to enter his two horses, he cleared a mere £60 for his win.) Robinson again won the Gold Cup on Camarine in 1832, in a most peculiar race. 'The horses went off at a walk for over a hundred yards, then Rowton (owned and ridden by Sam Chifney junior) broke into a slow canter, but there was no speed until the straight, when the mare ran or was forced out, and then straightened out to a terrible finish, both horses being severely punished, and both crossed the line together.' An objection was overruled and the race was re-run. Rowton was allowed to lead until close to the finish when Camarine 'crept up very cleverly and won by two lengths'.

George Dockeray was not a fashionable jockey but he was undoubtedly effective at Ascot where he won many races in the short period between his first Ascot winner in the Oatlands in 1825 and his last double in the Swinley Stakes and the Albany Stakes in 1830, after which he retired from the saddle because of his increasing weight problem. His biggest Ascot win was the Gold Cup on Chateau Margaux in 1826.

5

Then there was the Edwards family. The father was 'Tiny' Edwards, and he had many sons, of whom at least three made their name as jockeys. Brown wrote of the best known, the one-eyed Harry Edwards: 'He has a good seat, good hands and a good head, and is altogether an excellent rider.' It is doubtful if critics today would be as kind. Harry Edwards used to sit so far back in the saddle, with his legs so far forward, that he used to spur his horses *in front of* the girths! Unfortunately Harry 'would rather nobble for a pony than win a hundred by fair means'. His brother William rode first as a tiny featherweight, and ended as George IV's last trainer, with a lease of the Palace Stables at Newmarket (which are currently occupied by Bruce Hobbs). The third brother, noted for his courage, was George, who rode the winner of the New Mile at Ascot in 1827 and of the Swinley Stakes in 1829.

Amateur riders had their own races which were popular with the participants. In an atmosphere hectically linked with gambling the amateur events were not welcomed by regular racegoers. The undoubted stars of the amateurs were headed by the notorious Lord Barrymore at the end of the eighteenth century; Captain Durand in the early days of the nineteenth century; and in the 1820s Captain Bouverie, who in 1826 won three races at Ascot, one of them in 'a donkey canter'. These were good riders, but the general standard among amateur riders was less impressive. When in that year Captain Bouverie, riding Mr Kenyon's Habberley, won a race for a gold cup 'for horses not thoroughbred, *bona fide* the property of and rode by officers of the Household Brigade', *The Times* had some acid comments. 'After a tremendous time had been occupied in harnessing, the gentlemen jockeys started, and came in the style used in these fancy races, keeping a most respectable distance from each other, Habberley beating Squirrel by four or five lengths, the others fifty lengths behind, the fourth half a distance, and the last only about a head short of the distance post. ... We believe that the riders were more amused by the race than the spectators.'

Even Mr Hayne, rejoicing in the victory of his Rembrandt, on which he won an Ascot amateurs race on Friday June 29th, 1829, can hardly have been heartened to read in *The Times* on the following morning: 'The folly of gentlemen riding their own horses when opposed to jockies was evident ... Rembrandt was the best horse, brought to the course in beautiful condition by Coleman [but] when the struggle took place at the end, the gentleman jockey was rolling about like a ship in a storm, every body looking for both horse and rider to go down, nothing saved them but luck.'

The trainer remained a shadowy background figure for many years after jockeys were receiving the full flood of publicity. Their status was low, their names seldom given. Samuel Chifney senior names a few trainers who were his seniors or contemporaries, mostly with his usual contempt for all mankind. He called his mentor Fox, for whom he worked from 1771, 'the best training groom then on the turf', spoke with contempt of Warwick Lake, Neale and Casborne who managed the Prince of Wales' horses at the time of the Oatlands—he accused Casborne of administering 'poison balls' to the Prince's horses, including Escape. He also alleged that Frank More, who was training groom to Lord Sackville in the late eighteenth century broke into a stable to poison a horse, and that he was involved in *pigeoning* (rigging lottery tickets), at the time of the drawing of the Irish lottery. Chifney confirms that it was the training groom's duty to feed and work the horses, and to report on their condition and changes in running to his master.

In Brown's *Turf Expositor*, published in 1829, we get some insight into the change in the status of the trainer in the four decades following the Oatlands Stakes. The early term of training groom was dropping out of use, and the trainer, although far from reaching his present status, was emerging from obscurity. Brown did not have much use for the average trainer, and indulged in heavy sarcasm at his expense.

A modern trainer is a personage of the most mysterious and the utmost importance. His appearance is vulgar; but he makes up for this vulgarity in affecting a sort of semi-solemnity of aspect ... reverable, not to the *sublime*, but to the *arch* and the ridiculous; while, with slight, but significant, nods, ornamented by sententious oracles, he endeavours to impress on the minds of others his uncommon weight in the scale of creation, and the dignity with which he moves through infinite space!

... Trainers, generally speaking, are men with scarcely pretensions to a common village education; but from frequent contact with men of wealth and distinction, by whom, of course, they are principally employed and occasionally consulted, they conceive themselves beings of a very superior order, whose avocations they endeavour to convert into a profound and secret science.

... They are superlatively ignorant for the most part; but, skilled in cunning and trick, they are very rarely over-reached in driving a bargain.

I have conversed, or at least endeavoured to converse, with many trainers, and have found them ... men of low, vulgar minds, and many of them destitute of what is understood by the term *common sense*.

[The remarks are not intended] to include a class of men, who are what I call the domestic servants of those who keep racehorses and who attend to the stud, at least while they continue in the employment of men of character and distinction.

Certain trainers were excepted from Brown's strictures. 'Peirce of Richmond in Yorkshire . . . possesses not only much sound sterling sense but is capable of expressing his ideas in correct and expressive language. H (Harry) Edwards has lately commenced trainer: he is a man of good sense; he attended the Veterinary College in London, for some time; and I have frequently been pleased with his judicious observations . . . the highly respectable Mr Scholes, who superintends an extensive training establishment I do not include in the list of trainers . . . Scaife, trainer to the Duke of Leeds, is entitled to respectable notice, and the same remark will apply to John Smith, of Middleham . . . the King's Horses, I have no doubt, are very honestly trained, but either from error in system, or some other cause, they seldom answer expectation.'

As his reign progressed, King George IV's addiction to racing rivalled his youthful enthusiasm for the sport. He attended Ascot in considerable pomp. It is generally agreed that 1825 was the year in which the first Royal Procession took place down the course. It was indeed the first year that King George IV drove in semi-state down the course, but it had been the custom of George III and Queen Charlotte always to proceed to the Royal Stand along the course, followed by their numerous daughters and the ladies-in-waiting in carriages, and accompanied by their suite on horseback.

On the Tuesday of the 1825 meeting the King arrived precisely at one p.m. in a dark green travelling coach with four beautiful bay horses, attended by the Duke of Dorset, Master of the Horse, Lord Craven, the Lord-in-Waiting, and Lord Conyngham. But it was on the Wednesday that he made the first formal appearance of his reign at Ascot.

This day His Majesty came to the course, attended by Lord Maryborough (who was dressed in green, with the couples, as Master of the Staghounds) and a more numerous trail of outriders than we ever recall observing: in fact the whole of His Majesty's stud, by his express command, accompanied him. The Duke of Wellington sat on the right of His Majesty, and the Lords-in-Waiting opposite . . . His Majesty came on the course at the Straight Mile, thus giving a full view of his person and procession to all present. At three o'clock, precisely the races terminated, in ten minutes after which His Majesty, attended as before, left the course amidst the enthusiastic cheers of the spectators.

George IV swiftly acquired a large stable, containing many useless animals, as he was said to be a push-over for any horse offered to him, which he would 'buy' instantly. It was however considerably more difficult for the seller to get his money. Among the rubbish he almost inevitably did buy or breed some good animals.

Perhaps the King's favourite racehorse was his home-bred chestnut mare Maria, foaled in 1824, a daughter of Waterloo, a sire he favoured. In *Famous Horses* Maria is described as a beautiful little creature 'and her style of running quite captivating ... it was a saying of trainers that it would take twice round the Ascot Cup Course, at the very best pace, before Maria would blow out a rush light'.

Maria's first Ascot wins were as a three-years-old. *The Times* reports of her win in the Swinley Stakes, in which she ran in the name of Delmè Radcliffe; 'Maria was first by a length, amidst the acclamations of the populace. His Majesty, on being congratulated by the nobility in attendance on the success of the filly (Maria being of the royal stud), expressed himself highly gratified, as well with the result of the race as with the admirable jockeyship of that promising young jockey Arthur Pairs, who rode her.' On the following day, Thursday, Maria was started in the Windsor Forest Stakes at the forbidding price of five to one on, and was ridden by Robinson. The result was not as foregone as the odds suggested, and she only just won from Lord Mountcharles's bay filly by Tramp out of a Woful mare, ridden by Arnull. '... The loser, though a very promising filly, had never run before, which accounts for the odds being so high. They came off together, and kept so to the straight ground, when a beautiful neck-and-neck race commenced, and was kept up with extraordinary severity till a few yards from the judge's chair, when the King's filly shot ahead and won the stakes by three-quarters of a length with great difficulty.' In 1828 as a four-years-old Maria won the Oatlands Stakes. That year she also ran in a match at Egham, of which an account is given in *Famous Horses* (although the author was mistaken in saying that this was the last racemeeting attended by George IV).

[The King] came on the course in an open barouche with four splendid bays, and attended by Lord Albermarle, the Master of the Horse. Rising in his carriage, His Majesty turned towards the Ring: and, in loud tones, offered to lay £6000 to £4000 on Maria ... Robinson not seeing Lye on Tom Thumb, on making the last turn, the latter rushed past him like a whirlwind, Robinson being so amazed that he pulled Maria short up for a moment, and only won on the post by a short head by dint of the most resolute riding. The King was furious.

Later in the same afternoon Maria was started again in the King's Plate over three miles, in which she was again ridden by Robinson. 'Owing to a rope, which had been stretched across the course to keep off the spectators, not being taken down, the running horses ran into it. The King's favourite mare was thrown against the post, and her rider severely bruised. Mr Mabberley's bay horse Monarch was also forced off the course, but his rider managed to bring him back, and he completed the course and won the race.'

A contemporary alluded to the incident as a 'catastrophe' and continued '. . . the recent catastrophe had a palpable effect upon the manners of all parties . . . there was none of that hilarity usually displayed on occasions of this sort'. Fortunately, by the end of the week, *The Times* was able to report 'we are happy to state that Robinson the jockey is in a fair way of recovering from his late accident'.

In 1829 Maria returned as a five-years-old to Ascot, to run in a match against Lord Sefton's Souvenir, also a five-years-old mare, ridden by H. Edwards. In spite of George IV's displeasure at Egham in the previous year, Maria was again ridden by Robinson. The match was over two miles, Maria carrying eight stone one pound and Souvenir eight stone twelve pounds. Maria started as favourite at five to two on. The match attracted considerable interest. In the race Souvenir, in spite of giving eleven pounds to Maria, elected to make the running at a good pace, but at the distance Maria drew level and beat Souvenir easily by two lengths

amidst the acclamations of the spectators. The King observed the progress of the race with great anxiety, sweeping the entire course with his glass, and closely watching every inch of ground over which the horses moved . . . on Maria winning, which she did cleverly, after an excellent race, His Majesty seemed highly delighted, and was congratulated by some of the ladies about him, with whom he shook hands with every appearance of pleasure and satisfaction. The spectators took almost as much interest in the progress and result of the race as His Majesty himself and displayed the utmost enthusiasm, encircling the rider of Maria by acclamation and giving three cheers for his success . . . The King appeared much gratified, and acknowledging the loudly expressed congratulations of the assembly by uncovering and bowing repeatedly, in a manner the most gracious and condescending. He inspected very minutely through his glass, the grooming of Maria after the race.

But he did not go down to see his mare at closer quarters.

It was in the year of 1827 that George IV ran his horses in his own colours for the first time since he withdrew from the turf after the great Escape scandal of 1791. They were worn by Sam Chifney junior, when he finished second on Dervise in the Oatlands Handicap, won by Mr

Wyndham's Black Swan. *The Times* recorded that 'the colour is a light blue, elegantly embroidered in scarlet', but the colours registered for the King in that year are 'crimson body, gold lace, purple sleeves, black cap', which continue to be the sovereign's colours today.

In this same race poor Barnard, toiling along behind the field on 'the brother to Barefoot', found his way blocked by spectators crowding on to the course to see the finish, and was brought down and injured.

By the 1820s incidents in running were no longer taken for granted as part of the game, and there were objections for 'swerving and barging'. Many complaints concerned the starts, especially and understandably in the races for two-years-old. For example, in a two-years-old race in 1827

> the younkers were a considerable time before they could in the first instant be brought together, and when the word Off was given, not one seemed obedient to it. Some began to rear up and plunge, while others went off at a rattling rate till they found to return was imperative and after this false start a lapse of several minutes ensued: the word was again given—still no obedience—plunging, kicking and many pranks were played: in this way they went on for twenty minutes: but at last, after five or six false starts, off they went in the most magnificent style; a finer or more imposing sight has never been seen on the turf. They started nearly even, and instantly got at full speed, and continued, keeping a parallel line nearly from end to end . . .

The race was won by Mr J. Edwards' filly Starch by Woful, ridden by 'Young Edwards'.

King George IV's newly rekindled interest in racing led him to inaugurate a second racemeeting at Ascot in 1828 and 1829, the first attempt to introduce a regular second fixture since the mid-eighteenth century. *The Times* commented, not entirely accurately, when the second racemeeting was introduced in 1828: 'The Experiment of a second meeting at Ascot has never been tried before, if we except an occasion almost five or six years ago when the officers of the Life Guards had a day's sport for half-bred horses. When suggested by the King last year it was too late, but taken in ample time in the spring of the present year, His Majesty's suggestion has been acted upon.'

The experiment went off fairly well in 1828, but when it was held in early July 1829 it was a dismal failure. *The Times* reported: 'Dreadful weather, eighteen carriages, not a carriage or pedestrian seen on the way to the course. The booth proprietor professed himself pleased to have sold one bottle of porter. The roads were ankle-deep in mud, the course saturated. No King. One race only, the Gold Cup, off at 1.40 p.m. and finished at 1.52 p.m. The pace was wretched, yet it was a hard race from the home turn. The jockies came in literally covered with mud, and at least two pounds heavier.'

On the following day George IV *was* present. The Duke of Richmond's Hindostan, winner of the Gold Cup on the preceding day, ran again and won a race over the Old Mile. The King promptly bought the horse for 600 guineas, and had him started in a race over two and a half miles, which Hindostan, again ridden by Pavis, duly won.

'This was the SECOND year of two meetings, but the horses were inferior, and the stakes less valuable ... many of the proprietors who attend Hampden races having found that the expenses of removal were likely to render speculation doubtful (and so did not attend). It is only to those who seek the quiet enjoyment of a favourite amusement that it possesses any great attraction.'

In contrast, the 1829 principal meeting was the most brilliant in the reign of George IV, and it was the last he attended. The match won by the King's Maria was only part of a splendid scene, thus described in Cawthorne and Herod's *Royal Ascot*:

The crowd was intense, like the heat; splendid, genteel, grotesque; many in masquerade, but all in good humour ... dandies of men, dandies of women; lords with white trousers and black whiskers; ladies with small faces but very large hats; Oxford scholars with tandems and randoms; some on stage-coaches, transmogrified into drags—fifteen on the top and six thin ones within; a two-foot horn; an ice-house with cases of champagne; sixteen of cigars; all neckcloths but white; all hats but black: small talk with oaths, and broad talk with great ones, cooled with ice and made red-hot with brandy and smoke; all four-in-handers, all trying to tool 'em; none able to drive but all able to go with the tongue. An Oxford slap-bang loaded in London; Windsor blues freighted at Reading; Reading coaches chockful at Dorking; a Mile-End coach-wagon; German coaches; Hanoverian cars; Petersburg sledges and Phaetonees; St James's cabs; Bull-and-Mouth barouches, wagoned by Exeter coachmen.

... No place, no amusement, no holiday-making is so enchanting to the softer sex. Gentle and simple, grave and gay, all are on tiptoe of joy, and out jumps nature from both ends—eyes and feet. Lords' ladies tastefully costumed with roses and lilacs unstained or rather unpainted by Bond Street; farmers' daughters and farmers' wives sparkling in silks, rosy in cheek, tinted by soft breezes and bottled ale.

The most splendid day was, as usual, Gold Cup day. The fine field included two winners of the Derby, Mameluke who won in 1827 and Cadland who had dead-heated and won the re-run against The Colonel in 1828; The Colonel himself; Green Mantle, winner of the 1829 Oaks, and Bobadilla, winner of the previous year's Ascot Gold Cup. The value of the horses taking part was estimated at £45,000, a prodigious sum for those days.

The race attracted enormous attention. Vehicles were packed in lines parallel to the course, in places twenty deep. The best placed had taken up their positions overnight leaving their coaches on the course in charge of watchmen. Greville wrote in his diary, 'There was such a crowd to see the cup run for as never was seen before.'

On the morning of the race William Chifney offered Zinganee for sale. Zinganee, by Tramp out of Folly by Young Drone, had finished third only half a length behind the dead-heaters in the Derby in 1828. The horse was offered to King George IV, who had 'bought seven horses successively, for which he has given 11,300 guineas, principally to win the cup at Ascot, which he has never accomplished'. (Greville.) But George IV did not buy him, as he had a strong fancy for his own runner The Colonel. Two hours before the Gold Cup was run, Zinganee was sold to Lord Chesterfield, Greville acting as intermediary, for 2,500 guineas. George Augustus, Earl of Chesterfield, was then twenty-four-years old, a brilliant and wealthy young man.

To gratify the King, the horses were ordered to the front of the Royal Stand for Saddling, which ceremony took place just at the commencement of a tremendous storm, that lasted nearly an hour, and during which the jockies were parading about, exposed to the rain which soon altered the appearance of their gossamer apparel. The race made it still worse, the dirt being thrown over them so profusely that their most intimate friends could not have recognised them. After considerable trouble the horses were brought to the post, where two or three false starts threw the race back to a little after five o'clock.

The horses went off at speed and ran the legs off The Colonel, who however was making ground fast towards the finish, about twenty yards from home. Chifney [who was riding Zinganee] went off from them like a shot, and won with the greatest ease by a length leaving off with his horse full of running and with enough left in him to [have won by] ten or twenty lengths. We never saw anything more finished than the style in which Zinganee came in—nothing could live with him.

Mr Gully's Mameluke, ridden by Wheatley was second, followed in by Cadland and The Colonel, two lengths behind the second horse.

'At the close of the cup race the King made a slight movement with his arms, at the same time raising his hands, as if somewhat surprised.' (*The Times.*) Charles Greville recounts that the King was very disappointed, and complained that Zinganee 'had not been offered to him'.

There was an unhappy aftermath to the King's displeasure. In the following year the Ascot Gold Cup was closed against outsiders, specifically, it was said, to exclude Mr Gully, the owner of Mameluke. *The Observer* in March 1830 commented,

A new provision has this year been introduced into the articles for the regulation of Ascot races, to the effect that 'all horses must, at starting, be the *bona-fide* property of a member of the Jockey Club, of a member of the Upper or Lower Rooms at Newmarket, or of those Clubs in London where members may be admitted into the above clubs without ballot.'

The object of this regulation is said to be to exclude MR GULLY from entering a horse, and the cause of this exclusion is presumed to be his having excited His Majesty's displeasure ... At the race for the Gold Cup at Ascot last year, Lord Maryborough made an order that there should be but one start. When Mr Gully heard of it, after the horses were all brought to the post, knowing that his horse was of a fretful temper, he became apprehensive that he might lost this chance of the prize, and hastily rode in search of Lord Maryborough, to induce him to rescind the order.

In doing so, he passed the Royal Stand, and his thoughts being absorbed with apprehension from this new regulation, he forgot to take off his hat. The omission was observed, and felt both by His Majesty and his Court, at Ascot. Mr Gully was soon informed that he had fallen under the royal displeasure, and lost no time in writing to a nobleman then in attendance on His Majesty, expressing his deep regret for the omission of which he had unintentionally been guilty. He received a letter in reply, stating, that His Majesty was satisfied with the explanation. But though His Majesty was satisfied, his courtiers were not so easy to be placated, and the regulation above-mentioned was made to punish Mr Gully, by forbidding him again to run a horse in the Gold Cup at Ascot.

The Times, who quoted *The Observer* report, added, 'We are sure that the well-known generosity of His Majesty's disposition will correct this regulation – that is, on the supposition that it needs correcting.' But the restriction on entries for the Ascot Gold Cup remained in force in 1830 and 1831, and had a disastrous effect upon the race. In 1830 only four and in 1831 only two runners went to the post.

The programme for the four-day meeting of 1830, which was to be the last in the lifetime of King George IV was typical of the period. Tuesday opened with a match for 100 sovereigns over the Old Mile. This was followed by the Oatlands Stakes, which had sunk to a selling race, run over two and a half miles for a sweepstakes of thirty sovereigns each. The prestige race of the day followed, a valuable sweepstakes of 100 sovereigns, run over the Old Mile. Then there was the King's Plate, for four-years-old and up, over the old-fashioned distance of four miles, and the card was completed with three matches.

On Wednesday there were five races The Swinley Stakes over a mile and a half ended in a dead-heat between the King's Frederica by Moses and Lord Exeter's Green Mantle. There followed the Albany Stakes; a biennial; a walk-over for the Windsor Castle Stakes for three-years-old over the New Mile; and the day ended with a race for a Gold Cup for horses belonging to Officers of the Household Brigade.

Thursday was Gold Cup day. The card also included a two-years-old race, which in 1830 was confined to horses owned by members of the Jockey Club (had Mr Gully a promising two-years-old?); the Royal Stakes; a biennial and the Windsor Forest Stakes.

Friday's fare was pretty thin, with the exception of the ever-popular Wokingham Handicap. The King's Plate for hunters was run over two miles and a distance; there were two 100-guinea sweepstakes, both run over the New Mile, and proceedings concluded with an All-Aged Plate.

Time was running out for King George IV. Charles Greville gives a vivid picture of the state to which the King was reduced, shortly before the brilliant meeting of 1829, when he was living in the Royal Lodge in Windsor Great Park.

> The King complains that he is tired to death of all the people about him . . . he leads the most extraordinary life, never gets up till six in the afternoon. They come to him and open the window curtains at six or seven o'clock in the morning; he breakfasts in bed, does whatever business he can be brought to transact in the bed room, he reads every newspaper quite through, dozes three or four hours, gets up in time for dinner, and goes to bed between ten and eleven. He sleeps very ill, and rings his bell forty times in the night; if he wants to know the hour, though a watch hangs close to him, he will have his *valet de chambre* down rather than turn his head to look at it. The same thing if he wants a glass of water, he won't stretch out his hand to get it. His valets are nearly destroyed, and at last Lady Conyngham prevailed on him to agree to an arrangement by which they wait on alternate days. The service is still most severe, as on their days they are in waiting their labours are incessant, and they cannot take off their clothes at night, and hardly lie down.

When the time came round for the Royal Ascot meeting of 1830 King George IV was so ill that it was rumoured that racing would be postponed until the King was well enough to attend. The King however decreed that racing must take place as planned, and the meeting opened on Tuesday, June 8th, 1830. The meeting was in great contrast to the splendid spectacle of the previous year. The Royal Box was shut up and deserted. *The Times* reported, 'The accounts given on the health of the King were of the most gloomy kind, and induced apprehension that he would not survive the day.' Nor did the weather help. '. . . The deluge out of doors caused an overflowing of some of the hells.'

As the week progressed the news of the King's health became slightly better. 'It is positively reported that His Majesty was well enough on Tuesday to walk across his room,' reported *The Times*. The weather too improved, and brought out the crowds. On Gold Cup day 'the betting stand was one dense and black mass of sporting men, from basement to roof, and the public stand agreeably spotted and diversified with pretty women and gay dresses – the Jockey Club stand was full, and the smaller one at the side of it presented a good sprinkling of the female nobility.'

Yet another attempt was made to control the crowds who promenaded and rode on the course. It was announced: – 'No person shall appear on horseback within the lines except the Royal Family, their attendants, jockeys riding in the races, and individuals employed to do duty on the course. No carts or wagons shall occupy stations next to the rails for the space of twenty yards above the starting-post, or between the start and distance posts. All persons on the course are required to retire behind the cords upon the ringing of the bell for saddling, in order to prevent accidents and confusion.'

Ill though he was, George IV maintained his interest in the meeting, and by his orders a rider brought the result of each race separately to him shortly after the horses had passed the post. The news received by the dying King cannot have much cheered him. Yet again he failed to win the Ascot Gold Cup, either with his last year's runner The Colonel, which could only finish second, or with Zinganee, which he had belatedly bought from Lord Chesterfield. In the last race on Gold Cup day the King's Young Orion by Master Berry, ridden by Nelson, did prevail in the Royal Stakes, run over one mile.

Just fifteen days after the Ascot racemeeting ended, on Saturday, June 26th, 1830, King George IV was dead.

CHAPTER FOUR

The King and the one-legged sailor

GEORGE IV WAS DEAD; HIS BROTHER, THE DUKE OF CLARENCE, SUCCEEDED to the Throne as William IV. Charles Greville wrote:

> King George had not been dead three days before everybody discovered that he was no loss, and King William was a great gain. Certainly nobody was ever less regretted than the late King, and the breath was hardly out of his body before the Press burst forth in full cry against him, and raked up all his vices, follies and misdeeds, which were numerous and glaring enough.
>
> The King's good nature, simplicity and affability to all about him are certainly very striking, and in his elevation he does not forget any of his old friends and companions. He was in no hurry to take upon himself the dignity of King, nor to throw off the habits and manners of a country gentleman ... He says he does not want luxury and magnificence, has slept in a cot [at sea], and he has dismissed the King's cooks.

William IV decided that he should continue to support the turf, but that he would reduce the Royal Stud. He was not over-keen on horseracing, and it was said that he employed George Nelson as jockey solely because of his surname. Nelson had, however, ridden for George IV.

Queen Adelaide, who was now consort, although a plain woman was a beautiful rider with a good figure and looked well in the saddle. She must also have had a wonderful nature as she welcomed and was kind to her husband's enormous family of illegitimate children who lived with them. But Queen Adelaide preferred riding to racing, and offended the sticklers for etiquette by taking her woolwork to Ascot, and sewing during the long intervals between races.

Whether he enjoyed racing or not, William IV quickly made known his patronage of Ascot races. Quite unexpectedly he went to the very next racemeeting at Ascot, the minor second meeting inaugurated by

George IV, which took place on August 24th, 1830, less than two months after his accession.

> Soon after one o'clock the royal cavalcade made its appearance, and was hailed with great delight, it consisted of eight or ten carriages headed by Lord Maryborough, on horseback and dressed in green, and about a score of outriders. In the first carriage were Their Majesties and the Duke of Cambridge ... Their Majesties were loudly cheered as they passed along, and more so when they appeared at the window of the Royal Stand. The King was dressed in black, with a white waistcoat and the insignia of the Order of the Garter. The Queen was dressed with great simplicity having on a black satin bonnet, black silk frock, plain muslin ruff, and an India scarf. Indeed, the Court being still in mourning, the royal party did not make that dashing personal appearance which they usually do on such occasions.

William IV had the pleasure of winning the first race of this, his first racemeeting after his accession. The Colonel (so disappointing in the Gold Cup), which was ridden by Pavis, won the six-furlong Great Park Stakes in a canter. Later in the afternoon the King's Frederica, a filly by Moses, won a seller, in which she was ridden by E. Edwards 'who is not twelve years of age, and who required nearly two stone of dead weight to make up the six stone five lbs'. Small Edwards might have been, but it was reported 'whip and spur were plied unsparingly' until Frederica ran home, the winner by a neck.

The scandal of the meeting was the lenient handicapping of Lord Jersey's horses. His Glenartney won a race on each of the two days, ridden in both races by Robinson. *The Times* reported: 'That Glenartney won was not by any means, a matter of surprise to those who know anything of racing. Lord Jersey's horses for this and the £100 plate having been so favourably handicapped, that on Thursday evening, it was generally believed his lordship would walk over for both. Whoever fixed the weights must either have shut his eyes to the relative merits of the horses, or been lamentably deficient in judgment. Lord Jersey ought to consider himself under an obligation to him.'

In November 1830 William IV carried out his resolve to reduce the size of his stable. His horses were sold at Tattersall's, modestly catalogued as 'the property of one owner'. Zinganee, now a five-years-old, which had eventually been sold by Lord Chesterfield to King George IV for 2,500 guineas, was bought back by Lord Chesterfield for 750 guineas. The Colonel, which had cost George IV 4,000 guineas, was withdrawn unsold at 2,000 guineas. Altogether eleven horses were put up for sale, but the

King kept Fleur-de-lis, counted the best of the brood mares, and also the best of the young stock.

The Colonel ran in William IV's name in the following (1831) Royal Ascot, but broke down in the Oatlands Stakes so badly that he never ran again. He then went to the King's Stud. 'His Majesty has declared his intention not to part with a horse that was so special a favourite with his late Majesty, and that is so well calculated to improve the breed of English horses'.

With The Colonel unable to run the field for the Ascot Gold Cup, restricted to horses owned by members of the Jockey Club, was reduced to two. There was much criticism, both from press and public, and this was the last year in which a restriction on ownership was applied.

The raceweek royal festivities at Windsor Castle were very different from those in the previous reign. The hour of dining was put back to eight o'clock, to enable the Queen, who often outrode all her ladies, to enjoy her long rides. Charles Greville was a guest at dinner in the Castle.

About forty people at dinner, for which the room is not nearly large enough; the dinner was not bad, but the room insufferably hot ... The Castle holds very few people, and with the King's and Queen's immediate suite and *toute la bâtardise* it was quite full. The King drinks wine with everybody, asking seven or eight at a time. After dinner he drops asleep. Directly after coffee the band began to play, a good band, not numerous, and principally of violins and stringed instruments ... What a *changement de decoration*; no longer George IV, capricious, luxurious and misanthropic, liking nothing but the society of listeners and flatterers, but a plain, vulgar, hospitable gentleman, opening his doors to the whole world, with a numerous family [all illegitimate] and suite, a Whig Ministry, no foreigners and no toad eaters at all.

At the following Ascot in 1832 there occurred an incident of bizarre tragi-comedy, which linked the kindly King with a disgruntled and crippled veteran. And both were naval men.

'STONE-THROWING AT KING', read *The Times* headline. 'We lament that we are under the necessity of noticing an atrocious outrage committed on the person of His Majesty, by a ruffian, who, instead of expressing any feeling of regret, actually gloried in it.' Just after the first race William IV, who was standing at the window of the Royal Box, was hit on the head by a stone. A second stone followed, but hit the front of the box and fell to the ground.

Lord Frederick Fitzclarence, an illegitimate son of William IV and the actress Mrs Jordan, was standing beside his father when 'he was suddenly alarmed by hearing the sound produced by a stone striking His Majesty on the head. His Majesty exclaimed "Oh! God! I am hit!" ' The stone dented the King's top hat, but did not draw blood. The large flint with jagged edges was picked up by Lord Brownlow and handed to Lord Frederick, who afterwards produced it in court.

Meanwhile the stone-thrower, a wretched ex-sailor called Dennis Collins, had been seized. 'The indignation of the spectators was loudly and unequivocally expressed. His Majesty's appearance at the window two or three minutes after was most enthusiastically cheered by all classes.'

In the magistrates' court Collins 'appeared but little affected by his situation. His appearance was most wretched, and similar to those wandering mendicants who, in the tattered garb of sailors, are constantly imposing on the credulity of the public. He had a wooden leg of the most rude construction.' Collins was a native of Cork, and had served in the navy for many years, first in the *Kangaroo* and later on board the *Atalanta*, where he had lost his leg in an accident. He had been found a place as a pensioner at Greenwich but 'had misconducted himself towards his ward's man' and had been turned out in December 1831 without a pension or any means of support. All his efforts to be reinstated had failed, including a petition to the King. He declared, 'I might as well be shot or hanged, as remain in such a state.'

He determined to be revenged upon the King. He walked on his rough wooden leg the thirty miles from London, slept in a shed near Windsor on the previous night, and came to Ascot. There a gentleman had given him a shilling, with which he had bought beer, but he was not drunk.

After appearing at the magistrates' court at Ascot before Mr Elliott a magistrate of Reading assisted by Mr Roe, the chief magistrate of Bow Street, Collins was remanded in custody and taken in a post-chaise to Reading Gaol. He was committed for trial on the charge of high treason and was tried on August 22nd, 1832, at the Berkshire Assizes in Abingdon and found guilty. The savage sentence then passed on Dennis Collins was 'to be drawn on a hurdle to the place of execution, hanged, decapitated and quartered'. William IV immediately reprieved him from this fate, but Collins was transported to the colonies where, many years later, he died in exile.

Charles Greville wrote, under the date June 21st, 1832:

At Fern Hill all last week a great party; nothing but racing and gambling. The event of the races was the King having his head knocked with a stone. It made very little sensation on the sport, for he was not hurt, and the fellow was a miserable-looking ragamuffin. It, however, produced a great burst of loyalty in both Houses, and Their Majesties were loudly cheered at Ascot. The Duke of Wellington, who had the day before been mobbed in London, also reaped a little harvest of returning popularity from the assault, and, so far, the outrage have done rather good than harm.

The well-aimed stone, together with another incident at much the same time, illustrates how close the Royal Box must have been to the crowd, even though a sort of Royal Enclosure is said to have been in existence. William IV threw a sovereign to a poor gypsy woman who had attracted his attention in the crowd below the box. Immediately the people round her scrambled for the coin, and the old gypsy woman got nothing. The King saw what had happened and sent a servant to her with a £5 note. She then insisted on being brought before the King, to thank him in person. It would not appear that the King's aim was as accurate as that of the one-legged sailor! The stone-throwing also underlines a fact still evident today: only racing itself makes any lasting impression upon the racegoer. The stone was thrown on Tuesday; On the following day *The Times* reporter could write: 'the assault is wholly forgotten and has ceased to be a topic of conversation'.

The first re-opened Gold Cup, run in 1832, resulted in a fine race between Sir Mark Wood's four-years-old filly Camarine, ridden by Robinson, and Rowton, a six-years-old owned and ridden by Chifney, which had won the Oatlands Stakes on the Tuesday. The horses went off at a walk for a hundred yards, then Rowton broke into a slow canter, but there was no speed at all until the horses entered the straight. There the mare Camarine ran out or was forced out, but was quickly straightened and both horses fought a terrible finish, in which they were severely punished. At the line the judge could not separate them. Robinson objected to Rowton, but the objection was overruled and the race run off. In the run-off Rowton was allowed to lead, but Camarine crept up on him, and won cleverly by two lengths. The winner Camarine was a white-blazed chestnut filly with four white socks, by Juniper out of a daughter of Rubens, bred by Lord Berners. It was said 'she was required to run with her near leg first. If she started on her off one, she swung it round so much that unless she had been steadied and made to change, she would soon have been in distress'. Robinson, however, declared she was 'the very best mare he ever rode' and that he had never seen anything wrong with her action. The Cup on this occasion was 'a salver of large dimensions and was of exquisite workmanship'.

The Times commented: 'Sir Mark was a very heavy winner on the

6

Thursday's race; the Chifneys and the Sadler party were great losers. The betting on that race and the Oatlands were more than usually deep.'

Sir Mark Wood thus owned the winner of the Ascot Gold Cup in three successive years winning with Lucetta, Cetus and Camarine, all ridden by Jem Robinson.

The race for the Eclipse Foot was first run in 1832. The prize was one of the hooves of the chestnut wonder horse, magnificently set as a snuff-box in gold, and is today one of the treasures of the Jockey Club rooms at Newmarket. William IV presented it to the Jockey Club, together with £200 per annum, to be run for by members of the Jockey Club.

No act, however apparently altruistic or generous, will avoid criticism, even the gift of the Eclipse Foot. *The Times* wrote:

His Majesty's object was doubtless to encourage a noble national monument, but it is the opinion of those who are competent to speak on the subject, that the restrictions by which the gift is accompanied are ill-calculated to affect that end, they say, and with reason, that to promote a national sport, the prize ought to be national, and not confined to any body of men, however aristocratic or influential; that by the present conditions many of the most respectable noblemen and gentlemen, who are breeders of racehorses, and not members of the Jockey Club are shut out, that the Ascot Cup has manifested the impolicy of these invidious distinctions, and that to ensure the popularity of this magnificent prize, it ought to be thrown open to all challenges. We entirely concur with these objections, which derive additional force from the fact, that the challenge cup at Newmarket does not on average produce more than one race in six or eight years: moreover the entry for the hoof this year is confined to three horses.

The first race for the Eclipse Foot was run over two and a half miles on Thursday June 21st, 1832, the third race on the card — the Gold Cup being the fifth race. The Eclipse Foot was displayed and much admired 'for its chastity of design and workmanship' before the race. The race was won by Priam, the 1830 Derby winner, whose ownership had been transferred from Chifney to Lord Chesterfield apparently so that he could run in races confined to Jockey Club members. Priam was described as 'a mare-looking horse' by *The Druid*. He was a delicate feeder, and he had an extraordinary feathered coat from his ears to his withers, as though he had lain on it the wrong way.

The Eclipse Foot was won in 1833 by Galopade, owned by Mr T. Cosby, the owner's fifth winner in two days at Ascot, a feat attributed to 'the admirable condition in which his horses are brought to the post'. Cosby was an Irishman from Strabally Hall in Queen's County, in his day a well-known gentleman jockey, and a very popular man in racing circles.

In the following year Galopade again ran for the Eclipse Foot, but the race was won and the year's honours belonged to Glaucus, a bay colt by Partisan out of the Selim mare Namine, owned by Lord Chesterfield. Glaucus ran in the Gold Cup, as did Rockingham, winner of the St Leger, and Galata, the highly strung, fast winner of the Oaks. 'This race created the most extraordinary interest: vast sums were staked upon it, and the speculation never waned until the horses were off. At the Swinley Post, Galata, owing to the severity of the race, died completely away; and, when they reached the trees, Chapple brought Rockingham nearer the front, the pace still being severe, but Scott, holding Glaucus fast by the head, won with great ease.'

After an interval of only one race, Glaucus was started again over two and a half miles for the Eclipse Foot.

James Robinson, decked out in a brand new green and white silk jacket, was soon in the saddle, and Galopade gave one good kick-royal to let his supporters know he was all right and ready for the fray. As the two came up the course, Robinson was leading at a gentle hand-canter, three or four lengths from Scott and, in this way, they reached the Swinley Post without any alteration either in pace or position. Down the hill Scott made some advance; but at little better than a trot; but at the turn of the half-mile, away they came at utmost speed, Galopade never having the ghost of a chance, Robinson using neither whip nor spur, from the conviction that it was hopeless. Scott never stirred on Glaucus, who won in marvellous form, looking at the field he had beaten, over the same distance of ground, only an hour before.

That same year, 1834, two new races were introduced, which were to became part of the pattern of Ascot. The St James's Palace Stakes was run for three-years-old over the New Mile on the Tuesday. And in 1975 the St James's Palace Stakes is still held on the same day, still for three-years-old but is run over the Old Mile instead. It was worth 100 sovereigns to the winner in 1834: today the race, a Group 2 Pattern Race, has £10,000 added to the stakes.

The second new race, then known as the Ascot Derby, now known as the King Edward VII Stakes, was then run on the Tuesday, and today is incorporated in the Thursday card. But the conditions, for three-years-old over a mile and a half, remain unaltered. Like the St James's Palace Stakes, it is a Group 2 Pattern Race with £10,000 added to the stakes.

The Gold Cup in 1835 produced an unpleasant furore. The betting was thrown into confusion by the late withdrawal of the hot favourite, Mr Batson's Plenipotentiary, which had won the Derby in the previous year. Many bookmakers could not meet their commitments and welshed. Glencoe, owned by Lord Jersey and ridden by Robinson, was the winner from a field of nine.

> Rounding the turn, Chifney made his mighty rush with Shillelah, closely followed by Famine, but the severity of the pace soon beat them, as it did all the rest, scattered far and wide, Glencoe, Bran and Nonsense being alone left to contest the race. A glance at Robinson's seat (by those who know his style of riding) foretold the result. Next to the rails this superb horseman was skimming over the sod as light and graceful as the dolphin shoots away from the shark. At the betting stand, old John Day brought up Bran in the most resolute manner, and so gamely did Sir Edward's colt respond to the call, as nearly to get on level terms with Glencoe; but Robinson, mute and motionless as a statue, just slightly slackened his hold on Glencoe's head, and sent him in an easy winner.

Touchstone won the first of his two Ascot Gold Cups in 1836, beating Rockingham, who made the pace, by two lengths. The Herring painting of him shows a dark brown horse, with a large star or narrow blaze and one white sock on his off hind leg. *The Druid* wrote of him. 'The roots of his ears were the only coarse part about him . . . he was equally good for speed and stamina, though he required very fine riding, for he would instantly swerve if his jockey raised his whip.' Touchstone had a peculiar action. 'His near fore-ankle never was good; and at the first Ascot cup, it had almost risen to the dignity of a "leg", He had very fleshy legs, and turned out his hocks so much, and went so wide behind, that a barrel might have been placed between his hind legs when he was galloping.'

In 1837 Charles Greville, who had been so closely connected with Ascot for so many years, won three races at Ascot with his good horse Mango, by Emilius out of Mustard, who was by Merlin. The most important was the Ascot Derby, but the most exciting was a sweep over the Old Mile on the Wednesday. 'It was one of the closest races, short of a dead-heat, ever seen at Ascot.' In the lead at the distance, Mango swerved, but his jockey got him straight and he ran on to win 'by a very short neck'. Mango went on to win the accident-ridden St Leger that year, when the favourite fell soon after the start, and another fancied horse was brought down by a dog.

William IV's simple pleasures upon finding himself King died away. Politics perplexed him—the Reform Bill was causing violent controversy—and he became depressed. Greville recorded in 1835:

At Stoke for Ascot races. Riding on the course on Wednesday, I overtook Adolphus Fitzclarence [illegitimate son of William IV], who rode with me, and gave me an account of his father's habits and present state of mind . . . at half-past nine he breakfasts with the Queen, the ladies and any of his family; he eats a couple of fingers and drinks a dish of coffee. After breakfast he reads *The Times* and *Morning Post*, commenting aloud on what he reads in very plain terms, and sometimes they hear 'That's a damned lie', or some such remark, without knowing to what it applies . . . After breakfast he devotes himself with Sir Herbert Taylor to business till two, when he lunches (two cutlets and two glasses of sherry); then he goes out for a drive till dinner time; at dinner he drinks a bottle of sherry—no other wine—and eats moderately, he goes to bed soon after seven.

He is in dreadfully low spirits, and cannot rally at all; the only interval of pleasure which he has lately had was during the Devonshire election, when he was delighted at John Russell's defeat. He abhors all the Ministers . . . When Adolphus told him that a dinner ought to be given for the Ascot races, he said, 'You know I cannot give a dinner; I cannot give any dinners without inviting my Ministers, and I would rather invite the Devil than have any one of them in my house.'

William IV continued to attend the races, where he was popular, although *The Times* reported 'the king-seeing mania is over' (1834). It was becoming ever more likely, as Queen Adelaide's two infants failed to survive babyhood, that he would be succeeded by his niece Princess Victoria, the daughter of his younger brother, the late Duke of Kent. He delighted in showing kindness to the little Princess, and took her to Ascot, which she loved. The youthful Victoria thoroughly enjoyed the races, and even won in a bet with her uncle the King a chestnut mare which she named Taglioni.

Nathaniel Willis, the American writer, described the Princess in the Royal Box at Ascot, wearing a rose-coloured satin dress, with a pelerine cape trimmed with black lace and a pink bonnet, leaning over the balcony, fascinated by a ballad-singer, and by 'all the vociferous raggle-taggle of humanity'. Princess Victoria was, Willis decided, 'much better-looking than any picture of her in the shops, and for the heir to such a crown as that of England unnecessarily pretty and interesting.'

There were high hopes for Ascot at the beginning of the reign,

from the warm and personal interference of His Majesty, who lately expressed a desire to place Ascot, if not first, at least inferior to none among the stations of racing celebrity. Especially on Cup Day, the characteristics of Ascot are altogether distinct from those of any other meeting . . . in the beauty of the surrounding scenery, the number of no less delightful rides to the heath, and its proximity to the seat of Royalty, . . . there is a fascination which we in vain look for elsewhere, and which rarely fail of bringing together a brilliant assemblage of the highest rank of the country. Not the least of its recommendations is the presence of the Sovereign, who, throwing off the trammels and cares of state, enters into the amusements of his subjects with a fellowship of feeling which cannot prove otherwise than attractive to those who have no other opportunity of beholding him in his private circle.

But the King's lack of real interest in racing resulted in a falling-off of the standards expected at Ascot, where, in recent years, the amenities and the conduct of racing had been improved. Lord Maryborough, the Master of the Buckhounds, had supervised improvements carried out by Mr Jenner, the Clerk of the Course. In 1825 an elbow of the old course, 'from Swinley Bottom to below the King's Kennel' had been smoothed out and its steep contours modified 'keeping an even descent the whole length, and being double the width of the old course'. The draining had been improved in 1829, and £300 spent on preparing a training gallop for the horses, to avoid having the course used for work.

Matters were not made easier by a constant change of the Masters of the Buckhounds, the controllers of racing at Ascot. In 1830 Lord Maryborough was succeeded as Master of the Buckhounds by the brisk—some would say brusque—Lord Anson, whose special forte was the keeping of law and order. He insisted that there should be no riding down upon pedestrians on the course to frighten them off the track, no cracking of whips, and no disturbances on the course, and saw that order was kept by introducing a party of horse patrol.

He succeeded to the title of Earl of Lichfield, and in 1832 gave way to Lord Chesterfield, who was himself succeeded in 1835 by the sixteenth Earl of Erroll (spelt without the final 'l' in contemporary accounts). 'Although not on the turf, he seemed quite *au fait* to the business of the racecourse.' Unfortunately Lord Erroll, a Whig, was not in favour with the King, Greville said Erroll had behaved disgracefully towards the King, who did not invite him to the Castle even for Ascot races. Nevertheless Lord Erroll held office until 1839, two years into the reign of Queen Victoria.

The complaints, which were now snowballing, about the conduct of racing at Ascot concerned every aspect of events—the approach roads, the stands, the gambling hells, the beggars, the condition of the course, the planning of the programme, the prize-money, the delays at the start, the mismanagement of the homebound crowds.

The roads through the Park and Virginia Water were in a scandalous state and gravel sadly wanted. Once on the course the racegoers had to contend with 'an immoderate quantity of Irish beggars, in the utmost apparent state of misery and destitution, who annoyed by their unceasing importunities everyone within their reach. Many of them met with a recommendation that they should apply to their patron, Mr O'Connell' (the leader in the move for Catholic emancipation). 'Every carriage, as it arrives, was beset by a mob of vagabonds, forcing their services upon the occupants, and, in many instances, using the most disgusting language if their aid was refused.'

Another abuse, which was much resented, was the allocation of space for carriages along the edge of the course.

> Ropes are provided on each side of the course to prevent the carriages encroaching beyond a certain limit, and a space is thus preserved between the carriages and the rails within which, on the northern side of the course, the pedestrians are confined during the time the horses are running ... Around the stand to which the winning-post is attached a space between the ropes and the rails wider than any other part of the course, is preserved, originally intended to receive the hacks of the jockies sent up with their clothes immediately before each of the races. Carriages are placed, as in every other part of the course, around this space, and the view from there would of course be uninterrupted were it not for one great nuisance. Certain persons are permitted, it is said, by tickets from the Clerk of the Course, to bring their carriages within the ropes, and thus intercept the view of those who have secured their places by coming, some hours earlier, or by sending their carriages overnight.

This was a direct attack upon Mr Thomas Jenner, who had gained many golden opinions in the early days following his appointment in 1823.

'The course itself had deteriorated ever since the days of Lord Maryborough as riders were again being allowed on the course. 'The admission of horsemen on the course is also a great annoyance to the promenade. The huntsmen and whippers-in of the Royal Hunt render important services in clearing the course, and their aid is so well directed that no one is endangered by their horses; but the obtrusion of unofficial riders, with all their deficiencies in equitation, amongst a concourse of beautiful and well-dressed women, is too bad.'

Why, the critics asked, were the proprietors of the gambling hells not made to contribute handsomely to the prize-fund? The gambling tents included 'Le Merveille', the 'Royal Pavilion', in which French roulette was played, The Oxford Clubhouse from St James's Street and the

'Newmarket Clubhouse'. Thimble-rig men and pickpockets still flourished: 'the dull intervals between the races are enlivened by ducking pickpockets'.

Now that ladies were increasingly in evidence, there were complaints that they were being subjected to discomfort and bad language, while in 1833: 'One annoyance there was that the ladies must have felt particularly —the smoking of cigars, which was indulged in to excess by a set of young men, who evidently were not and could not be mistaken for gentlemen.' One lady who does not seem to have objected to the smell of cigar-smoke was the bold Lady Chesterfield, who sat at the select table under the betting stand, placing her own stakes.

The prize-money was derisory and totalled only £300 for the four days of the Ascot meeting, which was only a quarter of the current prize-money at Chester, Manchester and Doncaster, and only two-thirds of that given at a tiny new meeting held at Ramsgate.

Although the races were in general well-managed, Ascot always had a poor reputation for starting the races late. 'In the management of the races one fault only presents itself, and that is a serious one to those who have been accustomed to the clock-work regularity enforced by the Newmarket rules, and we allude to the want of punctuality in running. The last race on Tuesday being one and a half hours, and the last race on Thursday more than two hours after the time appointed for it.' (1834)

All these and other criticisms appeared in *The Times*, *The Morning Post* and other newspapers between 1833 and 1836, together with warnings that if nothing were done, Ascot would decline into a one-day country racemeeting. But *The Times* did not confine itself to criticism: On June 4th, 1836, it gave a lengthy and detailed review of ways in which the state of affairs at Ascot could be remedied. We have already seen that King William IV read *The Times* and the writer knew he was getting his ideas directly over to the King.

Suggestions for Reconstituting Ascot

In our notice of Tuesday we took occasion to advert to the poverty of the sums given as compared with those collected; the moderate character of the races on that and subsequent days prove to demonstration that unless something be done towards their improvement, or rather regeneration, they will come to nothing. Our remarks, we believe, have excited attention to the proper quarters, and an illustrious personage has been heard to express his surprise that the list should have been so unproductive of sport on the first day!

It is not too late to restore it to that pre-eminence which it formerly boasted, and, as we are quite satisfied that the disposition exists, we venture to throw out the following hints:

(1) The ground should be let by tender, the renter being allowed to take a small fee for each carriage placed in an enclosed space, next the rails; £500 or £600 at least might be obtained in this way, and there would not be any question as to the amount collected.

(2) An 'Ascot Club' should be formed on the basis of those at Goodwood and Heaton Park, the Master of the Buckhounds for the time being officiating as President. Of a club of this description His Majesty would no doubt condescend to become Patron, and we are convinced that there are many distinguished individuals who would willingly become members.

(3) There should be a free Handicap of 100 sovereigns each, half forfeit, three or four miles (as might be resolved upon) with 200 sovereigns added, the horses to be handicapped, and the acc. declared, in the month of March.

(4) and the Oatlands might again be made a sporting race by adding to it £100 or £200. (We are indebted to the Duke of Portland for the last suggestion.) The Portland Handicap, to which His Grace added the munificent sum of £300, created more interest at Newmarket than any other race since the famous match between Sir Joshua and Filho-da-Puta. We are the more inclined to press these two stakes, as there is at present too great a leaning towards short distances. Formerly there were six-mile courses, now the majority of our stakes are mile, half-mile and Two Year Course races (four furlongs at this period)! By and by we may look for them over the first half of a M(ile).

(5) Under the present regulation the Eclipse Foot can never become a race of importance, but as His Majesty wishes it to be select, would not the exclusion of objectionable people be secured by confining it to horses nominated by members of the Jockey Club? Or; if no alteration be deemed advisable, would not the £200 so generously offered by His Majesty, be more judiciously bestowed on the Oatlands?

(6) There should be a PLATE each day, and the entrance money, if exacted at all, be given to the owner of the second horse, as is required by the Act of Parliament.

(7) THE CUP articles should be altered so as to give inferior horses a chance.

(8) And the COURSE, at present in a wretched state, kept in proper order.

(9) Should a club, or failing that, a racing committee, be formed, and measures taken, embodying the spirit of our suggestions, we are convinced that ASCOT, now twenty years behind the times, may regain its popularity: one thing, however, is certain—viz, that unless the axe is laid to the root of the evil, it will be better not to touch it at all.

(10) KING'S PLATE.

His Majesty has been graciously pleased to give a free Plate of 100 guineas to the Egham races. Would it not be as well to withdraw the one from Guildford, where it is completely thrown away?

(11) The want of accommodation for the ladies at Ascot races has suggested the idea of a GRANDSTAND, on the same scale as that of Goodwood; if placed between the Royal and betting stands, it could not fail to answer. The profits might go to a race fund.

There is no doubt about the identity of the 'illustrious personage' who was interested. King William IV acted promptly. No doubt Ascot was discussed at the dinner he gave to the Jockey Club on June 8th, 1836. In any event the changes suggested in *The Times* were put into effect at once, and almost letter for letter. Changes in the management of the course were made. At the top, the Master of the Buckhounds, who had hitherto been the sole steward of the races, although he was not necessarily a racing man, would, during raceweek be assisted by stewards appointed by and drawn from the Jockey Club. The Master of the Buckhounds would, however retain his overall authority over the course throughout the year.

Mr Jenner the Clerk of the Course, was dismissed (Was this 'the axe laid to the root of the evil', suggested by *The Times* reporter, who was not on the best of terms with the Clerk of the Course?). Mr William Hibburd of Egham was appointed Clerk of the Course in Mr Jenner's place.

The Windsor Express on Monday, July 11th, 1836, carried a report, under the heading 'DISMISSAL OF MR JENNER', which ran 'The appointment of so active and efficient a person as Mr Hibburd to be Clerk of the Course, in the room of Mr Jenner, will give very great satisfaction to all lovers of the turf. Mr Jenner, who is highly respectable, and an old inhabitant of Windsor, has long held that office, but all who know that gentleman are aware that he was in no respect qualified for a post which required great activity, and a perfect knowledge of sporting (activity) – in fact a devotion to the turf.'

The suggestion made in *The Times* that the ground should be let by tender was agreed, and the Earl of Erroll, as Master of the Buckhounds, was instructed to let the ground in plots by auction, for the erection of booths; the spaces in the carriage enclosures were to be let by tender. The money thus raised was to be put to the prize-fund.

Progress was made with such exemplary speed that *The Times* was able to report in its issue of July 4th, 1836 only a calendar month after its original suggestions:

ASCOT-HEATH RACES

The Earl of Errol has commenced the reformation of these races, with a determination that cannot fail to be productive of the best results. Every individual formerly in office has been dismissed, and an active and efficient Clerk of the Course appointed in the person of Mr Hibburd of Egham.

A number of workmen are already employed in making the necessary improvements to the course. A new set of rails and posts will be put up, and a second line (commencing from the distance to beyond the winning-post) for carriages.

The money given away will be more than treble the amount of the last meeting, and will include a £100 Plate from the town of Windsor (its subscription this year was about half as many shillings), a similar one from the ground landlord of the betting stand, Plate from the county and borough members and other contributions, sufficient to ensure five or six races per day.

There are already 32 subscribers to the cup, and we have no doubt that the sporting world will show their sense of Lord Errol's exertions by sending their horses and in other respects doing all in their power to ensure the prosperity of the races.

The vigorous forward planning which followed the change of policy is shown by the publication of the races for 1837, which for the first time appeared as early as August, and are reproduced, in somewhat shortened form, from *The Times* of August 25th, 1836: 'The following list of stakes etc for next year will show that Lord Errol has carried his intentions into effect with a rapidity, vigour and effect altogether without precedent.'

PLANS FOR 1837

First Day

THE OATLANDS, of 30 sovs each, h. ft and only 5 sovs if declared the Saturday before Epsom, etc, with 100 sovs added.
THE ASCOT DERBY of 50 sovs etc etc. Winner of the Derby or the Oaks 5 lbs extra. Closed.
THE KING'S PLATE — the usual conditions.
SWEEPSTAKES of 100 sovs each, half ft., closed.
TWO-YEAR-OLD STAKES of 50 sovs each, six furlongs, closed.
THE ECLIPSE FOOT, under new regulations.

Second Day

THE SWINLEY STAKES of 25 sovs each. To close on March 1.
SWEEPSTAKES of 10 sovs each, with 50 sovs added, for 3 y.o. To close and name the Saturday before Epsom.
FREE HANDICAP of 50 sovs each, with 200 added, for four-year-olds and upwards, 3 miles.
THE WINDSOR TRADESMEN'S PLATE of 100 sovs, two miles.
A MAIDEN PLATE of 50 sovs, S.S. course.

Third Day

THE GOLD CUP, value 300 sovs etc, by subscriptions of 20 sovs each (conditions as usual) (32 subs) with 200 sovs added.

THE WINDSOR FOREST STAKES of 50 sovs each, half ft.

TWO YEAR OLD STAKES of 20 sovs each, 20 sovs ft. To close and name at the end of the Second Spring Meeting (Newmarket).

THE ALBANY STAKES of 50 sovs each, to close March 1.

SWEEPSTAKES of 100 sovs each, half ft. Closed.

BUCKHURST DINNER STAKES, etc closed.

Fourth Day

THE STAND PLATE of £100 Handicap. Once round and a distance.

A PLATE of £50 for the Beaten Horses, 12 furlongs.

THE KING'S PLATE FOR HUNTERS.

THE WOKINGHAM STAKES, 5 sovs each etc 45 subs. (conditions unchanged).

THE MEMBERS PLATE.

THE PLATE GIVEN BY INNKEEPERS AND POSTMASTERS.

making a total of public money of upwards of £1,300, about £1,000 more than the late management.

The Earls of Errol, Chesterfield and Lichfield, and Mr Greville, are stewards.

In Cawthorne and Herod's *Royal Ascot* there is an account of the courses at Ascot at this period.

. . . Races run on the New Mile Course started from the east end of the course, by Mr Fowler's Lodge, and, running straight up the course, ended at the winning-post; the Old Mile was from the north end up the Old Hill to its juncture with the New Mile, and then bearing to the right direct to the post.

The Swinley Course and Mile-and-a-Half ran from the Swinley Post and along the valley to the Old Mile, and through it to the winning-post.

The Two-Mile was similar, only that the horses started from the winning-post and ran down past the Swinley Post.

For the Two-and-a-Half Miles the horses started from the Half-Mile Post on the New Mile, and thence ran straight up to the Swinley Post, into the valley, and on the Old Mile, past the junction with the New Mile, and turning to the right, went direct to the winning-post.

The Four-Mile Course was the Two Miles run twice round.

The T.Y.C. or Two-Year-Old Course commenced at the starting-post near the union of the Old and New Mile, and ran straight up the course to the winning-post.

The exact distances were:

	Inside			Middle			Outside		
	Miles	Fur	Pls	Miles	Fur	Pls	Miles	Fur	Pls
The New Mile	0	7	26	0	7	25	0	7	25
The Old Mile	0	7	32	0	7	37	1	0	11
The 2-mile or									
Circular Course	1	7	24	1	7	36	2	0	8
The 2½ Mile	2	3	9	2	3	21	2	3	33
The 4-mile	3	7	8	3	7	32	4	0	16
The T.Y.C.									
(Two-Year Course)	0	3	19	0	3	19	0	3	19

When the next Royal meeting came round, with the first day Tuesday, June 6th, 1837, much of the planned renaissance had already taken place. The course had been improved, holes filled in, turf re-laid, and — for the benefit of horses trained locally — the old gallops had been repaired and new gallops made.

The arrangements for carriages had been revised:

Lord Errol, the spirited Master of the Buckhounds (who has in right of his office, the control of all the arrangements of Ascot races) determined to remodel the whole system. Instead of permitting an indiscriminate scramble for places between the carriages, the country carts and wagons, the go-carts and caravans of London costermongers, an outer line of rails on both sides of the course has been fixed, by which all but carriages are excluded, and their admission to the first or second rank is regulated by the price paid for their entrance within the said rails. This day the charge for the first rank was limited to 10s and the second rank to 5s.

Some carriages refused to pay, but there was a double line of carriages nearly to the turn.

Arrangements for policing the course had also been greatly altered. 'On the heath the most perfect regularity prevailed, chiefly through the exertions of the new police who, much to the credit of the new system, were substituted for the old "incapables", the local constables. Sir F. Roe was in attendance at the Royal Stand, assisted by Gardiner, Leadbitter, and Capes.'

The thimble-rig men arrived as usual, but did not like what they saw, and left. But theirs is a hardy breed, and some had crept back, and were apparently suffered to remain, by Cup day. As for the hazard and roulette booths, they still occupied a conspicuous and extensive line, 'but as they all contribute handsomely to the revenue of the course, we cannot entertain much pity for the flats who suffer from their chicanery'.

In fact, the red-waistcoated Bow Street patrol seemed to keep order by their very presence. 'Perfect order is preserved in the quietest manner possible, and the disturbances and squabbles which arose when the ground was policed by a collection of local constables sworn in for the occasion have been easily avoided.'

Leasing of the ground for the booths had produced an income of over £1,000, to which was added nearly £300 raised from the entrance fees for the carriages. The prize-money was therefore obtained, and with so much more money coming in, and so much effort put into the programme, racing at Ascot once more became lively and interesting.

There was one deepening shadow over the races in 1837. King William IV was unwell. His son told Charles Greville 'that it was bad enough, but not for the moment alarming; no disease, but excessive weakness without the power of rallying'. Queen Adelaide, bravely came to the course for a short time on Tuesday and Wednesday.

The weather was bad on Cup day. It was described as 'suitable for the pea-jackets, the Mackintoshes, even the umbrellas'. So concerned was Charles Greville, who was both clerk of the Privy Council and a steward of Ascot, with the approaching death of the King that he fails to record the Ascot triumphs of Mango, possibly his best horse.

On Wednesday it was announced for the first time that the King was alarmingly ill. On Thursday the account was no better, and in the course of Wednesday and Thursday his immediate dissolution appeared so probable that I conversed with Errol that I should send to the Castle at nine o'clock on the Thursday evening for the last report, that I might know whether to go to London directly or not. On Wednesday the physicians wanted to issue a bulletin, but the King would not hear of it. He said as long as he was able to transact public business he would not have the public alarmed on his account; but on Friday, nevertheless, the first bulletin was issued.

A week after Ascot races were over, on Friday, June 16th, 1837, Greville wrote in his diary:

Yesterday Lord Lansdowne sent for me to get in the first place that everything might be ready, and in the next to say that they were perplexed to know what steps, if any, they ought to take to ascertain whether the Queen is with child and to beg me to search in our books to find if any precedent could be found at the accession of James II. But they had forgotten that the case had been provided for in the Regency Bill, and that in the event of the

King's death without children, the Queen is to be proclaimed, but the oath of allegiance taken with a saving of the rights of any posthumous child to King William.

King William IV insisted on writing in laconic terms his own bulletins on his declining health. He sank gradually, and died at twenty minutes past two on the morning of Tuesday, June 20th, 1837.

Charles Greville wrote in his diary:

William IV was a man who coming to the throne at the mature age of sixty-five, was so excited by the exultation, that he nearly went mad, and distinguished himself by a thousand extravagences of language and conduct, to the alarm or amusement of all who witnessed his strange freaks; and though he was shortly afterwards sobered down into more becoming habits, he always continued to be something of a blackguard and something more of a buffoon. It is but fair to his memory at the same time to say that he was a good-natured, kind-hearted and well-meaning man, and he always acted an honourable and straightforward, if not always sound and discreet, part.

CHAPTER FIVE

The grandstand era

ASCOT SWEPT FORWARD INTO A NEW AGE WITH THE ACCESSION OF QUEEN Victoria. Not only was there a young queen on the throne, but by coincidence two of the greatest changes in the pattern of Ascot occurred at the same time. Queen Victoria succeeded to the throne in 1837, in 1838 the railway reached within ten miles of the course, and in 1839 the new grandstand was opened.

Ascot immediately ceased to be a Regency picnic and became a social occasion, centred upon the royal racemeeting. Gone was the dashing drive over dusty or muddy roads. Fast diminishing was the elegant discomfort of carriage-viewing. Gone was the titillating sight of George IV's mistress coquetting with him in the Royal Stand, or the sober view of Queen Adelaide bent over her embroidery, surrounded by her husband's affectionate illegitimate sons. Removed beyond the enclosures was the squalor and bustle of the mob.

Uniformity was impressed upon those who had entrance to the new grandstand. The racegoer was no longer distinguished by the sumptuousness and elegance of his travelling carriage, but only by the fashion of his wife's clothes, and that was less expensively achieved. With the level floors and orthodox dining-room of the grandstand replacing the dusty turf and the open-air luncheon, Ascot began to appeal to the towndweller, to those swelling middle classes who were beginning to enjoy the pursuits and pleasures which had belonged to the landowning aristocracy. But, in the snobbish progress of man, this in itself provided the basic reason for the subsequent development of the Royal Enclosure. As always, an inner circle of privilege is formed. When at last this is penetrated under the tireless onslaught of the climbing outsider, yet another inner circle is formed, which itself in time will suffer the same fate.

Even more far-reaching in its effects than the opening of the grandstand, was the arrival of the railway, the great leveller of the mid-nineteenth century. We can hardly appreciate today the immobility of the population

before the railway. Modest travel required planning long in advance, even
for the wealthy, while the vast bulk of the population lived and died within half a day's walk of their birthplace.

In 1838 the railway had reached Maidenhead, eight miles as the crow
flies and ten miles by road from Ascot, which immediately became a day
excursion for thousands. *The Times* recorded: 'A great number of lodgings
have been taken for the meeting at Windsor, Egham, Staines, etc, but a
considerable portion of the assemblage seen on the Heath yesterday were
merely visitors for the day, the opportune completion of the Great
Western Railway as far as Maidenhead having offered facilities for going
and returning which have never before presented themselves.'

The intrepid rail travellers found many obstacles in their way. Many
used Slough instead of Maidenhead, but Slough station was merely a halt
without facilities, for the bizarre reason that Eton College had protested
successfully against having a railway station so close to the school. (Yet
one of the line's first 'specials' was to take the Eton boys to see the Queen's
Coronation!) The Slough halt was totally inadequate to cope with the
racecourse crowds, and transport to the racecourse was almost non-
existent. 'Of the "railway division" hundreds, for want of accommodation,
were compelled to pedestrianise their way to the course; the same fate
awaited them at the conclusion of the races, and as the Slough terminus is a
good nine miles from the Heath, a considerable number were too late for
the last train, too late for the coaches, and too late to obtain "food,
raiment and lodging".'

Troubles on the railway continued for some time. There was a tremendous rush at Paddington for the trains, and at Slough for the omnibuses,
which were soon in short supply due to the scarcity of post horses, no
longer required after the railways took over. It was particularly difficult
during the ferociously hot weather of 1843. 'Hundreds were obliged to
walk from the racecourse to the Slough station, along a dusty road, as hard
and hot as the hearthstone of a kitchen fireplace . . . a long tail of pedestrians were flowing through Windsor and Eton till nearly eleven o'clock
at night, tired, wearied, depressed and chastened with the laborious bliss
of the day . . . The innkeepers made yesterday a very pretty thing of it.'
So did the Great Western Railway, which in 1839 carried over 5,000
Ascot racegoers, who paid over £2,000.

Simultaneously plans were being made for the new and important
grandstand at Ascot. The early history of the grandstand is recorded in a
Minute book bound in brown leather (on which is pasted a panel taken
from an even earlier Minute book bound in black morocco), which is still
kept in the secretary's office at Ascot.

7

The first Minutes are dated June 15th, 1838, and record that the Earl of Erroll, Charles C. Greville and Henry Seymour had been made Trustees of the Ascot Grandstand Company. The solicitor proposed that they should approach the Commissioners of Her Majesty's Woods and Forests for a grant or lease of ground, and that £10,000 should be raised in shares of £500 each. On July 20th, 1838, the Commissioners granted the Trustees a lease for sixty-one years at £5 per annum. The prospectuses were issued only three days later. Plans were already in existence: in 1828 three sets of architects had submitted drawings based upon the Goodwood Stand to Lord Erroll, and now, after being submitted for the opinions of 'four respectable Builders and several influential members of the Turf, the Drawings prepared by Mr W. Higgins were elected as the most eligible, from the increased convenience of his arrangements, and from the safety and solidity of the proposed structures'.

Originally the Trustees proposed to demolish the betting stand, owned by Wilfred Slingsby, builder of Eton and Mr Secker of Windsor, and to erect the grandstand in its place. Later the Trustees were satisfied that the grandstand could be sited 'so that it would not interfere in the slightest degree with the view from the Royal Stand and the Jockey Club stands'. Contrary to some accounts, the Slingsby Stand survived until 1859.

Work began on the site on July 28th, 1838, when Thomas Clark of Tottenham began excavating at 9d per cubic yard, having contracted to provide concrete at 7s 6d per cubic yard, and to sink a well for £135. The second prospectus of the Ascot Grandstand Company was issued on August 18th, 1839, followed by advertisements in *The Times* and *The Chronicle* on August 25th.

Then someone appears to have got cold feet, because on September 18th, 1838, all digging and concrete-laying was stopped, and the Trustees decreed that it would not be re-started until all the shares had been taken up. However, although it had proved impossible to contact Lord Erroll, who was in Scotland, work was resumed only nine days later. Estimates were received of £9,000 from Cubitt and £8,300 from Cuthill for constructing the grandstand, and the lower bid accepted. Although hardly any of the £500 shares had been taken up, it was bravely decided to add a £700 terrace walk to the plans. The foundations were completed before November 14th, 1838, when the Trustees held a meeting at which Charles Greville resigned as Trustee, possibly because of political pressures upon him at this time. It was at this meeting, however, that a suggestion was made that turned the tide in favour of the Ascot grandstand. It had already been decided that any member who subscribed £100 was to receive a silver ticket allowing him free admission to the grandstand: it was now proposed that the silver ticket could be deposited with the secretary, in which case the owner would be refunded the sum he would have paid for admission. At once, many subscriptions rolled in. The 100 silver tickets were provided by Garrards at a total cost of £27 5s 10d.

The money was raised in the form of a tontine, a method originally initiated by a Neapolitan banker, Lorenzo Tonti, as a financial scheme by which the subscribers to a common fund each received during his life an annuity, which increased as the number of participants was reduced by death, until the last survivor enjoyed the whole sum. At Ascot the numbers were reduced by eliminating five subscribers annually by ballot, when 'their names were indifferently drawn out and extinguished'. The silver badges remained valid.

The new stand was a fine building.

> The building is thrown well back ... It stands between the Queen's and the old betting stand, occupying the site formerly appropriated to six or seven wooden stands. The elevation from the ground is 52 feet, its length 97½ feet, or, including the balcony which extends beyond the building, 141 feet. The drawing room on the grand [sic] floor is 90 feet in length, and is provided with ten rows of benches placed above each other, both at the front and at the ends of the room. The windows extend from the ceiling to the floor, and slide up and down at pleasure. The roof is leaded, and will accommodate nearly 1,000 persons.
>
> There are several refreshment, retiring and play rooms. A very handsome balcony, supported by Corinthian pillars, extends the whole length of the building, the colonnade below it affording shelter from damp, rain, or heat to those who, for the convenience of betting, prefer the basement. The only entrance is at the back of the building, under an elegant colonnade, the carriage approach to which is by the great-Reading-road. To prevent confusion, there are distinct staircases to the ground-floor and to the roof.

The ground floor held between 1,000 and 1,200 people.

The whole sum of £10,000 had been raised in subscriptions. Moreover Cuthill, the builder was persuaded to reduce his estimate from £9,000 including the terrace walk to £8,100. The caterer was paying £300 for the hire of the dining-room, and £50 per annum for the concession. The private rooms had been let for £250. Financially, the grandstand was off to a good start.

On May 25th, 1839, Mr Skinner, the superintendent of the grandstand, took possession of the new building on behalf of the Trustees, only three days before the opening of the royal meeting. There was the usual rush to get the building ready in time. As all the iron fencing was not in position, wooden fencing was hurriedly erected. Mr Hibburd, the Clerk of the Course, found that his duties included ordering furniture for the ladies' retiring room.

The grandstand was first used on Tuesday, 28th May, 1839. 'If not quite complete in all its internal embellishments,' said *The Times* somewhat condescendingly, 'it is sufficiently so for the accommodation and comfort of the visitors.' There were complaints, of course. 'The seats on the principal floor and on the roof were not sufficiently elevated.' The Minutes recorded that the distemper used inside the building rubbed off on the racegoers' clothes. But the worst fault was at the entrance to the stand. 'The squeeze at the money-entrances of the grandstand was awful, insomuch that many elegant females were compelled to seek accommodation elsewhere.' The pay entrances were widened in 1840, only to be narrowed again in 1851.

The grandstand was an instant success. 'The ground floor was full of well dressed females', although new to racegoing, as little was thought of their knowledge of racing—they were said 'to fancy the horses with slender legs and very long tails'. Two years later *The Times* reported, 'The Grandstand absorbed nearly all the higher class of visitor, but many persons of rank, determined to look Royalty in the face, and at the same time enjoy their luncheons in the old-fashioned way, took their stand in the carriage enclosure, setting at naught both heat and dust, with the certainty of being at least one hour later off the ground than their neighbours.'

Sufficient money was raised and taken to pay the grandstand bills after the first meeting. The builders were paid £8,315 6s, plus £470 9s 9d for preparation of the site. Their account included such extras as the chimney-pieces, the engraved 'first' or foundation stone, installing the kitchen equipment, a silver trowel at five guineas, a deed box costing £1 12s and locks and keys at £1 0s 3d. Mr Higgins, the architect, received £400. Refreshments during the Trustees' inspection, which took place on Tuesday, June 15th, 1839, cost £12 6s 3d.

The tontine remained in force from 1839 until 1858, by which time the value of a £100 share had risen to £175 and the grandstand was entirely free of debt.

The grandstand's first housekeeper, at a salary of twenty-five guineas a year, was Frank Day, who lived in the building. He died soon after, and was succeeded by his wife Sarah, and on her death in 1840, by William Hibburd, who was also Clerk of the Course, and his wife Sarah.

The admission prices were 5s per person per day on Tuesday, Wednesday and Friday, doubled on Cup day. A ticket for the meeting cost one sovereign. The superintendent received £25 for his duties, and the moneytakers received £2 10s each in 1839, increased in 1851, when there were five moneytakers and thirteen moneycheckers, each of whom received £3 10s, plus £5 in all for refreshments.

There was a constant suspicion that the fingers of the moneytakers were inclined to be sticky; typically in 1848 'The secretary reported to the Trustees his conviction that at the last and many previous meetings a considerably number of persons had unduly obtained admission into the Stand, owing to the inefficiency of the present system of Check Taking.'

Improved provisions for betting were brought about at the opening of the new grandstand. 'Those who have been in the habit of attending these races must have noticed and perhaps felt the annoyance of the betting ring right in the centre of the course. To remedy this, and accommodate the speculators themselves, a space of 55 feet from the railing to the colonnade has been enclosed in front of the grandstand, for the use of betting men and others who have paid for admission; the ring is formed here, and business is carried on without requiring the services of police to disperse them, as was the case when they were driven into the sorry accommodation of the old betting stand. A spacious room in the basement was also set aside for betting when the weather was bad, an early predecessor to the enclosed betting hall at Doncaster.

Intermittently there was trouble with defaulters entering the betting rooms, and under the heading NOTORIOUS DEFAULTERS, an 1843 Minute reads: 'Resolved no person notoriously in default for either Stakes forfeits or Bets upon horse Races will be allowed to enter the grandstand at Ascot and if any such person should have obtained admittance he will be expelled by order of the Master of the Buckhounds.'

The gaming rooms in the grandstand were very busy and popular. Then on May 29th, 1844, Lord Rosslyn, who was Master of the Buckhounds, told the Trustees of a letter received from the Under Secretary of State, Home Department, which stated that no gambling in the grandstand should be permitted at Ascot Races. The Trustees therefore forbade gambling in any part of the grandstand during the forthcoming meeting. A letter from the Office of Woods and Forests, dated the day after the Trustees' meeting followed swiftly and a copy incorporated in the Minutes, stated: 'It had been represented to him [the Under Secretary] that in a portion of the Stand at Ascot Gambling Tables are usually kept, during the Races' and he drew attention to the fact that 'the grandstand at Ascot is erected on Ground belonging to the Crown, and that the lease was liable to cancellation on six months' notice'—a broad enough hint.

When the gambling rooms in the grandstand were duly closed 'the want of something to do seemed to be felt by a very large class'.

After the old betting stand was demolished in 1859 it was replaced in the following year by a new Iron Stand, with a membership of 200 subscribers, nearly all racehorse owners and betting men. Members were nominated by a committee appointed by the Master of the Buckhounds, and the subscription was a modest £3 to cover membership for three years. When the Royal Enclosure was barred to those who had been divorced, the Iron Stand was much used by men who had been divorced. The stand, which was entirely barred to women, was nicknamed the 'zariba', a term originally referring to a thorn-bush enclosure for Sudanese cattle but popularly used for a sanctuary. The Iron Stand exists today, and is so called, although it is that part of the concrete Royal Ascot Enclosure stand which is most convenient for the bookmakers' rails. Incidentally, it was quite unthinkable for any lady to place a bet, or even to undertake a wager for money. The currency used was 'a pair of gloves', and it was considered ungallant to make a lady pay for such a losing bet. It was a case of 'Heads I win, tails you lose'.

Racecourse catering was, as always, a vexed point. The grandstand catering was in the hands of James Careless of the Wellington Tavern, Cornhill, in the City of London, who paid £50 per annum for the concession from 1839 to 1844, when it went up to £60 per annum, raised in 1849 to £65 'in consideration of the use of the Ice House recently built' and then in 1851 to £100 per annum, payable in two instalments.

The Trustees, who did their best to cope with every crisis, gave long service. The most active of them in the early years was Captain Henry Seymour, born in 1802, the son of Lord William Seymour, until his death 'of an apoplectic fit while entering his carriage' at the age of sixty-five. Thomas Ward of Round Oak, Englefield Green and his close friend Matthias Gilbertson, who served until 1863, when he retired at the age of eighty-six, seldom missed a meeting and were closely connected with early grandstand policy.

Outside the ground leased by the grandstand company, the racecourse continued in the autocratic control of the Master of the Buckhounds of the day, who was also an ex-officio Trustee.

When Queen Victoria came to the throne, alterations were made to the Royal Stand, and a tent was erected behind it in which the Queen and her party took refreshment. This was prettily hung with 'elegant blue and white chintz, ornamented with Turkish festoons', and elegantly furnished and carpeted. Queen Victoria's first visit to Ascot as sovereign was in 1838. She arrived in a carriage drawn by six grey horses, in a procession of seven carriages and a pony phaeton, preceded by Lord Erroll in his green uniform and escorted by Yeomen Prickers.

Her Majesty immediately on her arrival in the Royal Stand appeared at the window and courtesied with great elegance and condenscion [*sic*] to the numerous company assembled in front. She was received with repeated cheers, and was in excellent health and spirits, appearing to enjoy the scene, and to enter into the sport of the racing. Her Majesty was dressed in a pink slip, over which a lace dress or frock; she wore a white-drawn gauze bonnet, trimmed with pink ribbons and ornamented with artificial roses, both inside and out. She repeatedly during the day conversed with great liveliness with those around her, and occasionally surveyed the scene through a double opera glass.

Smugly *The Times* remarked of Cup day, 'As ladies read newspapers as well as gentlemen, it may not be improper to say that Her Majesty was dressed in white muslin, trimmed with lace. Her bonnet was of leghorn straw with ostrich feathers and trimmed with French sarcanet ribbon having flowers (roses) on the inside.'

Charles Greville commented thoughtfully: 'A great concourse of people on Thursday, the Queen tolerably received: some shouting, not a great deal, and few hats taken off. This mark of respect has quite gone out of use, and neither her station nor her sex procures it; we are not nearer a revolution for this, but it is ugly.'

It is easily forgotten how gay and vivacious Queen Victoria was before the worthiness of Prince Albert subdued her. She was renowned throughout Europe for her passion for riding, and her beautiful seat on a horse. As far away as Russia, some dashing society ladies, who were indulging in a horserace, sported 'caps *à la reine* Victoria'.

Racegoers could approach close to the Royal Stand up to the year 1844. In that year a space stretching from the Royal Box down to the rails at the winning-post was enclosed, and gatemen were stationed at the only entrance. Admission was granted only to the Royal Household, members of the Jockey Club, subscribers to the Iron Stand and those persons nominated by the Master of the Buckhounds.

Before the meeting in the following June (1845) this enclosure was enlarged, and it served the dual purpose of a Royal Enclosure, entered only by those accepted by the Master of the Buckhounds, and a saddling enclosure-cum-parade-ring. Earlier, the horses had been saddled on the course. *The Times* commented on the 'enclosure of a large space in front of the royal and weighing stands, for the purpose of saddling, etc; it is objected to by the trainers and with some reason, as not being sufficiently extensive, but to counterbalance this defect, *it prevents the annoyance that Her Majesty has hitherto suffered from the constant assemblings of a noisy mob immediately under the window of the Royal Stand*, and besides enables the company to enjoy the promenade on the course for at least ten minutes longer than the old arrangement.' (Author's italics.) This then was the beginning of the Royal Enclosure in its modern sense, some twenty years later than the date usually given.

Saddling horses in front of the weighing room began in 1838, when trainers and jockeys were forbidden to ride on the course, but the regulation had been honoured in the breach. A number of improvements were made in that year. The old weighing room and judge's stand, which had been erected in the centre of the course, and which had interrupted the view of the racing from the stands were moved over. Six years later, the judge's seat was rebuilt, and behind it was constructed a building containing the weighing room on the ground floor, a first-floor stand for the stewards and their personal friends, and the roof, which was reserved for 'the use of trainers and jockies, who have good reason to be thankful for the pains taken for their accommodation'.

In 1838 horses were numbered on the race-card; a winner's board was introduced and the winner's number was hoisted on a board after the race. Ascot led the country in numbering horses, and this was so new, that a careful explanation was necessary. 'The list contains nine races, each horse having a number affixed to his name in the card; as the jockeys weighed, the numbers were exhibited on a black board placed conspicuously on the judge's chair, and on the termination of each race, the number of the winning horse (is shown), much confusion and trickery being thus prevented.' In 1841 the numbers of the horses weighed out were also exhibited on the number board before each race.

The judge's stand had deliberately been kept separate from the weighing stand and placed apart in a small enclosure of its own 'to prevent the annoyance of gratuitous opinions on the decisions of races.' from the trainers on the roof behind. The Clark family had the honour of providing the judge at Ascot. John Clark the elder, who combined judging with the design of racecourse stands, held the post from 1806 till 1822 when he was succeeded by his son John Clark the second, who was judge at Ascot from 1823 to 1852. John Francis Clark was appointed Judge in 1852, and he soon earned himself a high reputation for reliability and integrity. Indeed, *The Times* commented in 1855: 'to testify to the correctness of Mr Clark's decisions would be an act of superogation'. This third John Clark was also an architect, and in 1854 he designed the Master of the Buckhounds'

The Royal Drive passes the old stands.

ıblic coaches no longer
me from London, but
ınibuses plied to the
urse from the Great
'estern railway station
Windsor. Some guests
ove from nearby
untry houses in private
aches.

Even before the First World War, cars were beginning to take over: the car park in June 1907.

Early racing: Ben Alder unseats his jockey William Griggs at the start of the New Stakes, 1910.

A start at the old Golden Gates.

A rural scene out in the country. The Biennial Stakes of 1901, won by Fortunatis.

Persimmon in the winners' enclosure after his popular win in the Ascot Gold Cup for Edward, Prince of Wales, 1897. Note the jockeys' names.

Mrs Lily Langtry's Merman, after winning the Gold Cup of 1900; Tod Sloan in the saddle. (To modern eyes he does not seem to be riding very short.)

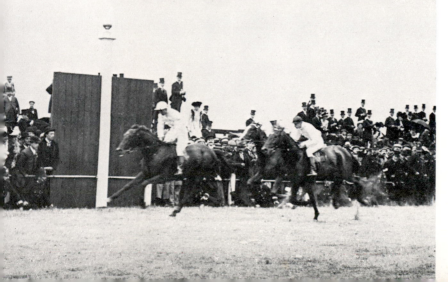

Santoi winning the Gold Cup of 1901, ridden by Fred Rickaby, who was killed in the First World War. He was followed home by Kilmarnock II (L. Reiff) and Forfarshire (D. Maher). The ground was exceptionally hard that year.

Jockeys and trainers descending the stairs of their stand, 1898.

Lt-Col Gordon Carter, Clerk of the Course at Ascot, in his office in 1922. He spanned the years from lavish Edwardian Ascot to the heart-breaking run-down of the Second World War.

Social stratification is illustrated in this 1907 Ascot scene.

Woman and child behind the carriages, 1907.

Crossing the course, 1907.

Elegant backs to the ladies' dresses, 1900.

The Royal Enclosure stand and lawn, 1905.

Paddock scene, 1908.

Black Ascot: in mourning for King Edward VII, 1910.

A last glimpse of carefree pre-war Ascot. Gypsy woman selling wares: June 1914.

Stand at Ascot. His son-in-law, Mr C. E. Robinson, succeeded him as judge in 1887.

Lord Kinnaird was Master of the Buckhounds in 1839; he was succeeded in 1841 by the genial Earl of Rosslyn, who had two spells of duty, from 1841 to 1846 and from 1852 to 1853. Lord Rosslyn, leaving the course in 1845, jumped a ditch near the kennel when his mare fell and rolled on him; at first he was thought to be seriously hurt, but the damage was slight. Earl Granville, who served from 1846 to 1848 was more interested in politics than racing. Then came the first of the three spells of duty of the painstaking and frugal Earl of Bessborough, a keen hunting man, who was Master of the Buckhounds from 1848 to 1852, from 1853 to 1858, and finally from 1859 to 1866. The Earl of Sandwich was briefly in office from 1858 to 1859.

The day-to-day conduct of the racecourse was in the hands of the Clerk of the Course. The Hibburd family was long connected with Ascot. William Hibburd had been appointed Clerk of the Course in 1836 and continued in that office until 1851. He was a huge man and very strong, renowned for 'great coolness and judgment and honesty of purpose'. Not only did he act as Clerk of the Course at Ascot, but also as starter, and he held many posts on other racecourses as well, sometimes as Clerk of the Course, sometimes as starter and sometimes as judge. In spite of his early strength, William Hibburd's health failed in middle life, and his death was accelerated by being knocked down by a racehorse at a Manchester meeting in the autumn of 1850.

William Hibburd's widow was appointed housekeeper on her husband's death. They had two sons connected with Ascot, Henry, born in 1831, who had acted as Clerk of the Course in 1850 and who often acted as starter, and Edward, who was appointed Clerk of the Course after his father's death. In August 1860 Edward Hibburd ran foul of both the Master of the Buckhounds and the Trustees, and was summarily dismissed. At the same time, 'it appeared expedient to the Trustees to terminate their engagement with Mrs William Hibburd as resident housekeeper and secretary'. They softened the blow by awarding Mrs Hibburd, by way of an annuity, the exact sum she received as a salary, which was £50 per annum. 'They did not ask her to vacate her apartments in the grandstand at once, but if she had left before Christmas 1860 they begged her further acceptance of six months' annuity in advance'. Edward Hibburd died in 1867.

The most famous starter associated with Ascot was the remarkable Charles Davis, who was Huntsman of the Royal Buckhounds for forty-four years, and who acted as starter at Ascot from the 1820s until 1845.

Charles Davis was born in 1788, and at the age of twelve became a whip to his father, who hunted the King's Harriers. When George III was hunting, because of the danger of highwaymen, he was always accompanied by armed guards, and young Davis became the King's pistol-boy. Later, he used to precede the King over the fences, breaking them down so that they were easier for the King to jump. As a huntsman 'His knowledge of his craft could hardly be exceeded, no detail concerning the runs of his stags, or the nature of his country was unknown to him. Not less notable than his practical skill, was the wonderful control he exerted with the surest and most effective tact . . . nature had endowed Davis with a demeanour which made impertinance impossible . . . he was seen at his best when he figured in the Royal Procession at Ascot.' In 1836 an engraving was made of Davis from a portrait painted by his brother, Richard Barrett Davis: the original was in the Dick sale of sporting pictures at Sotheby's in 1973. Charles Davis died in October 1867, having served four sovereigns with distinction.

T. McGeorge was another well-known starter, who became Jockey Club starter in 1860. He was a vigorous and energetic man, who used to walk on foot to and from the the start of every race, but he was a slow — a very slow starter. He died in 1885 when he was only forty-four years old.

There were certainly justifiable mutterings about the tardiness and quality of starts, of McGeorge and of the Hibburds. In 1860, at the start of the Hunt Cup 'considerable delay took place at the post, not owing to the fractiousness of any particular horse, but principally attributable to the perversity of certain jockeys, who obstinately refused to listen to the directions or obey the commands of the starter'.

In 1861 again there was trouble. 'The breakings away were as frequent and nearly every starter took part in them . . . even the most industrious speculator, who seldom likes to omit an opportunity of "laying", closed his book in sheer weariness, while the patience of that portion of the spectators who were indifferent to the mere racing was quite exhausted.'

The ever eagle eye of Admiral Rous turned upon the problem. In a letter to *Bell's Life* the predecessor of *The Sporting Life*, he wrote: 'It is an extraordinary fact that the art of starting racehorses on fair terms for short courses should be considered an arduous task. They are not ridden by sailors, or tailors, but by the most accomplished jockeys, who are assisted by well-paid officials, under the superintendence of stewards. Forty-nine horses out of fifty come to the starting-post like sheep. It is not until they have been ill-used and wantonly spurred that they become, like their riders, inclined to be mischievous.'

Surprisingly enough the gallant admiral did not himself make a very good hand as a starter. He was much criticised for his start of the St Leger of 1851; indeed Bird, his biographer, believed that he never again undertook the role. But in 1861, when there was an enormous field of thirty-three runners for the Royal Hunt Cup at Ascot, Admiral Rous insisted on starting the race. *The Times* wrote: 'Admiral Rous accompanied the starter to the post, and undertook the responsibility of getting so large a field off. His starting, however, was not so successful as his handicapping, and when he gave the signal, the horses were not in line. Buccaneer [the favourite and winner] was in front when the flag fell.'

The starts were eventually brought under control by the introduction of more severe penalties by the Jockey Club in 1863.

The condition of the course at Ascot continued to give cause for concern. It took a lot of wear and tear apart from racing. The royal party travelled along it, jockeys rode on it on their way to weigh out. Worst of all, it was the promenade for thousands of spectators between races. No wonder *The Times* commented in 1842: 'What is by courtesy "the turf" is at present so hard, slippery and dusty, that it is sufficient to break the hooves of all animals who are compelled to gallop on its perilous surface.' Yet in the *same* year the *same* correspondent was bitterly complaining about yet another regulation despairingly introduced to reduce the use of the track by spectators with the comment:

One [regulation] which appears to deserve more reprehension than compliments is the newly-imported practice of continually clearing the course, and allowing no time, as heretofore, for promenading. This is an interpolation at Ascot of the rule at Epsom, but it is one that ought at once to be repudiated and dismissed. The promenade at Ascot has for years been the principal inducement for thousands to attend . . . Whether this innovation is to be attributed to the caprice of any one or two persons in authority, or as a mode of forcing the whole of the better sort of persons who attend into the grandstand, where they are charged 5s a head for standing room, we know not, but this we know, that if such a practice be continued, it will make Ascot racecourse a very dull place and eventually degrade it to a mere *rendezvous* for jockeys, thimble-riggers and black-legs of all degrees.

Strong stuff this, about what appears to be a practical measure to improve the track. But it had its effect: the promenaders were back in the following year. The promenade was one of the sights of the London season, and Ascot assumed a special place in the social calendar. 'Devoid of the noise and confusion of Epsom, Ascot presents attractions which are all-powerful to Londoners which have the effect of drawing lady visitors to the Heath, as many a Benedict, instead of taking his spouse to the Derby, has to make a promise of accompanying her to Ascot.'

Descriptions of fashion are surprisingly late in appearing. Only the Queen's dress was described in the 1840s and 1850s, and references to individual women were rare. On Cup day in 1852, when it rained incessantly it was indeed commented 'a few adventurous ladies braved the showers, attired in waterproof cloaks from head to foot, a style of costume which attracted no little observation'. The problems of dress were reversed in 1856, when the weather was dry and the land parched. 'Ladies' dresses, however, were grievously damaged by the dust which the traffic and the wind raised in dense, blinding clouds, whitening the garments and spoiling the appearance of the visitors.'

One simile was almost certain to appear, year after year, in journal after journal; it was on the lines of: 'the many-hued dresses of the ladies glistened *like a tulip bed* of different shapes and dyes' (author's italics).

The ease of racegoing at Ascot was even compared sarcastically with the squash of the Courts.

> The platform [at Paddington] in London was made quite picturesque by the many-coloured dresses of the ladies who promenaded it, and who, as they were not attending a Drawing Room, but only required seats in a railway carriage, ran no risk of having their dresses torn and *toilettes* disarranged owing to a crushing crowd for which no provision had been made. Trains were despatched at frequent intervals, and from the excellent arrangements confusion was avoided, and the excursionists experienced little inconvenience or annoyance.

Once arrived at Ascot, 'ladies took their seats with as much ease as they would at the Opera, and their dresses were no more crumpled by the crowd than they would have been on a *fête* day at the Crystal Palace.'

Even with trains displacing carriages, there were enormous numbers of horses on the Heath during racing, quite apart from the racehorses. There were the hacks of officials, trainers and jockeys, the horses used in the Royal Drive, and of the mounted police, the vanners which brought provisions and supplies to the course, and there were the horses who drew the thousands of racegoers along roads from which rose ribbons of dust. Horses pulled 'four-in-hands driven by noblemen, horse-dealers, sharpers, black-legs and stage coachmen, brischkas, phaetons, gigs, tilburies, dennets ... besides omnibuses from Mile End, Paddington, the Bank, Blackwall, Kentish Town, the Borough.' During racing the horses were unharnessed and placed 'in tents and edifices of turves etc ... scattered over the Heath.'

At the time of the building of the grandstand the Trustees had sunk a well, and were successful in finding 'a fine spring of water flowing profusely' at a depth of eighty feet. Prior to this, water for watering the horses had had to be brought on to the course in water-carts and barrels and the going price had been up to 2s a pail. (The situation was even worse on the Downs at Epsom, where on Derby Day, up to 1s a quart was charged for watering a carriage horse.)

Shelters consisting of tarpaulins over wooden frames were erected annually at a cost of over £150 per annum to provide shade for the royal carriage horses. In 1843 these were replaced by two buildings in the west enclosure behind the Royal Stand, one to hold sixteen carriages and the other 100 horses, with small lodges for waiting-rooms for the coachmen, postillions and grooms at the ends of the building. No hay racks nor mangers were provided for the horses, as they would occupy the stalls for only a short while.

There continued to be much confusion during the arrival and dispersal of this vast assembly of horse-drawn vehicles, although the volume and the disorder gradually decreased as rail travel took over. In 1839 the arrival on the course of the Prince of Capua's carriage 'was beset by fifty or sixty cads and stablemen of the lowest description. They almost took possession of it, some pulling one way and some another, and but for the active interference of Bartlett, one of Her Majesty's hunting establishment, the carriage would not have arrived at the place intended for its reception.' Incidentally, a 'cad' was originally an unbooked coach passenger, whose fare the coachman had appropriated and later 'a confederate of a lower grade' (O.E.D.).

In 1840 a Colonel Cawthorn, driving with a friend to Ascot, behind a high-spirited horse 'the animal becoming restive started off furiously. Colonel Cawthorn leaped from the gig into the road and, pitching on his head, received a severe concussion of the brain'. A Colonel Bulkeley was more fortunate, losing merely his dignity. While raising his hat to Queen Victoria, his horse was startled and he lost the hat and nearly his seat. There was a fatal accident in 1851 during the running for the Queen's Vase, when a mare owned by Sir Joseph Hawley fell crossing the road and was galloping loose when 'she came in contact with a gentleman's coachman, who had run into the course when the horses had passed, and knocked him down, causing his death shortly after'. Ten years later Scrubbing Brush ridden by Challoner knocked down a woman with an infant in her arms. The saddle was broken, but fortunately jockey, woman and child escaped with a fright.

Elnathan Flatman, known as 'Nat', a famous jockey who was particularly successful at Ascot, had an incident-packed race in the Ascot Derby Stakes, at the royal meeting in 1852. He was riding the Duke of Richmond's Red Hind. The filly had started in an earlier race that afternoon, when she had been ridden by Bartholomew, but she had made a great fuss at the start, got off slowly and finished last. So Nat was put up in the Derby Stakes, with the hope of better things. 'In this race Red Hind, as usual, was restive, Nat being obliged to dismount two or three times before she could be induced to go to the post. A start was at last effected and the filly had at last taken the lead, when Red Hind fell over a dog opposite the stand, and rolled over on Nat's legs; he was speedily extracted, and happily escaped injury.'

In 1844 two jockeys had an unpleasant experience on the Old Mile course, when Roebuck ridden by Carroll and Mill Bolton, the favourite, owned and ridden by Mr J. Rogers, fell into the ditch at the side of the course. Carroll was uninjured but 'little Rogers' was much shaken, and was carried into the Brick Kiln farm.

Three years later Bartholomew, who was having only his second ride after a very bad accident at Goodwood in the previous year, was involved in a mishap in the Gold Cup in which he was riding Winkfield. Winkfield, who was trained at Ascot, bolted for the gate by which he usually left the course, and as Bartholomew was pulling him up his stirrup leather broke and he fell heavily to the ground, but fortunately he was comparatively unhurt. In the next race the New Stakes on the Two-Years-Old Course there was a more serious accident, when a horse ridden by Tyrol struck into the heels of the horse in front and fell, and the jockey was severely injured.

In 1861 James Goater was seriously injured when the filly he was riding to the start slipped and fell against the chains used to keep spectators off the course, rolling on Goater.

Ascot, with its undulating contours and short run-in, has always been a course on which certain jockeys have excelled. In the early part of Victoria's reign Nat Flatman was the outstanding jockey. Born in Suffolk in 1810, he was apprenticed to Lord Berners' Newmarket stable at the age of fifteen and thereafter rode an enormous number of winners. From 1834 to 1859 (the year of his death), Nat had at least one winner at Ascot in every year but three. Nat was a little man with large, luminous eyes, a hefty broken nose, a dimpled chin and long sidewhiskers. He was a better jockey than a stylist but sparing with his whip and a great match-rider. He was also a model of integrity and discretion.

Nat's first Ascot winner was in the Albany Stakes in 1834 on Charles Greville's filly Pickle, landing a gamble, as a racecourse rumour had been

whispered that 'the filly had a leg'. Nat won nine races at the royal
meeting in 1845, including the Emperor's Plate (which had temporarily
taken the place of the Gold Cup). Then he bettered his own Ascot record
in 1847 when he won a fantastic eleven out of twenty-nine races and
matches. He won three races on the Tuesday, the Trial Stakes on Lord
Orford's Prussic Acid, the Welcome Stakes on the Duke of Richmond's
Red Hart, and a sweepstakes on Mr Payne's Glendower. On the Wednesday he had an off-day with only one winner, which was in the opening
race on the Duke of Richmond's Reflection. On Cup day he had three
winners, the Queen's Plate and the Visitors' Plate on Lord Orford's
Footstool, and a sweep on Mr Mostyn's Crozier. Nat finished with a
grandstand flourish, taking the last four races of the meeting, a sweep in a
canter on Lord Stradbroke's Coningsby, the first class of the Wokingham
(the second class having been run earlier) on Lord Chesterfield's Pic-nic,
the Great Western Railway Race on the same owner's Lady Wild Air and
then the Borough Maiden Plate, again on Pic-nic.

James Chapple, a quiet, unassuming Devonian was also a great Ascot
jockey. He won many races there for Sir Gilbert Heathcote, the well-
known owner who was a perpetual steward at Epsom. Chapple was at his
best on a lazy horse, which had to be held up for a late pounce. His last
Ascot winner was in 1847.

Jem Robinson was an older man, born in Newmarket in 1794. A
melancholy man, with a long face and blunt features, he was respected as a
fine horseman and an upright man. Perhaps he was even better at Epsom,
where he won the Derby six times, but he also rode many fine races at
Ascot. He had a particularly good record in the Gold Cup, which he won
six times, on Lucetta in 1830, on Cetus in 1831, on Camarine in 1832, all
for Sir M. Wood; in 1835 on Glencoe, in 1839 on Caravan for Captain
Berkeley, and finally in 1843 on Ralph for Lord Albermarle. In all
Robinson won over fifty races at Ascot, before he entered the winners'
enclosure for the last time on Lord Clifden's Strongbow in his fourth
Wokingham Handicap win in 1851.

Sam Rogers who was born at Newmarket in 1818, where his father
was trainer to Lord Lowther, did not enjoy the same high reputation;
indeed he was warned off for several years after he was found guilty of
pulling Ratan in the notorious Running Rein Derby of 1844. His fall
from grace was a sad blow to his employer and supporter, Lord George
Bentinck. Rogers rode in races as a featherweight at the age of nine and
went on riding after he became a trainer. His last win at Ascot was in
1855 on the Duke of Bedford's Keepsake, after being unseated on the way
to the post. Roger's fondness for the whip was evident at Ascot as elsewhere,

as for example when he won the King's Plate on Mr Osbaldeston's Mic Mac, 'by whipping, stoutness and riding', and when he won the Ascot Derby in 1839 on Bloomsbury, 'not without a taste of the whip'.

All the many members of the Day family rode with success at Ascot. C. Day won several races on family horses in the early 1830s. 'Uncle Sam' Day, winner of three Derby Stakes and of several Ascot races, set up as a trainer at Ascot after he retired from the saddle. John Day the elder had around a score of Ascot winners between 1817 and the early 1840s, including four wins on Cup day 1839. Nor was his brother Sam Day of Danebury without his Ascot great victories.

William Day and John Day junior were the sons of John Day senior, and although they did well at Ascot, they were of dubious reputation and both were, at one time or another, warned off. It was the lesser-known Alfred Day, born in 1830, their younger brother, who was the most successful jockey of the family at Ascot, winning twenty-four races in all, including four in 1847 and the Gold Cup in 1854 on the first Triple Crown winner, West Australian, before his final Ascot winner in 1857.

Other notable Ascot jockeys in the early years of Queen Victoria's reign were the north country jockey Templeman; Frank Butler, a nephew of Sam Chifney junior; John (Tiny) Wells, who won at least one race at nine successive royal meetings in the 1850s, while 1855 was a vintage year in which George Fordham and Jim Goater each won his first Ascot race.

Bell, when a tiny shaver, wrote his way into the records when, after winning the Ascot Stakes in 1838, he was summoned before Queen Victoria, who asked him his weight. This he refused to tell her, saying, 'Please, Ma'am, Master says as how I must never tell my weight.' The Queen was much amused and presented him with a £10 note. Bell's secret was kept in the records, which gave his weight as the traditional 'feather', but it is said he weighed no more than four stones.

This young Bell must have had a mind of his own. In 1844 he was told to pull a horse Bloodstone in the New Stakes; he was to jump the horse off, 'get a taste of Old England', the likely favourite, and after a quarter of a mile to pull Bloodstone up and on no account to win, as the owner wanted to get good odds for him in later races, including the next season's classics. On the eve of the race, Bell told one of his regular owners about these orders, and took his advice to do his best to win the race. In the New Stakes Bloodstone got off to an excellent start, was soon in the lead, made strong running all the way, and won by six lengths. 'The incident is as creditable to the jockey as it is disgraceful to the owner,' said *The Times*. 'The stewards, we believe, do not mean to let it pass unnoticed.'

This was the second running of the New Stakes, for two-years-old, then run over half a mile, which continued under that name until 1973, when it was renamed the Norfolk Stakes, in honour of the late Duke of Norfolk, who had recently retired as the Queen's Representative at Ascot.

Other new or renamed races of the early part of Queen Victoria's reign, were the Queen's Vase, originally the Queen's Silver Vase, which took the place of the King's Plate, and the Ascot Stakes, which replaced the Oatlands Stakes in 1839. The Coronation Stakes for three-years-old fillies, run over the New Mile for the first time in 1840 took the place of the Windsor Forest Stakes for three-years-old fillies, which had been run over the Old Mile. The Fern Hill Stakes for two- and three-years-old over half a mile was first run in 1840. But the most important new race was the Royal Hunt Cup, a handicap over the straight mile, which was an immediate success from its introduction in 1843. It immediately became a big betting medium, and greatly improved the Wednesday card.

Among the races which slipped from sight was the Postmasters and Innkeepers Plate, run on the Wednesday and doomed by the advent of the railway. The Great Western Railway was eventually rather reluctantly persuaded to sponsor a race in its place, but that lasted only a short time. The King's Plate for hunters disappeared, and so did the Buckhurst Dinner Stakes. The biennial and triennial races, open to the same horses for two or three seasons over extending distances, flourished sporadically. Sir Joseph Hawley's Vatican won the second and third parts, in 1849 and 1850, of the first Triennial Stakes run at Ascot. The unhappy Vatican, who was later treated with unparalleled cruelty, even for those times, when he became unmanageable at stud, was of uncertain temper even then. The start for the last leg of the Triennial in 1850 was considerably delayed by Vatican's restlessness, but he won 'by a short half-length' from Lord Eglinton's consistent Elthiron, ridden by Marlow.

The Reform Bill notwithstanding, the Borough Members of Parliament continued to be considered suitable 'touches' for race sponsorship.

Many fine horses appeared at Ascot.

The delightful Beeswing won 'The Golden Cup' (as it was poetically termed that year) in 1842, as a nine-years-old. Her name was spelt in contemporary accounts as Bee's-wing, then for many years as Bee's Wing, but the *Stud Book* has now standardised its spelling as Beeswing. Beeswing stood only 15·2 and was light-boned, having been poorly fed as a foal. Beeswing was a well-advanced yearling before she 'rubbed her nose against an oat', as Theo Taunton described it. She had a lovely head, was strong behind the saddle, and ran looking as though she needed the race. She was Dr Syntax's best daughter, out of a big, unraced, lame mare by

8

Ardrossan. Beeswing was a tremendous kicker in her stall, but showed no vice whatever at the post, and although a hard puller before she settled down, was 'a most delightful mare to ride'.

In her Ascot Cup appearance she was ridden by Cartwright.

Eringo [a four-years-old owned by Mr Thornhill] was first from the post, and kept in front for a quarter of a mile. The mare then overpowered her jockey and went away, with a good lead, followed by Eringo, Lanercost [winner of the 1841 Gold Cup, the favourite] lying third, The Nob fourth and St Francis last ... in making the top turn the pace became severe, but no alteration in the places was observed until they reached the Brick Kiln, where Lanercost was beaten; and at the turn he was last in the race. Eringo held second place to the stand, where The Nob passed him and challenged the mare. For a moment he headed her, but the 'Pride of the North' resumed her position in a couple of strides, and after a fine race won by half a length.

The old mare had only one more race. She ran at Doncaster, where she went off at a rattling pace in front, which the other runners were unable to match, and won by six lengths. She then retired in triumph to stud, where she had two sons, Newminster and Nunnykirk, both by Touchstone. From her are descended, through Newminster, The Hermit, Lord Clifden, Petrarch, Hampton, Bay Ronald, Ladas, Ayrshire and their distinguished progeny.

Another great mare which distinguished herself at Ascot was Alice Hawthorn, a bay mare foaled in 1838, by Muley Moloch out of Rebecca, tracing back to the Bay Bloody Buttocks, foaled in 1729. Mr Martin Eversfield, author of the British section in *Thoroughbred Breeding of the World* (Podzun Verlag) has kindly traced her career:

Ran 3 times in 1841, won 2 (each of 2 miles).
Ran 9 times in 1842, won 7, distances up to 2 miles 1 furlong.
Ran 26 times in 1843, won 18 races up to 3 miles 1 furlong.
Ran 24 times in 1844, won 21 races up to 4 miles.
Ran 10 times in 1845, won four races, up to 3 miles 1 furlong.

In all, Alice Hawthorn ran in seventy-two races and won fifty-two of them, including the Chester Cup, the Goodwood Cup and the Doncaster Cup twice. At Ascot, on Tuesday, June 4th, 1844, Alice Hawthorn started at three to one on in the Queen's Vase, in which she was ridden by Hesseltine. She won as she liked — 'so hollow a race was never before seen at Ascot!'

On that occasion Alice Hawthorn had a distinguished audience. The race was run in the presence of the Emperor of Russia, Nicholas I, and the King of Saxony, though *not* of their hostess, Queen Victoria. The overseas visitors were escorted by Prince Albert.

> The Emperor was dressed in a plain blue coat, having no decorations whatsoever . . . The Emperor looked remarkably well, he had his hat off nearly the length of the stands, and bowed repeatedly to the persons assembled, who greeted his arrival. The Duke of Wellington wore Windsor uniform, with the riband of the Garter and several stars. Over them he wore a light Chesterfield frock coat.
>
> At the conclusion of the race for the Queen's Cup or Vase, which was won very easily by Alice Hawthorn, the Emperor of Russia, the King of Saxony and Prince Albert left the Royal Stand, and without any warning, came down upon the turf beneath to examine the winner, with whose points the Emperor seemed particularly pleased. On this occasion the police had much ado, from the suddenness of the visit, to keep back the public. The Emperor was loudly cheered, and evidently enjoyed the scene and the struggle of the spectators to get a close view of him . . . The Emperor patted Alice Hawthorn with obvious satisfaction.

The Queen attended on Thursday, which as usual was Cup day. She was 'in delicate health' — Prince Alfred later Duke of Edinburgh, her second son and fourth child, was born on August 6th — and in deep mourning. Her ladies were also in unrelieved black. The procession consisted of nine carriages, and 'an immense mob came close to the wheels of the carriage'.

It was an anxious time for the police. Wednesday's *Times* had reported: 'that a parcel of blackguards . . . purpose making a display and insulting the royal party.' In the event there was little trouble, and indeed great enthusiasm from the enormous crowds. The only demonstration was an unsuccessful attempt to distribute leaflets when: 'Some vagabonds, employed by persons of the same class as themselves, made an attempt in the earlier part of the day, to get up an expression of bad feeling towards the Emperor of Russia by scattering about bills, in which that Monarch is made to be a much greater tyrant than Nero or Caligula, and a farrago of lies and libels raked up denouncing his name.'

The Gold Cup was won by Lord Albermarle's unnamed chestnut colt by Defence, out of a mare by Reveller, ridden by Whitehouse, which started at ten to one. Lord Albermarle promptly and diplomatically named the colt The Emperor, a particularly apt choice as the Emperor of Russia had already signified his intention to give £500 a year, during his lifetime, for a Cup to be run at Ascot. Lord Rosslyn, the Master of the Buckhounds, had made the announcement on the Tuesday in the Stewards'

Stand, adding that, unlike the gift of the Grand Duke Michael at New-market, who endowed the Cesarewitch with cash, the Emperor wished to make his prize in the form of a piece of plate £500 in value, and that the first piece would be a shield with the Russian coat-of-arms on it.

It was decided that this Emperor's Cup would take the place of the Ascot Gold Cup. The Emperor's Plate was given by Nicholas I for nine years, until the outbreak of the Crimean war between Russia and England brought to a harsh halt the friendship between the Emperor and the Queen. The design of the Emperor's Shield varied from year to year and in 1845 took the form of a statuette of Falconetti's famous equestrian statue of Peter the Great, still to be seen in Leningrad. This is the statue in which the prancing horse is supported only by the hind-legs and the tail.

A particularly suitable winner of the Emperor's Plate was Van Tromp, winner in 1849, because the horse was afterwards sold to the Emperor of Russia (although he hesitated because of the horse's ewe neck), and became a great favourite of his. Van Tromp foaled in 1844, was an all brown son of Lanercost out of Barbelle, a mare by Sandbeck. He was a big, powerful horse. Struck into in the Derby, he could only finish third, but he got his revenge in the St Leger, which he won very easily.

In the Emperor's Plate Van Tromp was ridden by Charles Marlow, and owned by the popular Earl of Eglinton, who had bought him before his racing days. His principal rival was Mr Merry's bad-tempered grey horse Chanticleer, ridden by Nat Flatman. Van Tromp was the early leader, but as they turned into the straight Chanticleer challenged and almost got up, but Van Tromp answered the efforts of his rider, and drew away, to win by half a length. *The Druid* was inclined to blame Nat's judgment, declaring that if he had waited with Chanticleer until the stand, he would have got first run and beaten Van Tromp. It was, in any case, a most popular win with the crowds.

Lord Eglinton was so taken with Van Tromp that he had agreed with his breeder, Colonel Vansittart, to buy every perfectly formed foal of Van Tromp's dam Barbelle. As a result Lord Eglinton acquired The Flying Dutchman, by Bay Middleton out of Barbelle. The half-brothers were very similar in appearance: each was brown without a trace of white, with powerful, sloping shoulders, a little long in the back, and not quite so good behind as before the saddle. But the temperament of the two brothers was very different. Van Tromp was an exceedingly idle horse, who needed much hard work to get him fit. The Flying Dutchman went so freely and pulled so much that he never needed half the preparation of his brother, and was always galloped on his own. Both horses had irritable tempera-ments, and Van Tromp used to be trained in a muzzle.

The Flying Dutchman duly won the Derby and the St Leger and when, as a four-years-old he ran in the Emperor's Plate at Ascot in 1850, not surprisingly to modern eyes he started as odds on favourite.

Peep o'day [a bay mare owned by Lord Howth and ridden by Alfred Day] made the running, followed by Canezou [ridden by Frank Butler] and Little Jack, the favourite next and Jericho last. They ran at so capital a pace to the Swinley Post, where the mare took a strong lead, which she retained to the last turn. Here The Flying Dutchman, who had been drawing up from the Brick Kiln turn, went up, quitting her in an instant, and won in the commonest canters by eight lengths . . . we seldom remember so much general interest excited about any Cup race. To the surprise of all it turned out a most hollow affair.

Another son of Bay Middleton, out of the mare Jenny Lind, The Hermit, which was foaled in 1851, won the Queen's Vase at Ascot in 1854. The Hermit was owned by Mr Gully and ridden by Wells. To twentieth-century eyes it was a somewhat unusual race. 'When the flag dropped Hermit walked off, followed by Rataplan [ridden by Nat Flatman]. After proceeding 300 yards Hermit ventured upon a gentle trot, and so they went on until they arrived at the foot of Swinley Hill when a canter was raised, and after entering the Old Mile course, the pace was gradually improved, until the race began in earnest Hermit then made strong play, and at last won easily by one and a half lengths.'

The Hermit was the winner of the Two Thousand Guineas in 1854 in his first appearance on a racecourse, and was then third in the Derby. He should not be confused with the Newminster colt foaled in 1864, whose wins at Ascot in 1866 and 1867 will be recorded in the next chapter.

Rataplan, which came second in the 1854 Queen's Vase, but had won it in 1853, was a considerable character. A brother to Stockwell, he was foaled in 1850 on the day on which his breeder, Mr Theobald, died. He was a chestnut with a blaze, had an unusually marked half-white off fore-leg and a white stocking on his off hind-leg. He had a gentle temperament, and used to lie down while his mane was being plaited, go to sleep after feeding, and was for ever stumbling over his feet at exercise. Yet, when he liked, he could buck any boy or jockey off his back. During Rataplan's career he won more than forty races.

Another horse with an amazing record of wins was that great fighter Fisherman, by Heron out of Mainbrace, foaled in 1853 and bought as a two-years-old by Mr Tom Parr. Mostly in Mr Parr's puce and white colours Fisherman won sixty-seven races, including twenty-two Queen's

Plates, two Queen's Vases and nine cups. In the course of his long career he beat most of the good horses of his time. 'In after times,' said *The Druid*, 'Mr Parr loved to tell how he was wont to humour Fisherman either with a long gallop or a short one, but never left him long without work; and he constantly referred to the 65 lbs and head beating which Fisherman gave to Misty Morn [the winner that year—1858—of twelve races]; and which performance he regarded as Fisherman's greatest triumph in all his sixty-seven victories.'

Fisherman as a five-years-old won the Ascot Gold Cup in 1858.

In accordance with custom, [wrote *The Times*] the horses were paraded round the enclosure in front of the Royal Stand before proceeding to the starting-post . . . when the flag was dropped Princess Royal [a three-years-old ridden by Tuck] went off in the lead, which she increased to a hundred yards before reaching the grandstand, the rest headed by Arsenal and Warlock [Alfred Day] running in a cluster. On rounding the top turn Princess Royal was still further ahead, and on descending the Swinley Hill Commotion [Flatman] drew into second place, Arsenal and Warlock, nearly side by side, coming next, Glidermire going on fifth, and about three lengths in the rear was Fisherman. No further change occurred until reaching the Brick Kiln turn, when Princess Royal gradually 'came back' to her pursuers, Arsenal taking second place . . . and Fisherman well laid up. On entering the straight, Princess Royal was beaten [and Fisherman still in sixth place]. Before reaching the distance, Sunbeam was disposed of, and Fisherman soon afterwards took his place at Arsenal's quarters. At the half distance Wells called upon the old horse, who cleared Arsenal without any perceptible effort, and won by a length and a half.

Fisherman went on to win the Queen's Plate on the following day, 'in a canter', at the somewhat prohibitive odds of 100 to 6 on.

Blink Bonny, a rare female winner of the Derby, was another fine racehorse seen at Ascot during the period, although she merely 'walked over' for a sweepstakes. After she had cantered over unopposed, Queen Victoria asked to see her, and the mare was afterwards walked round the enclosure in front of the Queen's Stand, and was carefully looked over by the Queen and her suite.

Quite a number of the legends connected with Ascot proved apocryphal when contemporary verification was sought, but the most extraordinary story of all—that Queen Victoria had been so excited by the finish of a race that she had put her head through the glass window of her box—has proved to be entirely true. It happened on June 15th, 1854.

During the race for the New Stakes, an incident occurred which was fortunately attended with no other result than a hearty laugh. Just as the horses reached the Royal Stand, Her Majesty in her eagerness to see the race, not perceiving that the window where she had been standing, had been put down, leant forward rather hastily to look out, and broke a pane of glass with which she came in contact. The occurrence was perceived by only a few persons on the course, but it produced a great deal of merriment in the royal party, the Queen herself setting an example.

But the prejudices of Prince Albert were having an ever-increasing influence upon the Queen. He was totally uninterested in sport; indeed he did not much like an open-air life — which she did — and when they went riding together, he would be followed by a coach in which he took refuge if it began to rain. Sometimes Queen Victoria resisted his wishes during his life, and often she imperiously exercised her authority as sovereign; but all was to change after his death. Thereafter the Prince Consort's wishes took on the force of Holy Writ, as Queen Victoria dedicated herself to a long widowhood of perpetual mourning. After his death on December 14th, 1861, for the forty remaining years of her life, Queen Victoria never set foot upon a racecourse.

CHAPTER SIX

In the days of the Prince of Wales

ON THE WITHDRAWAL OF QUEEN VICTORIA INTO THE PERPETUAL GLOOM OF her widowhood, the royal influence at Ascot was carried on by her second child and eldest son, Edward, Prince of Wales. He was twenty years old at the time of his father's death, for which his mother always blamed him, the Prince Consort's original chill which terminated in typhoid — that disease of princes — had been contracted during an admonitory visit to his son at Cambridge. Edward had already been stigmatised as a sad failure. His parents, seeking to eradicate the admittedly appalling example of his great-uncles George IV and the Duke of Cumberland, had subjected him to a stern curriculum utterly foreign to his easy-going nature. It says much for the Prince of Wales's vitality that he survived it as well as he did.

Queen Victoria utterly refused, then and later, to her son and heir any share of what she called 'her dreary, sad pinnacle of solitary grandeur'. The Prince of Wales, deprived of any power, turned to society for his pleasures, and during the forty years of the Queen's widowhood there were two Courts in Britain, the gloomy one with the power, at Windsor, Osborne or Balmoral, and the gay, self-indulgent circle which centred upon the underemployed Heir Apparent at Marlborough House.

The Queen short-listed suitable brides for the Prince of Wales, and from them he chose Princess Alexandra, daughter of Prince Christian, afterwards King Christian IX of Denmark. Princess Alexandra came from an impoverished, informal, happy family. In her married life she had not only to contend with her formidable mother-in-law, but with her husband's constant infidelities. Yet such was her affectionate, fun-loving and ungrudging nature that she gained the respect and affection of all around her, not least that of her unfaithful husband, who jealously guarded her position.

If the country lost, Ascot gained from the idleness of the Prince of

Wales, and it became the brilliant setting for the rich materialism of the age.

But at first, of course, there was a period of mourning. Already in 1861 the Royal Stand had been shut up and its blinds down, in observation of mourning for the Duchess of Kent, Queen Victoria's mother. Again in 1862, some six months after the death of the Prince Consort, the blinds were down, the Box unoccupied. However the newspapers reported 'more than one member of the Royal Family was present incognito especially to see 'the great new race, to be called the Prince of Wales'' Stakes, a race for three-years-old which bids fair, in the opinion of many, very soon to rival the Leviathan of our summer events—the Epsom Derby.' The Prince of Wales's Stakes was run on the opening day of the meeting over a new course of thirteen furlongs, and was won by Mr T. Valentine's Carisbrook, ridden by Rogers.

'The great feature' of the 1862 meeting, according to *The Times*, 'which at first attracts notice is the completion of new post and rails for nearly a mile on either side of the straightest part of the course. It is constructed of a continuous hollow rail of iron running through solid oak posts; it is a light and durable fence, and must be deservedly popular with our fair visitors from the impossibility of damaging (*en passant*) the ample folds of their modern dresses (as, in the olden time, was frequently the case from the wooden splinters of their decayed predecessor), while the rail itself forms a most convenient lounge to the many who are anxiously watching the races on foot.'

It was in the following year, 1863, that all outsiders were rigidly excluded from the Royal Enclosure—a much later date from that usually given. 'The Royal Enclosure has been railed off, so that only a select few can obtain admission and all crush is obviated.' At the same time 'The Stand [grandstand] was crowded, not only in the Stand itself, but in the enclosure in front—so thronged that there was little more than standing room in any part of it. Even the minor and supplementary stands on either side were filled by one o'clock.'

In the following year (1864) a saddling paddock was set aside. It was pronounced 'a great improvement . . . is in the formation of a saddling paddock close in the rear of the Judge's chair, where the animals, before starting, can be carefully looked to by their trainers and owners, instead of, as heretofore, saddled anywhere on the course in the midst of crowds, so trying to horses of unequal temper, as the majority of racers generally are.' Tickets to get into the paddock area cost 10s.

This was the first year that the Prince and Princess of Wales were officially present at Ascot, a matter of two and a half years after the death of the Prince Consort. 'The Princess, who now wears half mourning, took her place at the window of the Royal Stand, and with a little book of the races in her hand, gave herself up to the enjoyment of the scene with the most vivid interest — an interest apparently as great in its way as that of the Prince himself, who stood beside her.'

The Princess of Wales immediately had two Ascot features named after her, a new Stand and a new race.

This new Alexandra Stand was designed to be 'the first, handsomest and most commodious Stand in the Kingdom . . . a model of what such a Stand should be, just as that at Epsom, may be said to be in the opposite category'. Yet this wooden stand lasted only fourteen years, and was demolished and the materials sold off by auction after the meeting in 1878.

The new race lasted longer. The Alexandra Plate was first run on Friday, June 1st, 1864, (a year earlier than the date given in Cawthorne and Herod's *Royal Ascot*) and was won by Anglo-Saxon, owned by Mr Lowe and ridden by H. Sharp. In the following year the three-mile race was won by Count F. Lagrange's Fille de l'Air, ridden by Harry Grimshaw, by a short head from Lord Glasgow's Strafford. £1,000 was added to the stakes, and the race was worth £1,315 to the winner — a very good prize in those days. Today the Alexandra Stakes is still run on the Friday and over much the same distance of ground — two miles, six furlongs and thirty-four yards — and is the longest flat race under Jockey Club rules. The Brown Jack Stakes, commemorating the gallant winner of no fewer than six Queen Alexandra Stakes, is run over the same distance of ground at the Ascot July meeting.

The Victorian era was obsessed with mourning, and the death of even a distant royalty might cause the cancellation of festivities or the withdrawal of royal patronage. For example, in 1880: 'the decease of the Empress of Russia, whose stay at the Villa des Dunes at Cannes last winter was productive of no permanent benefit, has placed the Court in mourning so that the charming array of colour for which the royal end is almost always remarkable, will be wanting and for the second time in three years we shall have a Black Ascot.' In 1885, the Royal Drive was cancelled because of the death of Prince Frederick Charles of Russia but it was noted, with surprise that mourning was *not* worn by the royal party. In 1888, more understandably, the illness of the Emperor Frederick, who was married to the Prince of Wales's sister, caused the cancellation of the Royal Procession. In 1892 the Prince's party was absent owing to the death in January of his son, the Duke of Clarence: the Princess of Wales appeared out of mourning for the Duke of Clarence for the first time on Ascot

Cup day in 1894. In 1895 the Court was in half-mourning for the death of the Czar of Russia. In 1896 there was again no Royal Drive because the Court was in mourning following the death of Prince Henry of Battenburg, although members of the Royal Family were present at the races.

Although Queen Victoria was seldom at Windsor at the time of Ascot races, she denied the use of the Castle to her son. This did not go unnoticed. The *Pall-Mall Gazette* commented in 1866: 'We are informed that the Prince of Wales has not hired Titness, formerly the residence of the late Mr Sampson Ricardo, and now the property of Lord Annaly. The noble proprietor of Titness, on learning that a difficulty existed as to obtaining suitable lodgings for the royal party in the neighbourhood of Ascot, has liberally placed his house at the disposal of his Royal Highness during the race week.' 'People would have been better pleased if on such an occasion the Prince had occupied Windsor Castle in some state,' commented *The Times* in the same year. 'One regretted this morning to see the bare flagstaff on the Round Tower.'

A branch line from Slough to Windsor had been opened by the Great Western Railway in 1849, and in 1856 the direct London and South-Western line from Waterloo to Ascot itself was opened. The Prince and Princess of Wales sometimes travelled daily to Ascot from London, and the Prince of Wales used to send his own horses and carriages by special train to Windsor, where they at least were accommodated in the Castle stables for the raceweek.

A letter in *The Times* about the Prince's special in 1864 gives a rather horrifying picture of the casualness with which the railways were being operated.

I came back from Ascot in a heavy train which was stopped unexpectedly at Twickenham. Another had been stopped already, and, as there was no more room in the siding, we were, after a certain amount of advancing and backing, moved on to the down or wrong set of rails. We had scarcely been one minute in position when between us and the shunted train, at a rate of thirty m.p.h., the royal train rushed through to London. A hitch of a single minute in the manoeuvring from the up to the down line of rails [might have caused] an appalling disaster.

Indeed a rail disaster did take place, involving an Ascot race train, that very year. *The Times* reported a railway accident which took place on Tuesday, June 7th, 1864, as usual the opening day of the meeting:

DREADFUL ACCIDENT TO AN ASCOT TRAIN

A fearful accident occurred last night on the South-Western Railway. One of the trains returning from the Ascot races—one of those long, un-manageable trains, heavily laden with holiday-makers, and such as are only seen at race times—ran into another train at the Egham station, destroying two carriages, killing five passengers almost on the spot, and more or less seriously injuring between twenty and twenty-five others. The accident occurred at about a quarter to eight o'clock, to the train which had left the races a little after seven, and which was followed as soon as safety, as it was thought, permitted, by *another* train equally long and equally heavy.

The races, due to innumerable false starts, had been running late, and the officials were getting the race-trains away as fast as they could. The train arrived at Egham shortly before eight o'clock.

Tickets were collected there, and a complaint was made about some card-sharpers, which delayed the train, which was just moving off when the next Ascot train arrived. Those on the platform called on the people in the carriages to jump clear.

The guard was in the break-van [*sic*], the last of all, and his experienced eye needed no warning, as he looked out and saw the next train coming on. He jumped out at once, though not a second too soon, as the crushed frag-ments of his van caught his coat skirts and tore them off.

The collision was very violent owing to the immense weight of the following train. It crushed the guard's van to splinters, crushed a second class carriage next to it, and partly crushed another beyond ... There was a horrible scene beneath the ruins of the broken-up second class carriage. From out of the wreck the bodies of four gentlemen were removed. A fifth died as he was being carried to the bank, and a sixth was so injured as to leave last night almost no hope of recovery.

A young man, unconscious, was carried in a bed in a chaise to Charing Cross Hospital, and about twenty-five slightly injured and bloodstained passengers were taken by train on to Waterloo. Among the dead was Mr Cockerell, clerk and confidential agent to the notorious moneylender Mr Padwick.

In spite of such setbacks the railways had become indispensable to Ascot. 'Never has the South-Western railway brought down such a heavy and fashionably-filled train,' wrote *The Times* in 1873, 'as that which left Waterloo at 4.40 on Monday afternoon and dispersed its contents over an Ascot radius of some half-dozen miles or more, while the afternoon trains on the Great Western had filled the royal borough with unwonted bustle and excitement.' There were three or more specials on the South-Western alone, as the guests for the house-parties assembled, accompanied by valets and ladies' maids and a vast impedimenta of luggage, which was piled on the platforms of the little country stations, and laboriously dispersed to the luggage brakes, sent in from the country houses.

Ascot could well have had two railway stations. The Windsor and Ascot Railway was under discussion in the 1870s. It was planned to run from the Great Western station at Windsor through Clewer, Winkfield and Sunninghill to an Ascot terminus 'on the north side of the Reading Road, by Hatchet Lane a distance of some eight miles.' Such a line would have been in direct competition with the London and South-Western line to Ascot. The Garrard family, which provided a Trustee of the Ascot Grandstand at this period, was closely connected with the London and South-Western while Charles Bulkeley, the son of the most active Grandstand Trustee of the time, Captain Thomas Bulkeley, was an original director of this Windsor and Ascot Railway Company. The Windsor to Ascot line was authorised by Act of Parliament in August 1898, and a considerable amount of land was bought up. Actual construction was never begun, although the company was taken over in 1905 by the Great Western Railway Company who showed the line as a proposed extension on their maps for years. Then, in 1911, a peace treaty was agreed between the Great Western Railway and the London and South-Western Railway, by which each railway retained its current sphere of influence. As a result the Windsor to Ascot line was never built. Finally, in 1924, an Act of Parliament gave the directors the power to sell some of the land they had acquired.

Meanwhile, in the big comfortable country houses of the prosperous neighbourhood, the house-parties were settling in for five days of almost non-stop activity. In 1882, for example, when the Prince and Princess of Wales were at Cowarth Park, Sunningdale, the Duke of Norfolk was at the Red House, the Duke of Portland at Armitage Hill, the Duke of Hamilton at Martin's Heron, Bracknell, the Earl of Rosebery at Englemere Wood, the Earl of Lonsdale at Frognal, Earl Compton at Wardour Lodge, Sunningdale, and Sir J. D. Astley at Ascot Heath House.

The Prince and Princess of Wales generally drove down the course in semi-state on the Tuesday and Thursday. The Prince was always, and the Princess sometimes, present on the other days as well, but there was no Royal Drive. Sometimes the royal party was allowed to use the Queen's carriage horses for the drive, which were neatly described as 'a well-appointed and handsome cortège, amply sufficient to mark royalty, though diminished enough to prove it did not mark the sovereign'.

Now that the Royal Enclosure and opposite it the carriage enclosures for the Four-in-Hand and other Coaching Clubs were rigidly reserved for the few, society had the setting and the space for its luxurious display of elegance. *London Society* in 1862 exclaimed, 'Ascot is filling, not with dusty vehicles and hilarious folk seen at the Derby, but for the most part, with people so spotless in costume and calm in manner that, to all appearances sake, they might be driving to church with a liberal supply of prayer books in the hampers.'

Coaches and carriages increased in snob value as they decreased as a necessary form of transport. Hosts sent their carriages to Berkshire from far afield and drove in them only a few miles at most from the country houses which they had rented for the week at vast expense, to the race-course, there to act as private grandstands, and the centre of splendid picnics. 'The roofs of the coaches, from one end of the Club Enclosure to the other, afford one huge banquet', ran one report.

> . . . the show of coaches was one of the features of the week, and their arrival and departure were regularly waited for, especially by the ladies, as one of the sights of the meeting. There were eighteen or nineteen coaches of the Four-in-Hand Club and fourteen or fifteen of the Coaching Club, present on each day, and each provisioned as only coaches on a racecourse can be;

> . . . No doubtful teams and overladen vans, no 'gay' animals with vicious eccentricities, no jibbing brutes, capable of infinite entanglement with the traces on the shortest notice; and always ready to back into the stream of vehicles behind. In their stead were the well-kept barouches or stately four-in-hands crowded inside with ladies, whose overflowing toilettes bloomed out of the windows in soft piles of ineffable millinery, looking in brightness and in colour like the loads which are despatched by nurserymen to take first prize at a Flower Show. (1877)

There was meticulous order in the enclosure set aside for the Coaching Club, which was opposite the lower end of the stand. There the drags were drawn up under the eagle eye of the club's honorary secretary Colonel Armytage, 'not one barely an inch before the other, bars, poles and chains arranged in order'. After Colonel Armytage retired in the 1880s, it was never quite the same again.

Outside these exclusive enclosures the lines of vehicles stretched away, three or four deep 'as close as pins in a paper' on both sides of the winning-post through the descending order of family carriage, brougham, jobbing clarence, stage coach, 'bus, 'shay', tax-cart and 'wan'.

Those in society who did not picnic on or by their own carriage would accept an invitation to a Club tent. 'The tents of the soldiers provided another agreeable incident, and the Grenadier Guards, Caribiniers, Royal Artillery and some three or four Regiments added their quota to that lavish Ascot hospitality which was never more unbounded than this year' (1877). The lavishness escalated, and twenty years later *The Times* commented:

> The most remarkable feature, so far as the social side of the meeting goes, is the gradual increase in the number of clubs which pitch their tents on the Heath and dispense an elaborate hospitality of which the racing world had no conception fifty or even twenty years ago. There is now a long line of tents, some fifteen or twenty in number, in which luncheon may be enjoyed in the most perfect tranquillity, and prominent as ever among these is the marquee of the Guards Club, the first to set this good example, though nothing could be more luxurious than all the appointments of White's, and of the Cavalry Club, while those of the Bachelors', the Tiffin Club, the Badminton and the Grosvenor are also extremely good.

Fashion in dress had now become of the first importance. Consuelo, Duchess of Marlborough, wrote in her memoirs: 'I found Ascot week very tiring . . . Fortunes were yearly spent on dresses selected as appropriate to a graduated scale of elegance which reached its climax on Thursday; for fashion decreed that one should reserve one's most sumptuous *toilette* for the Gold Cup day . . . We spent our mornings donning various dresses in accordance with the vagaries of the weather, and by noon we were apt to be not only cross and tired but also probably attired in the wrong dress.'

As early as 1864 we had to be reminded that 'Ascot . . . is not entirely a question of new bonnets (though they do enter largely into the scheme), elaborate toilettes and Fortnum and Mason.'

Among the early newspaper descriptions of dresses, was that from 1871 quoted in *Royal Ascot*.

> The Princess of Wales wore amber satin and black lace, with a bonnet to match. The handsome Duchess d'Ossima, in a *manteau de cour* of brown satin striped gauze over yellow silk, attracted general admiration, as did the beautiful Lady Mary Dawson in pale primrose muslin (flounced), the Countess of March in bright yellow satin, and the fascinating Madame Bechevé in dark blue velvet, over which was worn a pearl white *poult de soie* polonaise, without sleeves, the petticoat of which was trimmed with rich point d'Alençon. The exquisite rose silk, trimmed with lace, of Mrs Sloane Stanley, with parasol to match, was admired by many present. The Marchioness of Westminster was easily recognised by her rich Indian

mantle of claret and gold, and the new half shawl of *point avère* coming greatly into vogue. An attractive group on the rustic seat, beneath the Royal Saloon, included the Duchess of Manchester, in pink silk, Lady Royston and her sister, Lady Feodorowna Wellesley in silver grey, with hats to correspond, but with contrasting streamers of violet and cerise velvet.

In 1874 'Isabella, the favourite flower-girl of the French Jockey Club,' arrived at Ascot, dressed in chocolate and red, the colours of Boiard, which won the Gold Cup. She was not permitted to enter the Royal Enclosure.

Of course, from the very beginning of the Queen's withdrawal from Ascot, there were already voices raised declaring that it was not the same as it had once been. In 1868 *The Times'* correspondent declared:

> How greatly Ascot has changed within the last fifteen years, what distinctive characteristics it has lost, and how it has been absorbed into the common run of great racemeetings, few among us now pause to remember. It certainly enjoys in a peculiar manner royal patronage, and our aristocracy flock to it pretty much as they did a quarter of a century ago; but it has long lost all claims to exclusiveness, and with them have gone much that no doubt rendered Ascot the pleasantest of racemeetings.
>
> It is a huge metropolitan gathering, becoming each year more Epsom-like in character, retaining, indeed, some of the old *prestige* in the scarlet liveries of the royal party and the select circle in and about the Royal Enclosure, but in all other aspects an Ascot of the people, imposing in its numbers, and with a certain magnificence pertaining to it which no other country can show.

For those who had to make do with the grandstand, into which one could enter by mere payment, there was considerably more congestion. Ascot, like society, was stratifying. The mix-up of noblemen and mob which had been tolerated in Georgian days was disappearing. The climate of Ascot was becoming ever more fastidious. 'The Ascot is to the Derby what genteel comedy is to broad farce. All London goes to the Derby, only the West End goes to Ascot ... At Ascot the gypsies make more money selling bouquets than tips, broad ditties are cleaned up into songs of irreproachable propriety and dullness' (1863).

The gypsies were kept outside the grandstand enclosure. But especially on Wednesday, which was the big betting day, and when entrance was 5s against 10s on Cup day 'The reduction of the price of admission ... had the effect of filling the enclosure with an enormous number of welchers and other disreputable characters who endeavoured with more or less success to entrap the unwary, and whose language, besides being unparliamentary, was by no means fit for the ears of the ladies who occupied benches and chairs on the lawn.'

In the mid-1860s the price of admission to the grandstand was levelled off at 10s, on each of the four days, the first increase since the grandstand had opened nearly thirty years earlier.

With the rapidly expanding middle class the pressure upon the grandstand accommodation was always increasing. The Trustees received complaints about the 1864 meeting, and 'the great inconvenience arising from the yearly increase of Members in their enclosure and the almost utter impossibility of providing even standing room for visitors on the principal day — also the deficiency of accommodation generally and of the difficulty of access to the refreshment and ladies' room in the body of the stand.'

It was difficult even to get into the grandstand, through traffic congestion outside the stand, caused by setting down grandstand patrons, and also at the junction of the Reading and London roads. In 1865 the Horse Patrol were engaged by the Trustees to control the traffic, and if possible to prevent the drivers of hackney carriages from indiscriminately plying for hire.

At the same time, the Trustees obtained about half an acre of additional ground behind the grandstand at a nominal rent from the Master of the Buckhounds, where they made a lawn and built a pavilion for light refreshments. James Careless, who had succeeded his father as caterer, and who claimed a worn-out stove had contributed to catering deficiencies, did no better when a new stove was installed, and was dismissed in 1865. The Trustees decided to appoint in his place Mr Browning of Conduit Street, Westbourne Terrace, but the claims of Mr Baily of the Ascot Hotel were warmly supported by Mr Weatherby, and it was only after somewhat acrimonious exchanges that Browning's appointment was confirmed for seven years, at an annual payment of £300. The flower garden at the back of the stand was hired from 1862 for several years by a Mr Tod Heath for a private party, but his request in 1864 for a permanent refreshment pavilion on the site, was turned down.

But the grandstand patrons were not too badly off for refreshments. 'The private luncheon rooms in the grandstand are the scenes of many pleasant parties, and the large dining-halls on the lawn at the back of the grandstand claim a fair share of patronage, and during the luncheon hours proper are full to overflowing. In the balcony, which is kept cool by running water flowing over it, private tables are reserved, while lighter refreshments are served in the pretty Japanese tea room.'

The Trustees had a long-held suspicion that they were not reaping their full harvest from their numerous patrons. Mathew Skinner was appointed housekeeper in 1864. He may have been a relation of the Mr Skinner who was appointed grandstand superintendent in 1839: he may even have been the same man. However he was soon in hot water. In 1866 he was explicitly forbidden to continue to take any commission whatsoever on work done for the grandstand, while his salary was raised to £200 per annum in compensation. At the same time he was asked to supervise more closely the disposal of the entrance check-tickets 'with the object of detecting any person who should fraudulently dispose of same', a task which, he said, was impossible—'an opinion in which the Trustees did not concur'. That same July two of the check-takers were tried and convicted at Reading, the one for stealing and the other for receiving check-tickets, each receiving a sentence of four months' hard labour. Another man received the same sentence for counterfeiting tickets. There was a similar case of stealing check-tickets in the following year, when a policeman and another man were convicted and received the same sentence. But this time Mathew Skinner was in real trouble: he had stood bail for one of the convicted men, and a special Trustees' meeting was called to consider whether he should be dismissed. He apologised abjectly, and got off with a severe reprimand, but two years later was again under suspicion in connection with a check-ticket discrepancy. Again he was reprieved and— Mathew Skinner was nothing if not a trier—put in at once for a rise, which he did not get. However he kept his job until January 1874. Even then he was granted an annuity of £25 for past services.

In the context of the times Ascot was a very good employer. There are a number of instances of old servants of the Grandstand Company being retired on their full salary as pension. For example, in 1870, 'it having been reported that John Blake, who has been in the service of the Trustees for thirty years, but was too old to do much work, it was resolved that he is paid for the future eight shillings a week and that he is to work at the stand when his health will permit him to do so.'

The most important achievement of the Grandstand Trustees at the time was the negotiation of a new lease for extra ground at the grandstand formerly occupied by 'Mr Roberts' stand' when on July 14th, 1860, they accepted the offer from the Office of Woods and Forests of a new lease of 'one acre, one rood and two perches' at the rate of £20 per annum for thirty-nine and a half years from April 5th, 1860. A further twelve perches were added, for an additional £13 per annum in July 1861.

The Iron Gazebo on the Ascot lawn was on their ground, but there was a complaint when building was begun before the plans had been approved by the Office. They also complained that three-year membership was being offered to members when the building was on a six-month termination notice. In a typically circumambulating civil servant's letter, paragraph one sought to raise alarm and despondency, while the final paragraph magnanimously declared that a new clause would be introduced, raising the term of notice to three years. The contractors were lent £500 by the Trustees, so that they could start work. At the request of Lord Bessborough a committee was formed, consisting of Baron Meyer de Rothschild, Admiral Rous and Captain Seymour, to select the 200 members, who would each pay £3 for a three-year membership. When the original cost was paid off, the profits were handed over to the Grandstand Trustees, 'and dealt with as other surplus'.

By this time, Ascot was in some ways the leading racecourse in the world. *The Graphic* reported in 1878: 'The added money at Ascot was £11,000 and the total value of the Stakes no less than £28,890 – sums beyond any which have ever been run for at any racemeeting in the world. The total number of starters for the twenty-nine races in the four days was 197.'

At this time a long and increasingly bitter difference of opinion was beginning between the Grandstand Trustees and the Jockey Club over entrance fees and concessions. The Trustees raised funds which were handed over to the Jockey Club, through the Master of the Buckhounds, to provide prize-money for the racemeeting. Basically, the Trustees wanted to plough back part of the proceeds into improvements, while the stewards, all members of the Jockey Club, wanted the entire sum allocated to prize-money. The stewards complained they did not even attend the meetings of the Grandstand Trustees, but the Trustees pointed out that the Master of the Buckhounds was an *ex-officio* member. A courteous letter was sent by the Trustees to the Jockey Club members in 1860, and addressed to Admiral Rous, the Duke of Beaufort and the Earl of Portsmouth, who did in fact attend a meeting.

An idea for raising more money was put in a letter from Admiral Rous, a Jockey Club Steward, to Captain Henry Seymour, a Trustee, written on May 10th, 1861 and is bound into the Minutes.

My Dear Seymour,
    Why should we not have a second Ascot Meeting of two days on Wednesday & Thursday the 24th and 25th of July – it would pay well, the horses going to Goodwood would take it en route & the London season not being over we should fill the Stand.
    ... £600 would be ample for all the Prizes, & if well managed, which it shall be, we might establish brilliant second Meetings – think it over my good friend.

The second meeting duly took place, but the amount taken at the grand-stand was only £258. Expenses totalled £54 15s. It was minuted that the stewards of the Jockey Club, who had been unable to attend, had been notified of the poor financial result, as the entire receipts had barely covered working expenses, and £800 for the prize-money was still due to Messrs Weatherby. The accounts for the year show the receipts were £4,174 10s for admission to the grandstand, and that Mr Careless, the caterer, paid £150 rent. The balance at the bank stood at £5,096 8s 1d.

When the debt on the building of the grandstand had been paid off, the one-third of the income, which had been set aside for this purpose, became available. By an omission it had not been made clear in the original documents what was to be done with this money. The Trustees – at the same time patting themselves on the back for their liberal interpretation – decided to apply this newly-available fund, like the other two-thirds, to the prize-money fund. The legality of this decision was afterwards questioned, and the Trustees took the matter to court to obtain a ruling. The case was held before Vice-Chancellor Wood on January 19th, 1864, 'when he, by his Decree (subsequently enrolled) directed the Trustees to stand prepared of the one-third of the Surplus Income Upon Trust to pay the same to the stewards of Ascot Races'.

Some silver tickets were still outstanding, and the holder of the day could claim free entrance to the grandstand. The Trustees had bought back silver tickets whenever they could, at a cost of between £5 and £10 a badge, but at a meeting on May 26th, 1870, they decided to refuse free admission to silver ticket holders in the future, after advertising their intention in the newspapers.

Loosely enclosed in the Minute Book is a torn, unidentified newspaper cutting, dated June 21st, 1879, which reads:

> The Ascot 'silver ticket' holders claim a grievance and we think they have one. The management (that is, Captain Bulkeley and son-in-law) maintain that they have law on their side, but they are guilty of a breach of contract morally, if not legally. The understanding with their customers was 'free admittance to the Stand for sixty-one years' of which twenty have yet to expire. On the faith of this understanding many persons, in no wise connected with the original contract, have purchased these tickets for considerable sums, and justly deem themselves in the position of men rooked.
>
> A large number of these tickets have been in recent years purchased by the management themselves at no small cost. Now, if Brown, Jones and Robinson claim a right of way over our land, and we pay off Brown and Jones, but shut out Robinson, is not that rather tough on Robinson?

The Grandstand Trustees served for long periods. Mr Ward died in 1863, Mr Gilbertson, then aged eighty-eight, although not well enough to attend the meeting in that year, had 'at some personal inconvenience gone through and approved the annual accounts': he retired later that year. Mr Thomas Bulkeley of Clewer and Mr Robert Garrard of Wokingham replaced them. Captain Seymour, who had been a staunch worker for the grandstand, died in 1867. His son Harry was appointed a Trustee in his stead but resigned, apparently after a disagreement, two years later. Captain Bulkeley became the leading figure among the Trustees. Born in 1807 he went to Harrow and served in the Life Guards for over twenty years. He was a keen and progressive Trustee, responsible for most of the improvements right up to his death in 1882.

Captain Bulkeley brought in Mr Robert Garrard, born in 1793, a member of the well-known firm of jewellers and silversmiths. Mr Garrard had undertaken to give financial help when there was some shortage of money at the time. His brother was chairman of the Staines and Wokingham railway line, which was built mostly with Garrard money, and which was the means of opening up the Ascot district.

There was a slightly farcical ritual at the annual meeting of Trustees, when the firm to make the Gold Cup was selected. Robert Garrard the silversmith and jeweller very properly withdrew from the meeting – and desired that the fact that he did so be recorded in the Minutes. The remaining Trustees then selected Garrards to make the cup, and Mr Garrard returned, to receive instructions from his fellow Trustees as to its design. Robert Garrard resigned in 1874, and for the first time an election was necessary, there being two candidates. Captain Robert Garrard was elected.

The wisdom of the Garrard representative withdrawing when the goldsmith was selected was proved in 1877, when the Trustees favoured Garrards, and the Master of the Buckhounds preferred to order a cup elsewhere. It is minuted in June 1877:

A misunderstanding having arisen with regard to the selection of the Ascot Cup for 1877 (in consequence of which two cups were ordered by the Trustees) it was decided that the Gold Cup manufactured by Messrs Handcock should be run for at the Ascot Meeting of 1877 and the Silver Cup by Messrs Garrard at that of 1878. It was also decided that in the future the Trustees of the Ascot Grandstand shall meet at the earliest possible time after the annual Ascot Racemeeting to arrange as to the Cup for the following year, and to select the firm by which it shall be supplied.

When the next cup was needed, for 1879, it was resolved that it should be made of *Gold* and that it should be made by Messrs Garrard. Lord Hardwicke, the Master of the Buckhounds and Captain Bulkeley undertook to order the Cup — 'The Earl of Hardwicke to order the Hunt Cup where he pleases.' In the following year Hunt and Roskell were appointed to make the 1880 Cup to the value of 1,000 sovereigns, and that Garrards should make the Hunt Cup, whose value was to be increased from £300 to £500. In 1881 Lord Cork succeeded Lord Hardwicke as Master of the Buckhounds, and Garrards made the Gold Cup.

Captain Robert Garrard, born in 1835, who had served with distinction in the Grenadier Guards during the Crimean Wars, remained an active Trustee until his death in 1895. He was a keen hunting man, and owned several racehorses, although they did not run in his name. When Captain Seymour resigned, his place was taken by Captain Bulkeley's son-in-law, Colonel W. S. Ewart, who was also a Grenadier veteran of the Crimea, and who served until he died in 1890, when he was succeeded by another of the Bulkeley clan, Colonel Rivers Bulkeley. After some rather short-term Trustees, Colonel Victor Van de Meyer, of New Lodge, Windsor, was appointed in 1892. The son of a Belgian Ambassador to England, he was educated at Eton, married an Englishwoman, and became an ardent supporter of every Berkshire activity.

Mr J. R. A. Clement was appointed secretary to the Trustees from January 1st, 1881, at a salary of £500 per annum, plus £100 for a house, increased in 1884 to £700 per annum, plus £300 for a house. An assistant secretary, with a salary of £250, was appointed at the same time, but when he left in 1895 he was replaced by 'a clerk who understands Type Writing & Shorthand' who was paid only £150 per annum.

The atmosphere between the Trustees and the Jockey Club, as represented by the Master of the Buckhounds, became ever more strained. For example at a meeting in September 1892 the Trustees had awarded themselves £1,000 divided among them, in place of the £120 they had hitherto received for expenses. Lord Ribblesdale, the Master of the Buckhounds, was furious. He called a meeting at Durrant's Hotel on November 21st, 1892, at which, according to the Minute which he signed, 'he called attention to the fact that the Remuneration had been raised ... at a meeting held early in September at which the Master of the Buckhounds was not summoned, and which was not called by the clerk of the Trustees, who himself was not present and knew nothing of the business transacted. After some conversation on the subject, Lord Ribblesdale declared his intention of consulting the Law Officers of the Crown upon the legality of this transaction and how far the Institution of the Trust is affected thereby.' The Trustees' cheques were returned within three days, and at a further meeting held at the grandstand on December 1st, 1892, the usual sum of £120 for expenses was divided among the Trustees.

There was continuing friction between the Grandstand Trustees and the Stewards of the Jockey Club on the subject of prize-money versus improvements. The Trustees wished to build a new and better Alexandra Stand, and estimates and drawings were called for in 1877, with Captain Thomas Bulkeley in charge of proceedings. The plans were submitted to the Trustees at a meeting in May 1878, and in July the tender of £7,900 submitted by Hollis was accepted, 'subject to Captain Bulkeley's attempts to get the price brought down'.

The new Alexandra Stand, partly built on ground used by the old, small stand, was completed in time for the 1879 meeting. It was erected on the same level as, and adjoining the grandstand. The new stand held twenty-eight boxes, and there were 391 stall seats on the roof. At the back there was a large refreshment hall, 60 ft x 20 ft, with a terrace, reached by a flight of stairs. It also contained three private luncheon rooms. In the basement were the cellars and storerooms.

The expenses of this much-needed extension caused some friction with the Jockey Club. Again the bone of contention was the amount of money available for prize-money. The Jockey Club was reckoning on a larger sum at its disposal than the Trustees would have available. The Trustees met on July 9th, 1879, when Captain Bulkeley reported to the Trustees (but not to the Minutes) the upshot of a meeting with Lord Hardwicke, the Master of the Buckhounds, who was not present at the Trustees' meeting. The Minutes read: 'It was resolved that the Trustees of the Grandstand at Ascot will not be responsible for any sum of money advertised to be run for at the races at Ascot unless the amount so advertised has previously received their sanction, and that this resolution be communicated to the Jockey Club.' The resolution was signed 'Cork', presumably at the next meeting, when the Earl of Cork, who had meantime succeeded Lord Hardwicke as Master of the Buckhounds, was present.

The sums involved were considerable. In 1885 the Master of the Buckhounds received the sum of £14,200 'to defray expenses for Cups and Stakes'. In 1890 the sum passed over for prize-money and cups was £14,500; for 1894 £17,600; for 1897 and 1901 £22,400 apiece.

Minor improvements continued.

At the same time that the new Alexandra Stand was opened new saddling stalls and boxes were erected on the south side of the paddock, with their backs to the main road. The wooden palings which had surrounded the paddock were replaced with rails, and the jockeys' changing-room was doubled in size. In 1881 the Press Box was moved, to allow the Master of the Buckhounds Stand to be enlarged. The slope of the Royal Enclosure lawn was increased, to improve viewing from ground level.

In the forty years between the death of the Prince Consort and of Queen Victoria, British bloodstock reached what was perhaps the peak of perfection. Paradoxically it was also the period when the British thorough-bred was first challenged and beaten by the French, and when British jockeys met the shock of defeat by the Americans. It was the time of Admiral Rous; of George Fordham, Fred Archer and 'Monkey' Sloan; of Mat Dawson and John Porter; of the Marquess of Hastings, hell-bent on self-destruction; all were connected with Ascot, like nearly all the equine and human racing characters of the time, but only a few of the innumer-able racing dramas from the Ascot scene can be described.

Many modern races had their origin at this period. The Prince of Wales's Stakes, was introduced as a thirteen furlong race for three-years-old in 1862, is now a mile and a quarter, three-years-old and up. It is a Group 2 Pattern race and in 1975 was worth over £10,000 to the winner. Another new race of 1862 was variously called the Royal Stand Plate or the Queen's Stand Plate, but was run not as a sprint as the King's Stand Stakes is today, but 'from the distance Post, once round and in', a distance of around two and a quarter miles. The Alexandra Plate, now the Alexandra Stakes, first run in 1864, is now (together with the Brown Jack Stakes, run over the same ground) the longest flat race under Jockey Club rules. The Ascot Plate was instituted in 1871 and was run over a mile and a quarter on the Friday for a prize of 300 sovereigns and the stakes. It was suggested that it should be called after Lord Cork, then Master of the Buckhounds (whose name, however, is now preserved in the Cork and Orrery Stakes, a Group 3 Pattern sprint over six furlongs, which provides the opener on Cup day). The Rous Memorial Stakes, first run on Cup day 1878 over the New Mile, is now a handicap sprint for three-years-old and up, run on King George VI and Queen Elizabeth Diamond day at the big July meeting, and in 1975 had £1,600 added to the stakes.

The Hardwicke Stakes, named after the Master of the Buckhounds from 1874 to 1879, was introduced in 1879 over the mile and a half of the Swinley course, and was a valuable weight-for-age with 2,000 sovereigns added. Today the Hardwicke Stakes, still run on the Friday, has increased its importance, but is no longer open to three-years-old nor to geldings. In 1975 together with the King's Stand Stakes it was the second most valuable race at Royal Ascot, second only to the Gold Cup (which had £25,000 added), and worth £15,000 in added money.

The Bessborough Stakes commemorates the well-known Master of the Buckhounds who held office three times between 1848 and 1866. The Coventry Stakes, named after George, ninth Earl of Coventry and a most successful Master of the Buckhounds, was first run in 1890. It is still run on the Tuesday, and is still for two-years-old, although the distance has been extended from just under four to six furlongs. It is now a Group 2 Pattern race, and had £5,000 added in 1975. The Chesham Stakes is named after the last Master of the Buckhounds, Charles, third Baron Chesham, who succeeded Lord Coventry, but was serving overseas in the South African War and was never actually in control of an Ascot race-meeting. Viscount Churchill, who afterwards became the King's Representative at Ascot, acted for him.

Before the photofinish camera dead heats were much more common, but even so it was unusual to have a dead heat for the Ascot Gold Cup in 1863 and again two years later.

The powerful field of six for the 1863 Gold Cup included Caller Ou, the strong, ewe-necked daughter of Stockwell which won forty-nine races out of ninety-eight starts including the 1861 St Leger, and Hurricane, winner of the One Thousand Guineas. But the dead heat was run between Buckstone and Tim Whiffler. Buckstone, foaled in 1859, by Voltigeur out of the Touchstone mare Burlesque, was owned by Mr James Merry. He had been fancied for the previous year's Derby, but had not acted on the course and finished third. Tim Whiffler, owned by Lord W. Powlett, had demolished Buckstone in the Doncaster Cup, in which he gave him seven pounds. In consequence Tim Whiffler, said before the race to be 'another Eclipse in his speed and powers of staying', started favourite for the Cup at five to four against, with Buckstone at nine to four. It was a fast-run early race Buckstone taking up the running at the foot of the hill, when the pace began to slacken. At the road Tim Whiffler took the lead and seemed to have the race won when 'shouts of *Whiffler wins* were speedily superseded by the shouts of the partisans of the yellow jacket and black cap'. In the run-off Tim Whiffler started at seven to four on. *The Druid* recalled 'In the decider Tim Whiffler seemed to fly over the turf; but, at the stand, Buckstone collared him and won, beating West Australian's time. The pace was terrific.'

The second dead-heat was between Ely and General Peel in 1865. Ely, foaled in 1861, was a bay bred and owned by Mr W. S. Crawfurd, and was something of an Ascot specialist having won the Triennial at two, three and four years, as well as the Prince of Wales's Stakes as a three-years-old. General Peel, also a four-years-old, was a bay colt by Young Melbourne out of an Orlando mare, and was owned by the eccentric Earl of Glasgow. He was trained by John Scott and had won the Two Thousand Guineas, and run second to Blair Athol in the Derby and St Leger.

In the race Ely was ridden by Custance and General Peel by Fordham. Ely seemed to be winning fairly easily when 'General Peel answered in the most surprising way to pressure. In three of his enormous strides, he recovered nearly a length, the first took him opposite to Ely's saddle girth, the next well up with his shoulder, the third neck and neck and had there been time for a fourth his victory was assured.'

Great excitement and considerable betting was centred on the run-off. As soon as the dead heat was declared 'there was a rush at once to ascertain the condition of the horses, and to the delight of their respective supporters it was found that neither was touched by the spur, though one less fortunate in the race had been opened up about the shoulder. The white foam was promptly combed from the coats of the favourites, and as soon as they had recovered their wind, which Ely was the first to do, they were led away to their stables, the decisive heat being postponed until the other races had been run.'

The re-run lived long in the memories of those who witnessed it. 'General Peel waited upon Ely to the turn, where he drew up to the leader, but on reaching the enclosure he put down his ears, and shortly after gave in, swerving across the course and denying all Fordham's efforts to keep him straight. He was beaten disgracefully by a dozen lengths.'

Years later Charles Lund, travelling head lad for John Scott, recalled the famous outburst of temper of Lord Glasgow to John Rascliffe (*The Life and Times of John Osborne*).

Of all the storms of temper he showed I never saw him in a worse one than when General Peel was beaten after his dead heat with Ely at Ascot.

After the dead heat I took General Peel back to his stable, which was close to the stand. Lord Glasgow came to the stable and saw the horse dressed and made ready for the deciding heat. The horse was a picture of health, and he was sent out to run the dead heat as clean as a new pin, and as fresh as if he had never had a gallop.

But he cut up the biggest coward in the decider that ever was saddled in the ring; he tried to do everything but win, and would have run into the ring if he could have got in. Lord Glasgow broke into a towering rage, and his language was 'beautiful' when we took the 'General' back to his quarters. Nor was John Scott himself ever more disappointed than at the horse's cowardly display in the race.

In between the Gold Cup dead heats, in 1864 came a race which sounds strange to modern ears, the race for the Royal Hunt Cup, in which the first past the post was Gem of the Sea, ridden by H. Grimshaw. Gem of the Sea and Mr Merry's Crisis, ridden by the kindly George Sopp who was afterwards a champion rider in Germany, repeatedly cannoned into each other 'from sheer distress': the objection by the second to the first for 'alleged foul riding' was overruled.

But the thoughts of modern racegoers might be with Lord Exeter's Amelia, ridden by Loates, a four-years-old carrying six stone three pounds. *The Times* reported laconically, 'half way up the hill . . . the ranks were thinned by the retirement of Amelia who, despite the bottle of whisky administered to her prior to starting, shut up like a coward when awakening from its effects'.

The tragic road to ruin of the Marquess of Hastings was temporarily halted by his success with Lecturer in the Gold Cup of 1867. Lord Hastings, crazily addicted to gambling, was being harried by the notorious money-lender Padwick (the same whose confidential clerk had been killed in the Ascot racetrain crash). Lecturer was a four-years-old bay colt by Colsterdale out of Algebra bred by Sir Tatton Sykes. Ten runners went to post, after the usual parade in the Royal Enclosure. Hippia owned by Lord Rothschild and Lecturer were joint favourites. 'The Marquis of Hastings' horse had slightly the call of the mare, who struck us as not looking so bright in her coat as at Epsom, while Lecturer, who was stale at Bath, here looked more in his last year's form.' In the race Hippia was beaten in the straight but Regalia, an outsider owned by Mr Graham and ridden by Heartfield was going so well

> that her name was shouted as the winner; but Fordham, creeping up next to the rails, gained on her at every stride, and coming with one of his rushes approaching the Royal Stand, landed Lord Hastings' colours a gallant winner by a length and a half.
>
> There was considerably more than the usual cheering. Lord Hastings, it is no secret, was a heavy loser on the Derby, and being one of the most plucky of spectators, and bearing his losses bravely, as an English gentleman should, there was considerable satisfaction at his success.

Later his Lady Elizabeth won the New Stakes in a canter, and on the Friday, Lecturer won the Alexandra Plate of 1,000 sovereigns over three miles. But it was only a blink of sunshine in his owner's misfortunes: in 1868 Lord Hastings died, ruined in health and fortune, at the age of twenty-six.

The Derby winner Blue Gown entered at the post for the 1868 Gold Cup, which he duly won. A hard bay by Beadsman out of the moderate Bas Bleu, he was bred and owned by Sir Joseph Hawley, and was ridden in the Gold Cup by Cameron. Reputedly the most docile of horses—after winning the Derby he walked away with a stable lad hanging on to his tail—he showed temper before the race at Ascot.

In the following year Blue Gown was among the five runners for the Ascot Gold Cup. Before the race 'they are paraded round the Royal Enclosure according to the time-honoured custom, but the ladies we are happy to say, kept their seats, firmly resisting the pressing entreaties of an official to retire, and Blue Gown led his four competitors in and out of the gay toilettes in a perfectly composed manner, without the slightest danger to life or limb'. In a slow-run race, where the pace quickened only at the Lime Kilns, Blue Gown ran gamely, but could not get up and was beaten a length by the Oaks winner Brigantine, owned by Sir Frederick Johnstone. The third horse home was Thorwaldson, but on returning to scales his rider Hudson could not draw the weight and was disqualified.

In the late 1860s the French horses began to make their mark at Ascot, as elsewhere. Count Lagrange's remarkable Gladiateur, winner of the French Grand Prix, the French St Leger (then Prix du Prince Imperial) and the English Triple Crown, carried off the Gold Cup in 1866. Then in 1871 Monsieur Lefèvre's Mortemer was followed home by the French-owned Verdue. This produced a comment to be echoed many more times, 'And so in one of our chief Cup races, and over the severest course in England, we have to stand by and see French-bred horses first and second. No one grudges the honour to our neighbours, who deserve all they have gained, but we trust the lesson it inculcates may not be thrown away upon our breeders. Fields are small, Cup races are unfashionable, and today our Derby favourites and our Cup winners are beaten by the foreigner.'

This Monsieur Lefèvre, who came over to England at the outbreak of the Franco-Prussian War, was a prolific owner of winners: indeed his record of 105 winners in England in 1873 in one season stood until 1969, when it was beaten by Mr David Robinson. Whereas Count Lagrange was welcomed by the aristocratic world which ran racing, it was quite otherwise with Monsieur Lefèvre, who was cold-shouldered when he first arrived in England. According to Sir George Chetwynd,

Gentlemen had held aloof from Monsieur Lefèvre on his first appearance at Newmarket, because several French visitors circulated rumours prejudicial to him; but no one could ascertain anything for certain about these stories, and at last Mr Payne took the bull by the horns, went straight to Count

Lagrange and others, and simply said, 'What is it you have against Monsieur Lefèvre? Tell me, otherwise I shall certainly be introduced to a man who runs his horses so straightforwardly, enters them in every available race, and whose friends say he is in all respects a worthy associate for a gentleman.'

He could ascertain nothing definite, and accordingly was introduced to him, as were many prominent members of the Jockey Club, and we all constantly dined with him. The detrimental rumours were supposed to be about his Stock Exchange transactions, but I only desire to speak of him as a notable figure in the turf-world of his age; I found him a straightforward gentleman, always good-tempered and pleasant in spite of being a martyr to gout, which I believe is saying a great deal.

In 1874 the Ascot Gold Cup was again won by a French horse, Monsieur H. Delamarre's Boiard, with another French horse, Monsieur Lefèvre's Flageolet, dead-heating for second place with Doncaster. John Osborne, although not himself connected with the finish, reckoned this as one of the greatest races he ever saw. *The Times* account ran: 'but six runners, [Boiard] the acknowledged best horse France has produced for some years; the winner of last year's Oaks; and the first and second in last year's Leger, Kaiser and Gang Forward, who were so close together last year that it was almost impossible to separate them; and Flageolet, that good horse, who had measured his strength with Boiard on more than one field'. Boiard, by Vermouth out of La Bossue was ridden by Carver; Flageolet by Fordham; Mr Merry's Derby winner Doncaster by F. Webb. Kaiser was ridden by Maidment, Gang Forward by Challoner and Mr Merry's second runner, Marie Stuart by T. Osborne. Boiard was two to one favourite.

All appeared well in the paddock. Marie Stuart had a decided thoroughpin on one of her hindlegs, but which did not seem to interfere with her action. The horse that looked most improved there was understandably Gang Forward, who has grown into a very grand horse, a trifle high on the legs perhaps, but with a faultless top. Boiard and Kaiser both looked remarkably well ... In the march-past to the Stand Flageolet headed the procession, followed by Gang Forward, Boiard and Kaiser, Mr Merry's pair bringing up the rear. No declaration had been made about these, but it is known that Mr Merry had backed both ... They were not long at the post, and when the flag fell, Flageolet went to the front, and up to the top turn the lot went on in Indian file fashion at a slow pace; but then Fordham slipped his horses, and down the hill into the Swinley Bottom led them at a much merrier one. His immediate followers were Gang Forward, Boiard, Kaiser, Doncaster, with Marie Stuart in the rear, and they continued in this order until entering the straight, when Boiard passed Gang Forward, and at the heels of Flageolet,

came up the last half of the New Mile. Opposite the stand Boiard headed
Flageolet and the race was over, for, despite Fordham's efforts, Flageolet
was beaten very cleverly by three parts of a length.

The great Isonomy won the Ascot Gold Cup in 1879 and again in 1880.
Foaled in 1875, a bay son of Sterling out of the Stockwell mare Isola
Bella, he was such a moderate two-years-old, that his owner Mr Gretton
did not run him in the Derby, but kept him for the Cambridgeshire, in
which he duly obliged. He won both Ascot Gold Cups in a common
canter, beating a good field including the Oaks winner Janette in 1879,
but in 1880 his reputation had driven off all the runners except Lord
Beresford's Chippendale and Count Lagrange's Zut. 'Isonomy had
proved himself such an exceptional horse, so good at all distances, and had
won all his races under the most unfavourable conditions in such style,
that it was useless expecting anything to lower his colours even in such a
good horse as Chippendale. The latter made the running, and Isonomy
waited on him, shaking him off when they came to the Stand, and winning
easily by a length. Isonomy again proved himself the wonder of modern
times and Mr Gretton's collection of cups will soon want a plate room to
themselves.' This particular Gold Cup of 1880 was a gold vase depicting
in high relief the labours of Hercules 'while the handles are formed by
groups representing his education by the centaur'. It was designed by G.
A. Cater and made by Hunt and Roskell. The trophies had lost the purity
of line of Georgian days, and the enormously detailed workmanship was
more notable than the artistic merit. Themes were mostly taken from
Greek or Roman mythology, or occasionally from the works of Sir
Walter Scott.

The rivalry between George Fordham and Fred Archer came to a head
at Ascot. George Fordham, born in 1837, was exactly twenty years older
than 'The Tinman'. He too had been an infant prodigy in his time, and
had won the Cambridgeshire at the age of fourteen riding at three stone
twelve pounds! Roger Mortimer in his *Encyclopedia of Flat Racing* says of
Fordham: 'As he grew older and stronger his skill increased and in his
prime he was inferior only to Fred Archer, and very little inferior at that
. . . His style was by no means graceful but it was undoubtedly effective.
His sense of timing was superb and again and again he got up in the last
strides to win by inches. He used the whip far less than most of his contemporaries.' George Fordham's winning career at Ascot spanned twenty-
nine years, from his first win on Mr T. Parr's Coroner in the Trial Stakes
in 1855, until his last on Wild Thyme in the New Stakes in 1883. In all
George Fordham won ninety-nine races at Ascot. He won the Gold Cup

four times, the New Stakes seven times, the Queen's Gold Vase six times, the Ascot Derby five times, the Royal Hunt Cup three times and the Wokingham Stakes twice.

Fred Archer was born in 1857, two years after George Fordham had ridden his first Ascot winner. Archer's first Ascot winner was Mr C. S. Hardy's Merodach, when carrying six stone ten pounds in the Wokingham Stakes in 1873: reported as 'a fine race, won by a neck'. Fred Archer's tragically abbreviated career covered only fourteen Royal Ascot meetings, from 1873 to 1886, during which time he had eighty Ascot winners, many of them in the sprints he rode so well. Fred Archer never won the Ascot Gold Cup. He did however win the Royal Hunt Cup twice, the Fern Hill Stakes five times, and the Wokingham, the High Weight Stakes and the Queen's Gold Vase four times apiece. Archer won twelve races in 1878 at the one royal meeting, and ten winners in 1881 and again in 1883. What his total would have been in a career as long as that of George Fordham one can only guess.

There was a great tussle between Fordham and Archer in the 1875 Ascot Derby over the Swinley course. George Fordham rode Gilbert, owned by Monsieur Lefèvre, and Fred Archer rode the favourite Spinaway. Sir George Chetwynd described the race. 'Knowing that his mount, Gilbert, wanted a pacer he [Fordham] made the whole of the running till he rounded the turn, and then eased his horse with a cunning that was not perceptible to lookers on. Archer took up the running on the favourite, Spinaway, closely followed by the Earl of Dartrey. Everyone thought the race was confined to these two when to general astonishment, in which no doubt Archer joined, Fordham, who had apparently dropped back beaten, came with a rush on the inside and won three-quarters of a length. It was one of the most remarkable of his many stolen races.' In John Osborne's opinion 'Archer would win races with ten pounds in hand and make it appear he had got twenty-one pounds in hand. Fordham would win a race with ten pounds in hand and make it appear that he had got home by the skin of his teeth.'

There was no love lost between the two men. George Fordham was dignified and respected, the soul of discretion and honour, and he did not take kindly to what he considered the impertinence of his brilliant junior. As it happened, it was at Ascot that Fordham's resentment against Archer boiled over, and again it was at Ascot that he took his revenge. The story is told in *Asghill: or the Life and Times of John Osborne*.

One of several tussles Osborne had during his career with Archer revealed the fact that when it came to fine, resolute handling, 'The Pusher' was as

good as 'The Tinman'. . . Archer about this period had been carrying everything before him, and became so conceited that no man believed more in
Mr Archer than Fred Archer, the jockey. He was heard to say that there was
no steward who dare suspend him. He had the bad taste to hector George
Fordham at the starting post for the Royal Hunt Cup. 'George' took it
very quietly. 'You have taken a liberty with me, *Mister* Archer', he said
'and I will teach you to act differently. I may not do so now; I shall probably
wait until you are on something that you fancy yourself about; you must
not take a liberty with George.'

    The right moment came in the Hardwicke Stakes at Ascot in 1879,
Osborne was riding Lord Bradford's colt Bradford, and Archer was riding
Lord Falmouth's Silvio, then a five-years-old, a favourite mount of Archer's
[on which he had won the Derby]. Fordham made all the running. Presently
Archer came up on Silvio and called out, 'Pull on one side.' Fordham did
not pull on one side. Archer then tried to come round, but Fordham saw, he
thought, some better going in the middle of the course and made for it.
In all he did there was not the slightest room for objection, and yet he most
effectually prevented Archer winning the race . . . 'I do not think Archer
will ever take a liberty with "George" again', said Fordham as he dismounted
from Chippendale.

Archer's genius is well illustrated in the often-told tale of Peter at Ascot in
1881. Peter was owned by the popular Sir John Astley, nicknamed 'The
Mate'. Ridden by Wood, Peter started favourite of three runners in the
Queen's Gold Vase on the Tuesday. His official odds were five to two on,
but he seemed such a sure thing that it is said he carried bets of three
hundred to one on. After turning the Swinley bend and opposite the
Ascot Hotel Peter suddenly dug his toes in and began to kick. Herod and
Cawthorne recount in *Royal Ascot*: 'A groan of astonishment arose from
the backers of the favourite. Wood tried persuasion and coercion, but Peter
was like his namesake – firm as a rock. By this time the others were in
the Swinley Bottom, and poor Wood had to bring the refractory Peter
back to the paddock, where he was met by his owner who, true sportsman as he was, sympathised with his jockey, merely remarking to the
horse, "So he wouldn't go past his stable, eh?" '

    Peter appeared next day in the Royal Hunt Cup, with Archer replacing
Wood. *The Times* wrote: 'Though the twenty runners were at the post
in capital time, more than half an hour was wasted owing to the vagaries
of Peter. Peter was seen so much in the rear on the stand side that it
appeared he had been left at the post. Such, however, was not the case,
but he had shown temper after going a short distance. When over the
hill he took heart apparently and raced after his field. Opposite Tattersall's
ring the race seemed to be between Sword Dance and Petronel, but

Peter got on terms here, and caught Sword Dance fifty yards from home, got his head in front, and won easily.'

Royal Ascot takes up the story. 'Deafening shouts greeted the final struggle, and Sir John Astley, as well as his jockey, received quite an ovation in the paddock. But this was not the last of Peter. He was entered for the Hardwicke Stakes, worth over £3,000, and Archer was engaged to ride him. As the starting-post was just below where Peter had stopped to kick on the Tuesday, Archer got Sir John to approach the stewards, and obtained permission to take him down on the reverse side, and arriving at the starting-post as the flag fell, led him past his favourite stopping place and won by eight lengths'.

Strangely enough the wayward Peter's own brother, Timothy, a chestnut colt out of Lady Masham, winner of the Ascot Gold Cup in 1888, was described as 'a charming colt who had a perfect temperament'.

Many people have tried to analyse the genius of Fred Archer. He was a great starter. Osborne commented: 'At the fall of the flag he would "set about" his horse directly, and that was how he was great in short races.' Archer never seemed to know fear, and he would take chances and bring them off, which no other jockey would have attempted. Tall and cadaverous, the relentless punishment he gave his body, and the domestic tragedy in which he lost his young wife, are well known. How great Fred Archer must have been, to carve such a reputation so young. He was only twenty-nine years old when he died by his own hand.

Although Fordham and Archer were giants among jockeys, there were other bright stars in the Ascot firmament. John Osborne might prefer the north, but he won twenty-nine races at Ascot including one on objection, between 1853 and 1889. He won the Ascot Gold Cup on Apology in 1876, on which he had won the Coronation Stakes two years earlier. He won the Jubilee Cup of 1887, run over the New Mile, for Mr Vyner on Minting, but perhaps Minting's greatest race was the Hardwicke Stakes of 1887 in which he finished second.

The struggle for the Hardwicke Stakes was invested with an importance never equalled in the stirring history of this race. Minting, four years, 9 stone 10 lbs with Osborne up, succumbed to the mighty Ormonde, four years, 9 stone 10 lbs, piloted by Tom Cannon, the other runners being Bendigo, aged, 9 stone 12 lbs, and Phil, three years, 7 stone 12 lbs. The betting was 5 to 4 on Ormonde, 7 to 4 against Minting, 100 to 8 against Bendigo and 100 to 7 against Phil. The excitement while the son of Lord Lyon and the son of Bend Or were fighting out the last fifty yards of the battle was painful in its intensity, a relief only being felt when the Duke's colours flashed past the post with the advantage of a neck.

Corlett wrote in his 'Life' of John Osborne:

John Osborne, who never rode a better race in his life, and who, not-withstanding he had celebrated his jubilee, can still teach the youngsters something, sent Minting along as hard as he could pelt with the obvious intent of finding out the weak spot in Ormonde, should it exist. Bendigo, meanwhile, though always upsides with the other twain, never gave one the impression of actually going to win, though many of those who said so felt queer when he made his final challenge.

Minting had kept his forced lead till past the bottom turn, where Ormonde came up and overhauled him. It is just possible that Osborne kept a little bit up his sleeve at the point, for the ways of the 'Old Pusher' are marvellous, and it was undoubted that Minting looked like coming away again 200 yards from the finish. At the same moment, Bendigo made his effort, but the two juniors went away from him at once. The Duke's colt came again under Cannon's velvet hands, not to mention the very vigorous application of the 'gaffs', while Minting got a couple of rib-benders that he would not forget in a hurry. Ormonde, however, running on as straight as possible, won by a neck.

Why on earth a usually phlegmatic crowd of Britons took occasion to go stark, staring mad is rather more than can be readily explained. Certain, on this occasion, the British public took leave of its senses, and did a good old fashioned yell and bellow and general kick-up, tearing around in a way that would not have discredited an excitable crowd on the Champ de Mars or Donnybrook Fair. Old gentlemen skipped like young rams; elderly and otherwise staid, matrons leapt in the air in a way calculated to rejoice the hearts of the hatters; and altogether there was the most unexampled pow-wow and jamboree that has ever been witnessed by the present generation of turfites. Not only was Ormonde mobbed, but Minting and Bendigo were surrounded by the excited, cheering crowd. Never on any racecourse had been such tumultuous enthusiasm as at the finish of this Hardwicke stakes.

Tom Cannon was, of course, a superb horseman. He was a shrewd tactician, a wonderful judge of pace, and had marvellously light hands. Born in 1846, he was the father of those great riders and great jockeys Mornington and Kempton Cannon, and thus the direct ancestor of Lester Piggott. He rode forty-six winners in all at Ascot.

Tom French was something in the mould of Tom Cannon. French was an unassuming, modest man, a fine horseman, although plagued by lung trouble, who rode for Lord Falmouth, and who won four races at the 1870 royal meeting.

Admiral Rous was seriously ill at the age of eighty-two, when the

Ascot meeting took place, and racegoers exchanged anxious news of him on the racecourse. He seemed to be rallying, but sank again and died on June 20th, 1877. It was hard to imagine British racing without him. The race named in his memory, the Rous Memorial Stakes, was first run over the New Mile on Cup day 1878.

> There was a great struggle for the new race, the Rous Memorial Stakes with 1,000 sovereigns added — a rich prize worth the winning, and with Thunderstone, Insulaire, Petrarch and Dalham among the runners, it could not be said that it was unworthily contested. Petrarch and Dalham were, however, the only two in it, and singling themselves out from the others at the distance, and close on the rails, they fought out the race inch by inch, Petrarch always having the best of it and winning by a neck ... he walked away as if he had broken down. If it should turn out to be his last appearance, it has been a brilliant one, for he was giving Dalham, about our speediest miler, five lbs.

Petrarch was described by Theo Taunton as 'an exceedingly handsome and blood-like son of Lord Clifden, who won the Middle Park, his only two-years-old appearance, from a field of thirty, and on his reappearance won the Two Thousand Guineas in a canter. Only fourth in the Derby, he won the Prince of Wales's Stakes at Ascot in 1876, then the two and a half mile Ascot Gold Cup in 1877, before reverting to one mile in his final race, the Rous Memorial Stakes.'

In 1883 the King of the Netherlands presented a cup to Ascot, which was called the Orange Cup, and valued at £600. It was won by Barcaldine, a bay son of Solon bred in Ireland in 1878, and a very good horse indeed. Barcaldine was a strong, rangy animal with one white hind sock and a scraggy tail. In 1883 alone he beat Tristan in the Westminster Cup at Kempton Park, won the Cup at Epsom, the Orange Cup in which Archer rode him at Ascot and although unfit cantered home in the Northumberland Plate at Newcastle before retiring unbeaten to stud. His stock improved as they grew older, but mostly suffered from temperament.

St Simon was another great horse seen at Ascot. Foaled in 1881 by Galopin out of the King Tom mare St Angela he was, of course, barred from the Classics because the entries became null and void on the death of his owner Prince Batthyany, St Simon was acquired for 1,800 guineas by the Duke of Portland, and won every race in which he ran. When St Simon ran in the Gold Cup of 1884, he started at odds of seven to one on. Ridden by C. Wood, 'St Simon came with such an easy swing up to the leaders that when the line for home was fairly reached, he was fairly treading on the heels of Tristan. From this point the race was virtually over, as St Simon in his own inimitable style, strode gaily to the front, and won easily by twenty lengths.'

This Tristan, foaled in 1878, by Hermit out of Thrift and owned by Monsieur C. J. Lefèvre, was a considerable Ascot specialist, although he did not win a race there until he was four. In 1882 he carried off the Queen's Gold Vase followed by a stakes race over the Old Mile on Cup day, and rounded off a tremendous Ascot by winning the Hardwicke Stakes on the Friday. As a five-years-old he won the Gold Cup, followed by the Hardwicke Stakes. As a six-years-old, although beaten into second place in the Gold Cup by St Simon, he again took the Hardwicke Stakes for the third year running. He was ridden in his earlier races by Fordham and later by F. Webb.

In those days, when horses frequently came out to win two races at one royal meeting, even occasionally two races on one day, winners of three races at Ascot were not unknown. For example, the good race mare Geheimniss by Rosicrucian out of Nameless by Blinkhoolie, won the Trial Stakes in 1883 and the All-Aged and Queen's Stand races in the following year. She was owned by Lord Alington and had the assistance of Fred Archer.

St Gatien won four races at Ascot, the Gold Vase, the Gold Cup at odds-on, the Alexandra Plate in a canter by six lengths and finally, in 1886, the Rous Memorial Stakes. The great Ormonde won three races at Ascot, the Hardwicke Stakes 'with consummate ease' in 1886 and as a four-years-old with trouble developing with his wind, the second Hardwicke Stakes already described and the Rous Memorial Stakes.

The Prince of Wales's first flat-racing horses were owned in partnership and ran in other people's names; he had shares with Captain Machell in horses in the early seventies, and in Geheimniss, which ran in Lord Alington's colours. His first runner in the familiar purple, gold braid, scarlet sleeves, black velvet cap with gold fringe was a 13.3 Arab pony which ran in a match at Newmarket in 1877, and was beaten by thirty lengths. His first Ascot winner was not until 1891, when The Imp, by Robert the Devil out of The Martyr II, won the Ascot High Weight Plate, a handicap over a mile and a quarter run on the Friday. The Prince of Wales's flat racehorses were trained at Kingsclere by the great John Porter, and his first Ascot winner was ridden by G. Barrett, but at the end of the 1892 season his horses were moved to Richard Marsh at Lordship, Newmarket so that the King would have better opportunities of seeing them in training. Success came to the Prince of Wales with the sons of Perdita II, bought for the Prince by Porter. The first of these was Florizel, which in 1894 won the St James's Palace Stakes and a Triennial race at Ascot. Florizel II was the only one of the Prince's six horses in training to win a race that year, and when his new trainer was asked his opinion of the other five he replied with emphasis 'Awful!' Florizel II duly took the Gold Vase at Ascot in 1895, but the year was really distinguished by the debut of his full-brother the great Persimmon, which won the Coventry Stakes, which had been introduced in 1890 to commemorate that Master of the Buckhounds.

The following year, 1896, was the greatest that the Prince of Wales experienced on the turf. Thais narrowly won the One Thousand Guineas and Persimmon carried off the Derby, amid scenes of enormous enthusiasm. But the Prince of Wales failed to win a race at Royal Ascot, although Thais was second to the Duke of Westminster's Helm and Florizel II, now a five-years-old with dicey legs, ran a gallant third in the Gold Cup.

In 1896, the Court was in mourning for the death of Prince Henry of Battenberg, and the royal party was in black, although the Royal Enclosure was a blaze of colour. There were bright hopes of a royal win in 1897, when Persimmon contested the Cup. The Prince and Princess of Wales remained at Marlborough House, travelling by train to Windsor and thence by carriage to the course. There was even a rumour that Queen Victoria, in residence at Windsor Castle six miles away, might attend. *The Times* wrote: 'the baseless speculation that the Queen would drive over from Windsor had its effect upon attendance, the crowd being greatest at the extremity of the New Mile, up which the Royal Procession ascends to the Queen's Stand.'

There were four runners for the Gold Cup:

The Prince of Wales's Persimmon	4 years	9 stone	J. Watts
Mr J. C. Sullivan's Winkfield's Pride	4 years	9 stone	M. Cannon
Mr Hamar Bass's Love Wisely	4 years	9 stone	S. Loates
Lord Hindlip's Limasol	3 years	7 st 4 lbs	F. Allsopp

Persimmon was quoted at eighty-five to forty, Winkfield's Pride at four to one, Limasol at eight to one and Love Wisely at a hundred to six.

Cawthorne and Herod in *Royal Ascot* recounted:

The stalwart band of Metropolitan Police and detectives, under the direction of Superintendents Beard and Swanson, are in their places. and at the word of command the Course is cleared as if by magic. Preachers, prophets, hawkers and cardsellers are going in a moment, and everybody crowds to the barriers to see the moving bit of colour that has come into sight from the gates at the end of the New Mile. At a fair trot the Royal Cavalcade sweeps up the Course. Preceded by the Royal Huntsman and the whippers-in comes the Master of the Buckhounds [the Earl of Coventry], splendidly mounted, in full regalia and distinguished by his silver couples—the mark of his office. Following him are the mounted outriders, dressed in scarlet. Then come four or five carriages, roomy landaus with cane-faced sides, and drawn by four horses with postillions. All heads are uncovered, and a long roll of cheering announces that the Prince and Princess of Wales have arrived. Neither does the applause cease until the party are safely ensconced in the Royal Stand . . .

After luncheon we either hurry back to our seats to follow the next race, or wind our way to the paddock. All the morning people have been passing and repassing through the tunnel that leads from the Grandstand lawn to the grassy paddock, where one has an opportunity of inspecting the candidates for the various races.

Let *The Times* take up the story:

Persimmon, who had been sent to Ascot in the pink of condition, reflected the greatest possible credit on the care and skill of his trainer, who had him perfectly fit for the race in which he had to run, and though he cannot be described as a model of symmetry, he quite overshadowed such commoners as Love Wisely and Limasol, whose respective victories in the Ascot Cup last year and in the Oaks a fortnight ago may be regarded as illustrating 'the glorious uncertainty of the turf'. The only possible danger for Persimmon was the Irish colt Winkfield's Pride, who had run well in handicaps, but had never given evidence of being a stayer . . . The four runners were, as is customary in this race, paraded past the Queen's Stand before being started.

In the race itself . . . Persimmon like Gladiateur in 1866, lay last for the greater part of the way, only coming to the front at the last turn. Directly, however his jockey sent him going he won his race in a few strides, and sailed home the easiest of winners by eight lengths from Winkfield's Pride, who could make no sort of impression on him.

It was a great performance and if Persimmon had belonged to the humblest of racehorse owners he would have been loudly cheered as he passed the post, so that it was easy to understand the enthusiasm which his victory in the Prince of Wales's handsome colours evoked. The demonstration was, in its way, as remarkable for its spontaneity and its warmth as that which attended his Epsom triumph, for the whole of the vast multitude turned, as with one accord, to the Royal Enclosure, cheering, for several minutes. The Prince came forward to acknowledge the compliment, and the cheering was continued until Persimmon had been led back to scale and his jockey duly weighed in.

The triumphs of Diamond Jubilee were to come (though not at Ascot). Persimmon was the Prince of Wales's last Ascot winner before his accession.

There were some racing excitements to come in the last years of Queen Victoria's reign. Flying Fox, foaled in 1896, by Orme out of Vampire, a mare of most uncertain temper, made his racecourse debut in the New Stakes in 1898. 'Flying Fox ran somewhat green, but he answered his jockey's call very gamely and won rather easily at last. He is a very good-looking colt with more substance than his half brother [Batt, second to Jeddah in the 1898 Derby], and gives every promise of developing into a worthy bearer of his yellow jacket, black cap.' Flying Fox went on next year to win the Triple Crown.

A humbler horse which made his mark at Ascot was Eager, owned by 'Mr Fairie' [Mr A. W. Cox] and trained by Ryan which won races at Ascot for five consecutive years from 1896 to 1900 inclusive. Eager, by Enthusiast out of Greeba, was foaled in 1894. As a two-years-old he won the first leg of a Triennial, at three the Rous Memorial Stakes over the New Mile, and again won the Rous Memorial at four. As a five-years-old he reverted to six furlongs and won the Wokingham Handicap with Mornington Cannon in the saddle. His last victory at Ascot at the age of six was in the Queen's Stand Stakes over the even shorter distance of five furlongs, at which time he had changed hands and stables, and was owned by Mr L. Neumann and trained by Gilpin—but he was still ridden by Morny Cannon. 'Eager, who had won at Ascot in four successive seasons' wrote *The Times*, 'and who came out full of life and spirit after the long rest which Mr Neumann, who purchased him from Mr Cox after the fiasco at Newmarket last autumn, let the old horse have ... won with extreme ease yesterday, though Sloan got second with a two-years-old bred in the States.'

The Gold Cup was won in 1900 by Merman, owned by Lily Langtry, who raced as 'Mr Jersey', and ridden by Tod Sloan, whose monkey-on-a-stick style was sweeping away the old, upright English classic style. Merman was a chestnut by Grand Flaneur out of Seaweed, foaled in Australia in 1892 and trained by W. Robinson. There was afterwards a rumour that the Cup might be taken from him on a technicality. Merman was expected to start later in the week for the Alexandra Plate, thought to be at his mercy, but 'Mrs Langtry had sent orders that he was not to run ... Had he run he would assuredly have won, and his absence from the post after being seen in the paddock, seemed to give colour to the report that there was an objection lodged against him for the Cup on the ground of some informality in the nomination. It is to be hoped, however, that there is nothing in this surmise, and that this stout and honest horse may be left in possession of this, the greatest of the many racing trophies he has won.' Merman kept the Cup.

In 1900 the tide of success turned strongly for the American jockeys, who won seventeen of the twenty-six races at Royal Ascot. The meeting was held in a strange atmosphere, as the Boer War was going far from well. *The Sphere*, under the heading THE MOST FASHIONABLE RACEMEETING OF THE YEAR, described the scene:

The veldt has been responsible for short-comings of every kind at home, and it has certainly affected the turf, for Ascot has rarely been quieter than it was this week ... the habitués of the meeting were engaged in the more serious business of battle. Thus, for example, Lord Rosslyn, whose father figured conspicuously at Ascot when he was Master of the Buckhounds, and who himself carried off the Gold Cup in 1892 with Buccaneer, was probably engaged with Lord Roberts' forces against Botha when 'all London' was streaming to the course ...

Of course everybody who was anybody, and could be there, was there, including the Duke of York, the Duke of Cambridge, Prince Christian, the Portlands, the Devonshires, Lord Coventry and his son-in-law Prince Victor, Dhuleep Singh, the veteran Sir Harry Keppel and the no less distinguished Captain Lambton of Ladysmith fame, while Mr Lowther and Mr Chaplin represented the best sporting figures in the House of Commons. There was no Royal Procession on the third day, the Princess of Wales having gone to Sandringham.

The feature of the first day's racing was the success of the American jockeys, who won four out of seven valuable races ... On the second day the Americans carried off three first and three seconds in seven races, Master Reiff becoming the hero of the day by riding Mr Drake's Royal Flash (rather an outsider) to victory for the Hunt Cup. As a matter of fact the cup consists of two tankards valued at £500, the work of Messrs Hancocks of Bruton Street and New Bond Street. They are fine specimens of chased repoussé work in silver, descriptive of a classic feast in the ancient city of Pompeii.

Royal Flash has had a strange career ... he was entered in a race at Manchester. The owners had overlooked the fact that there was a selling clause attached to the race, and the horse then became liable to be claimed at a tithe of his value by the owner of any horse finishing in front of him. He was claimed by Mr W. F. Lee, who in turn sold him to Mr Wishard, one of the American trainers now over here.

American jockeys also figured conspicuously on the third day, winning five out of the seven races; and it was Sloan who won the Gold Cup with Mrs Langtry's Merman. In view of America's somewhat chilly reception of the lady, American citizen though she be, this triumph for her colours was not without a certain ironic touch.

The Prince of Wales and Princess Anne on their way to Ascot.

The Royal Procession of Queen Elizabeth II passes through the winners' enclosure, 1974.

The Queen riding on the course, 1975.

The Queen presenting the bronze trophy sculpted by Elizabeth Frink to Mr Nelson Bunker Hunt after his filly Dahlia had won the King George and Queen Elizabeth Stakes for the second time. (*Left*) Sir Philip Oppenheimer, chairman of the sponsoring De Beers Consolidated Mines Ltd: July 27th 1974.

Royal Ascot triumph . . .

. . . and disaster

Great horses that have run—and won—at Ascot. The incomparable Brown Jack with—
of course—Steve Donoghue up.

Aureole, ridden by Eph Smith, won the King George VI and Queen Elizabeth Stakes
in 1954 for Her Majesty the Queen. Here ridden by W. H. Carr.

Ribot, unbeaten in sixteen races, won the King George VI and Queen Elizabeth Stakes in 1956 for the Marchese Incisa della Rocchetta; E. Camici up.

Mill Reef, owned by Mr Paul Mellon, trained at Kingsclere by Ian Balding and ridden by Geoff Lewis, won the King George VI and Queen Elizabeth Stakes in 1971.

Lester Piggott has the best Royal Ascot record since Fred Archer. Piggott winning the 1972 Queen Anne Stakes on Sparkler, owned by Mrs M. Mehl-Mahlens and trained by his father-in-law, F. Armstrong.

Joe Mercer on Lady Beaverbrook's game Bustino (*left*) and Pat Eddery on the brilliant Grundy (*right*) the winner, fight out a memorable duel in the King George VI and Queen Elizabeth Diamond Stakes, 1975. Grundy was owned by Dr C. Vittadini and trained by Peter Walwyn. Bustino was trained by W. Hern. Dahlia (Lester Piggott), who finished third, is seen between them.

The Toffee Man: for fifty years Nat Yardley has handed out toffees in summer, sherbets in hot weather, cough sweets in cold to the jockeys. Here he is seen at Ascot with Paul Cook, 1973.

Bill Garland (Press Association) who books the jockeys' rides, consults his book beside one of the lions presented to Ascot by the Duke of Norfolk.

The first race for lady riders run at Ascot was the Cullinan Diamond Stakes on July 28th, 1973. Twenty-nine lady riders went to the post, and the race was won by Miss Caroline Blackwell, riding for the first time under Rules, on Hurdy-Gurdy.

Extravaganza: some of Mrs Gertrude Shilling's Ascot creations.

Meanwhile, behind the scenes, the Grandstand Trustees were running into stormy waters. True, their alteration in 1897 of the space given over to the bookmakers to move them further from the private boxes had met with general approval from the grandstand patrons. Nor were they directly concerned with the complaints which followed the enlargement of the Royal Enclosure at the expense of the unsaddling paddock in the same year, about which *The Times* complained: 'The Royal Enclosure has been provided with additional accommodation for getting some view of the racing, but as this has been affected by taking a little off the unsaddling paddock, it is a change which does not commend itself to those who are interested in seeing the winning horse after the race.'

It appears to have been at Ascot in 1897 that number cloths were first introduced; at least it was at Ascot that the experienced racing correspondent of *The Times* had first seen them: 'One modification which commands universal approval is that by which the horses about to run are provided with a number, which is attached to their quarter-sheet, so that people can at a glance distinguish the various competitors without having to pester the attendants with questions. It is strange that so obvious a method as this has not been adopted before – it is to be hoped it will now become universal.'

But the Jockey Club was again moving in to the attack, with a view to obtaining a larger share of the grandstand receipts for prize-money. Weatherby and Sons, then as now the Jockey Club secretariat, wrote from 6 Old Burlington Street in October 1899, asking that the stewards of the Jockey Club should be shown the Ascot Grandstand accounts for 'the past two or three years'. The Trustees promptly replied, stating: 'The Stewards of the Ascot Races are represented on the Trust by the Master of Her Majesty's Buckhounds, who has access to the accounts at all times, and in the circumstances the Trustees regret that they find themselves unable to comply with the wishes of the stewards of the Jockey Club.'

The Trustees took Counsel's opinion on the request. A copy of Counsel's opinion, dated December 21st, 1900, and signed A. T. Lawrence, is kept in the Minute book. It read:

> I am of the opinion that the stewards of the Jockey Club have no rights whatever in the matter. The stewards of Ascot races are the persons to whom the surplus funds of the Trustees are properly paid, but they are not *cestui que trustent*. No one who is not a *Cestui que Trust* can call upon the Trustees to render accounts except the Attorney General on behalf of the public, See Skinner's Company v The Irish Society, 7 Beeavan 593.
> In my opinion the course the Trustees should take is courteously to inform the agents of the Jockey Club that they are advised that the stewards of the

Club have no *locus standi*. Further that the stewards of Ascot Races have through the senior steward the Master of the Buckhounds all the information to which they have any rights.

That under these circumstances the Trustees cannot accede to an application which might have the effect of hampering them in the administration of their Trust.

The final outcome of the battle between the stewards of the Jockey Club and the Trustees of the Ascot Grandstand is recorded in the next chapter.

CHAPTER SEVEN

Edwardian splendour

KING EDWARD VII CAME AT LAST INTO HIS OWN WITH HIS ACCESSION TO the throne. At the age of sixty, for the first time, he could live without the disapproving shadow of his mother falling upon him. Buffoonery dropped from the elderly playboy, who showed he possessed courage and enterprise far beyond anything his detractors – or even his friends – thought he possessed.

The first Edwardian Ascot was held during the period of mourning.

> The whole of the lawn below the King's Stand had been railed off, and no admission was allowed to it, the consequence being that the number of vouchers issued by Lord Churchill, the Acting Master of the defunct Buckhounds, had, perforce, to be restricted . . . The race programme was encircled in black, and it was intimated that the holders of tickets must all be in black, or some hue almost as sober. Access to the bookmakers in Tattersall's ring was also made more difficult for the occupants of the enclosure, and the shutters of the King's Stand were all closed.

Nevertheless twenty-four special trains were run from London on the opening day. The luncheon tents were numerous and well patronised, although there were fewer carriages than usual. A reaction became apparent from the imposition of mourning, which had been so omnipresent in Queen Victoria's reign. On Wednesday there was 'scarcely a touch of colour', but on Cup day 'it was clear . . . that a number of ladies who were in black on the first two days had assumed a more modified form of mourning, as there were many dresses of white, lavender and mauve, although not enough to impart any colour to the scene'. On Friday 'there were more white and lavender dresses in the Royal Enclosure than on previous days.'

Both this Ascot and the Ascot following the death of Edward VII (when mourning was spontaneously worn and rigidly adhered to) were called at the time 'Black Ascot'. It was a mourning Royal Ascot that inspired Cecil Beaton to create the lovely dresses in black and white for *My Fair Lady*. Incidentally in the stage version, the horses ran the wrong way round the course, as that was the way the stage revolved.

There was a rare criticism of lack of attention to detail in 1901. 'It was lamentable to see a lot of dirty paper flying about the paddock and frightening valuable horses which were being led about there. It surely would be easy to employ a man to pick up all the débris, and this should be attended to at once, or there will certainly be a bad accident before the week is out.'

The new reign brought new administration. The Queen's Buckhounds were given up. Racing was put under the control of the Earl of Coventry, whose father had been in control as Master of the Buckhounds in 1886.

Viscount Churchill had acted on behalf of Lord Chesham who had been unable to take up his appointment as he was fighting in South Africa. He was now placed in charge of applications for the Royal Enclosure and the Iron Stand. Lord Churchill was a formidable personality. Born in 1864, he served Queen Victoria continuously from 1876, when he was made a Page of Honour, until her death. His many business commitments — he was a power in the Great Western Railway — never kept him from a detailed surveillance of the Ascot scene. He personally selected those eligible for entry to the Royal Enclosure, sorting the letters into three baskets labelled 'Certainly', 'Perhaps' and 'Certainly Not'. Once, after allocating the vouchers for a Royal Ascot, he said, 'Now I am the best-hated and the best-loved man in the country.'

Lord Churchill's memory was prodigious: in 1912 he saw in the Royal Enclosure a lady to whom he had refused a voucher. Enquiries were made, and an interim juncture followed, restraining a Miss Meadows from selling vouchers for admission to the Royal Enclosure. 'It was a grave social impropriety that persons who had applied for and had obtained invitations to the Royal Enclosure, should seek to make money out of them, and sell the privilege that had been extended to them,' commented *The Times*.

When Lord Hamilton of Dalzell was appointed the King's Representative at Ascot by George V, on the death of Viscount Churchill in 1934, the King decided that the issue of vouchers for the Royal Enclosure should be made by a department of the Royal Household and he asked the Master of the Horse, the Earl of Granard, to be responsible for entries into the Royal Enclosure. Lord Granard was no more popular than his predecessor with those to whom he refused a voucher, and one unsuccessful society woman commented tartly: 'Lord Granard decides whether you are a fit and proper person to have a little ticket with your name on it, which will take you into the Royal Enclosure.'

King Edward VII was not present at Ascot in 1901, nor were his colours seen on the racecourse, but he did in fact have an Ascot winner. His horses ran during the period of mourning in the famous straw colours of the Duke of Devonshire, and one of the King's horses, Lauzan, a three-years-old bay colt by St Simon, ridden by Mornington Cannon, won the St James's Palace Stakes.

At this meeting the American sportsman Mr W. C. Whitney was by far the most successful owner, winning the Trial Stakes, the Fern Hill Stakes, the Alexandra Plate and the Windsor Castle Stakes, all with horses trained by a popular American trainer Huggins and ridden in the American style by one or other of the Reiff brothers. The Gold Cup was won by Santoi, owned by Mr George Edwardes and ridden by F. Rickaby, a horse which had also won the Jubilee Stakes at Kempton Park.

The Ascot meeting of 1901 took place in a behind-the-scenes atmosphere of tension and drama. The meeting opened on Tuesday, June 17th, and the Coronation of King Edward VII was fixed for Thursday, June 26th. Naturally London was packed with overseas dignitaries and sightseers, and Ascot was crowded. On the Saturday before Ascot the King and Queen were at Aldershot for the Coronation Review of troops. Reginald, Viscount Esher, deputy Governor of Windsor Castle, wrote in a letter that the King was not well when he went to Aldershot 'and the damp and misery of the Royal Pavilion, plus the Tattoo produced violent pains'. After a terrible night and day, he was brought home to Windsor on the Monday, feverish and feeble. On the Tuesday he seemed somewhat better and the Queen went to Ascot. On Wednesday he was much worse. Racegoers at Ascot had been told the King was suffering from lumbago, but uneasy whispers were circulating that the illness was serious. Yet on Cup day Queen Alexandra again drove in state along the course. The Royal Procession came slowly up the course, to avoid cutting up the wet turf. For the first time (and in the future), instead of drawing up in front of the Royal Stand, the carriages were driven past the Judge's Stand and through gates off the course into the yard behind the Royal Stand, where the Queen alighted from her carriage. She stayed only a short time. On the Wednesday and Friday other members of the Royal Family were present at the races, dissembling a confidence they were not feeling, but withdrew early, and without ceremony.

On the Friday Lord Esher saw the King. 'He sent for me and received me in bed. He was looking feverish and flushed, but was quite cheerful. He was lying in his charming bedroom, very bright and gay, overlooking the East Terrace. Jack, his terrier, was lying on the bed, and when I kissed his hand, growled at me . . . The doctors warned me not to bother him with questions, so I did not transact much business. He postponed the Eton Gala, then gossiped . . . he was very friendly and gentle.'

The King's temperature soared and dropped.

The possibility of the coronation being put off was fast becoming a probability, but Edward VII declared he would rather die in the Abbey. 'The difficulty now will be to avoid all the tiring receptions *before* the Coronation of Thursday,' wrote Lord Esher. 'After that we need not care . . . The King's popularity—his personal popularity—is extraordinary. There is no doubt that, in spite of the Queen's presence, Ascot was *manqué*.'

Over the weekend the King became rapidly worse. Appendicitis—in those days a frightening, almost unknown disease—was diagnosed. On the Monday following Ascot the coronation was postponed and on the Tuesday, exactly a week after the opening of Royal Ascot and only two days before the coronation should have taken place, the King was operated upon. A letter quoted in *Queen Mary* by James Pope-Hennessy conveys the atmosphere of those anxious days. 'I have never felt anything like the physical and mental oppression . . . in London. It was hot and airless and muggy, the decorations flapped about in an ominous manner—and gloom and consternation were in every face.' The operation was a complete success, and the King recovered remarkably quickly: the postponed coronation, without the foreign representatives, took place in a spirit of heartfelt thanksgiving on August 9th, 1902.

No longer was King Edward VII forced to entertain for Ascot from a rented house. During the meeting he lived in regal state at Windsor Castle. The King was genial, but he was a stickler for complete adherence to correct dress and procedure, and there was nothing slipshod about any occasion with which he was connected. At the same time he was a kindly man, and did not like to make a culprit feel ill-at-ease.

The German, Daisy, Princess of Pless described her stay at Windsor Castle for Royal Ascot.

June 18th, 1909, Windsor Castle

Quite sad that tonight is the last night here. Today is Friday and we arrived on Monday and it really has not been too long. I was afraid at first it might be stiff and boring but it is not only a magnificent palace but a charming house to stay everything most comfortable and the servants so obliging. Hans and I have breakfast together in our own sitting room, and at a quarter past twelve have to be ready for the races; before that, and after the races, one could do what one liked; dinner is at half past eight or a quarter to nine. We always go back very late, so I was only able to rest the evening of the one day the Queen and Princess Victoria did not go, as we went in motors, and therefore got back sooner. After tea I took a walk with Soveral [the Portuguese Minister, a close friend of Edward VII and Queen Alexandra, nicknamed 'The Blue Monkey' on account of his swarthy complexion], whom I consider to be almost a dangerous fanatic in his feelings against Germany, the danger to England, and so on . . .

Today I did not go racing as the Queen asked me to go on the river; as she and Princess Victoria, Princess Murat, Mrs Standish (a charming elderly lady, French by birth, who is here with her niece), Soveral, Mensdorff, the Austrian Ambassador, Sir Harry Legge, in waiting, and Lord Anglesey, young, about twenty-eight; all went on a steam launch from here to Cliveden; we left at one o'clock and got home at seven; frightfully sleepy, and I must say it is tiring to sit facing one another and trying to be amusing and agreeable for six hours with only the meals for a break. We had lunch and tea on board. At Cliveden all the ladies were landed on one side of the river and the gentlemen on the other. Soveral arranged it; it was most extraordinary and very pointed! I felt quite shy afterwards, as we simply stopped, I think, for this purpose . . .

Soveral and the Queen sitting always side by side, I am rather afraid he is a snob . . . All my clothes have been a great success and Hans said I was the best dressed woman at the races. All very simple and draped; one day a big bunch of pink lilies and my scarab turquoises. Then I twice wore Fritz's gold coat which made a great effect and looked lovely.

A feature of the court of Edward VII were the enormous meals. The King's feats as a trencherman were fabled. Colonel J. P. C. Sewell, who edited King Edward VII's *Personal Letters*, wrote:

His Majesty no doubt required considerable nourishment to maintain his amazing energy, and he was famous throughout his life as a great eater. He had a glass of milk at seven; at ten (after dealing with a mass of correspondence) he enjoyed a large breakfast of boiled eggs, bacon, fish, potted meats and coffee; at luncheon numerous dishes with, if possible, lamb and chicken. He consumed a large tea, and at dinner, which was generally served at a quarter past eight, he disposed of five or six courses, drinking Rhine wine or champagne, and liqueur brandy.

When at the Hôtel de Palais at Biarritz towards the close of his reign, he once sat down to table after declaring that he was not very hungry. Nevertheless, course after course was served and eaten by him with relish until finally, when all the other guests were gasping for breath and had long since lost all interest in food, fruit was passed round. Thereupon the King looked up and exclaimed in disappointed tones, 'Is there no cheese?'

At Buckingham Palace and at Windsor Castle the menus were remarkable mainly for the large number of meat and sweet courses they included; quails followed by lamb, turkey and chicken figure, for instance, on the menu of a banquet at Windsor, and there were no fewer than three sweets; peaches with cream, soufflés and Venetian ices.

. . . After his meals and far too often during the day to please his physicians, His Majesty thoroughly enjoyed a good cigar. It was a sign of favour to be offered one of the Corona Coronas or Henry Clays which he carried in a large leather case.

King Edward VII was also an ardent supporter of the new phenomenon bursting upon modern life, which was to have such far-reaching consequences—the internal combustion engine. He first drove by car to Ascot on Tuesday June 20th, 1905. That year 'it is a sign of the times that a special enclosure should have been arranged for the use of motors at the back of the grandstand, while at least fifty more automobiles were drawn up in the main road. None of the cars were allowed on the Heath, where, for the present at all events, the horse remains supreme.'

A most unusual incident regarding the King and his car at Ascot is told in *What I Know* by C. W. Stamper, who was motor expert to the King:

On his return to England His Majesty went to Windsor, and from there, on the 17th of the month [June 17th, 1908] I took him to Ascot. We returned by way of Sunningdale, and in the car with the King were two ladies and an Equerry. Before we started for the Castle, the latter desired me to go through the Rhododendron Drive when we entered the Park, but I told him I was afraid the ground would be too wet. However, he said that it was His Majesty's wish and that I had better try, so no more was said at the time. When we came to the drive I told the chauffeur to stop and turned to the King.

'I'm afraid the ground will be too soft for us, Your Majesty.'

'Go on as far as you can,' he replied.

With that we entered the drive. We had not gone very far when we came to a bad dip, and again I stopped the car. The Equerry was sitting just at my back, and I showed him the hollow and said that if we went down into it, I very much doubted if we should be able to get out again. He only told me to go on. We slid down somehow, but, just as I feared, we could not get out the other side. I asked His Majesty to alight, and he and the others did so. Of course, they were all dressed for Ascot, and it was terribly wet under foot, but there was nothing else to be done.

With great difficulty we managed to turn the car, but when we tried to get out of the dip on the side on which we had entered it, we fared no better.

The wheels sank into the thick, wet moss, and it began to look as if the car would have to remain where it was, till assistance arrived. Then the Equerry pushed on one side, and we made a few inches, but the wheels started slipping, and we had to desist. I asked His Majesty to wait while I plucked some branches, and this I presently spread in front of the wheels, making a track on which they could get a grip. I then laid hold of the spokes of one front wheel, while the Equerry took hold of the other and—though I did not know it—the King and the ladies started pushing behind. The chauffeur let in the clutch. Round span the wheels, flinging up mud and moss in great quantities. But the car began to move, and after a minute or two the wheels found the bracken and we scrambled up the side of the hollow.

When he stood up, I saw that the Equerry was in a terrible state, with mud all over his gloves and his clothes, where the wheel had brushed them; but when His Majesty and the ladies appeared from behind the car, they were all in the most awful state imaginable. They were simply covered from head to foot with the moss and mud which the hind wheels had thrown up and their clothes were in a shocking condition. However, they all re-entered the car, and after slipping and sliding about, we managed to struggle out of the drive and on to the road once more.

The type of car involved is not specified, but at that time the King owned several forty hp Mercedes cars, which were driven by chauffeurs seconded from the Metropolitan Police.

At Ascot the first motor-garage opposite the entrance was done away with in 1910, and replaced by 'making a turning place for motors in front of the grandstand entrance, a very considerable improvement ... for the convenience of the public'. In the following year a new entrance was made for motor-cars, and the new garage, which had replaced the original, leased to the Royal Automobile Club for three years. Such was the growth of motor-traffic that in 1913 extra men in uniform were employed, just to open and shut the doors of the cars arriving at the entrance to the Grandstand Enclosure.

Railway patrons were not forgotten: in 1911 a delightful rustic path was made, leading down to the special platform for the reserved specials returning to London, and this was in use until recently.

At about this time Ascot began to take its traditional stand against photographers, who have never been popular on the course. Before the Royal Meeting in 1911, it was announced: 'A good many complaints have indeed been received by the authorities from people who resent being "snapped" at unexpected moments by the camera fiend,' and restrictions were introduced, to be followed in 1920 by a total ban on cameras, which were ordered to be impounded. Ascot was alive to the value of racing photographs: it was photographs of individuals which were (and are) frowned upon. Moving pictures were tolerated, and as early as 1912: 'Special facilities to take bioscope pictures, from the most advantageous points, of all the principal races next week, together with scenes of the paddock and a full view of the Royal Procession' were announced.

On the whole, there were only minor changes in the year-to-year running of Ascot during the reign of Edward VII. Viscount Churchill tidied up the small stands, and the replacements had a little more room, including viewing space on the roofs. The number of seats in both the Royal and Grandstand Enclosure was considerably reduced, and those seats remaining were marked 'Free' and could not 'be reserved by placing cloaks upon them'. Prices went up. The cost of a voucher to the Royal Enclosure was raised in 1903 from £1 to £4, and the cost per day of reserved stalls in the grandstand rose to £1 10s for a covered and £1 for an uncovered stall.

The Grandstand continued in the control of the Trustees, who in 1905 appointed a remarkable man to be secretary. He was Colonel, later Sir Gordon, Carter, whose erect military figure and keen eye were known, feared and respected by all who knew him. Born in 1852, he enlisted in the First Life Guards in 1872 and rose from the rank of trooper to that of Lieutenant-Colonel in the same regiment. For fifteen years, he was Adjutant of the Life Guards, and he took part in the relief of Kimberley. He was nicknamed 'Troops', and that was his telegraphic address.

Colonel Carter had been appointed Clerk of the Course in 1901. Throughout the year he daily walked round the buildings, and rode round the course at Ascot, minutely inspecting every nook and cranny. He would accept nothing less than perfection—for example, there was a long, thick and prickly holly hedge bounding the course: every single fallen leaf had to be picked up and removed.

Ascot week was the peak of his year. Sir Gordon's establishment beside the racecourse was kept at the standard he demanded by his butler-cum-valet for twenty-one years, Mr Alex Mabey. (A childless widower, he had married in the 1880s, but his wife died while he was in South Africa.) Sir Gordon was called every day at six fifteen a.m. with a cup of tea, by which time the bath water had to be hot, and the shaving water boiling. Sir Gordon was precisely punctual: he used to say that a man who came before his appointed time was as big a nuisance as one who came late. He was fastidious in his dress. His shoes were mirrors of polished leather. His bootlaces were removed each day from the shoes, washed and ironed! If they were leather laces they were removed and pulled through a polish cloth.

During Royal Ascot Sir Gordon would be on the course, in riding kit, at seven in the morning. Later he would change into a lounge suit at his office. At noon he crossed the road to his home, to change into morning dress. When the Royal Procession came down the course, he stood always at the gate where the Procession left the racecourse. It was at this spot that his ashes were scattered after his death.

After the first race, which was at one thirty p.m., there was a break of one hour for luncheon. Sir Gordon Carter and his house party always took luncheon in a private dining-room on the course. After the racing, his valet brought another lounge suit over to the office into which Sir Gordon changed. He changed again, for the fifth time that day, into evening dress for dinner, an eight-course affair of iced melon, soup, fish, entrée, water ice, saddle of lamb, sweet, savoury and dessert, followed by coffee, liqueurs and cigars.

Especially in his younger days, Sir Gordon Carter was intolerant of delay or inefficiency, and not a little short-tempered—a sign that the storm was about to break was that his ears used to go very red. But he was as hard on himself as he was on anyone else, he was absolutely genuine and he never went back on his word. He inspired absolute trust and great respect.

There are many stories about him. He went on a treasure-hunting expedition in the Cocos Islands in the Indian Ocean, unfortunately without success. Every morning, whatever the weather, he went for an early morning gallop over Ascot Heath. He was a strict, but fair disciplinarian, and expected his work-force to work any overtime at 1s an hour. He was fond of little notices, some of which read:

> Smoking during working hours is strictly forbidden. *Any one caught disobeying this order will be immediately discharged.*
> Smoking is permitted in the Bothies during the time allowed for meals, but at no other times or in any other buildings.

Another notice read:

> Painters will be allowed to leave work five minutes earlier, in order to enable them to wash their hands before partaking of their meals.

It is somewhat surprising to find that Sir Gordon was also very superstitious. He always took off his hat to a new moon. If he saw one magpie he would wait and wait until he saw a second. And he believed it was vital for the rooks to nest each year in the trees near his home, and that if they did not come it portended a death. One year the rooks did not nest; there was an unspoken but perceptible lightening of tension when one of the gardeners died.

Sir Gordon Carter lived too long. He maintained his beloved racecourse at its incredible state of polish and perfection right up to the outbreak of the Second World War, but his heart was broken by the inevitable wartime deterioration which then set in. He died in November 1941.

With the arrival of Colonel Carter the Minutes of the Grandstand Trust became more detailed. In 1901 the caterers Browning and Company had gone into liquidation. The Trustees considered getting Mr Browning to continue to run the catering under the direction of the liquidator, or even running the catering themselves, but eventually decided to put the catering contract to tender, and 'it was unanimously resolved that Messrs Letheby and Christopher's offer be accepted subject to a guarantee and security'. The grandstand catering remains in their hands to this day (1975).

The grandstand was completely repainted in 1905, and compensation for paint damage to the ladies' dresses was paid out after the meeting. An attempt was made to reclaim this money from the painters, Cooper and Sons of Windsor, but was abandoned

In spite of the modern belief that all was rosy in those far-off days, the Trustees had considerable difficulties in making ends meet. Annually the sum of about £22,300 was passed over by the Trustees to the Jockey Club, for the provision of stakes and cups. Yet the Trustees had an overdraft, and in 1905 had to sell Consols to the value of £3,539 to cover it.

There appeared to be a shortage of stall-seats. The Trustees appealed to those who had reserved but not used seats for the past seven years to give them up, and in 1906 they built 250 more stall-seats in the Alexandra Stand, making room by raising the stand roof. But this was not the answer, and the new stalls did not fill. Fifty boxes (for which there was a constant demand) were then built out of one block of new stalls, and a further block released for free use by the public. This left for sale 542 covered and 370 uncovered stalls, and now the balance was right.

It was possible to report after the 1909 meeting, 'Splendid weather attended this meeting, which was most successful and may be classed as a record'. Money taken, including admission to the paddock, totalled £32,217 10s. Grandstand receipts were up by over £5,000 and paddock receipts by nearly £1,700. Badges sold totalled 24,228, an increase of 612 weekly and 5,312 daily badges. (It was found cheaper to use cardboard badges with a strong pin on the back than paper tickets — they cost only £5 per thousand from Oxley and Son.) The organisation was good too, 'owing to the arrival in quick succession of the special

trains, there was once during the meeting, for a short time only, a slight
delay in the issue of badges at the main entrance'. Sales of stalls were
still down, except on Cup day, when they were sold out. 'The portion
of the Alexandra Stand thrown open to the Public in lieu of the space on
the lawn taken to build more boxes was much sought after and greatly
appreciated.'

In the previous year, 1907, a detailed assessment of the area occupied
by the racecourse was compiled for Income Tax and Corporation Tax
purposes and showed:

The Grandstand	3¼ acres (afterwards increased to 5¾ acres)
Race Course	24¼ acres
Jockeys Room	1¾ acres
Stand	¼ acre
Carriage enclosure	13½ acres
Racecourse and Lodge	9½ acres (New Mile)
Total	52½ acres (increased to 55 acres)

The Gold Cup was stolen during the race in 1907. It was on display just
behind the grandstand, guarded by two policemen and two Ascot gatemen. According to the account in the newspapers — which paid the incident
little attention — as the bell rang, as the horses turned into the straight and
the roar of the crowd heralded the finish, the men on duty looked through
an opening on to the lawn in the hope of seeing the runners. When the
horses had passed and they returned to the table, the Gold Cup had gone.
An elderly gateman, who said he had been present, told the author that a
lady fainted, or feigned to faint and the men looking after the cup had
hurried to her assistance. When they looked round the cup had vanished.
It was never found. But later that summer, King Edward VII was hugely
amused when a man in the crowd called to him, as he arrived at Kempton
Park for a racemeeting 'What've you done with the cup, Teddy?'

The cup was specially made for the 1907 race by Garrards, who were
apparently still the owners at the time of the theft. The Trustees of the
Grandstand and the Royal Enclosure authority each paid £100 to Garrards
as 'an Act of Grace' with the proviso that in future the cup was to be
fully insured and properly guarded.

The race itself was unusually exciting. 'In the last two furlongs the race
was confined to the French horse Beppo and The White Knight, and
from the beginning of the stands, where Beppo was beaten, Eider came
out from the rails right on The White Knight, and the pair ran on
literally [sic] locked together, the judge being unable to separate them at

the post.' After an enquiry the race was awarded to The White Knight, but the stewards exonerated the rider of Eider, which they described as 'a big handful'.

The American invasion of jockeys had been as successful at Ascot, as it was elsewhere. Tod Sloan had come and gone before Edward VII succeeded to the throne, but the Reiff brothers continued to take their toll of victims from the English riders. Lester Reiff was the older, and a very fine rider, although he had trouble with his weight, and with his reputation. His first win at Ascot had been in the Queen's Stand Stakes of 1896, in which he rode Wishard owned by a man of that name. He only had eleven wins at Ascot, but that included four on the same day, Friday in 1901, when he carried off the Alexandra Plate, the Windsor Castle Stakes, the Hardwicke Stakes and the King's Stand Stakes, three of the races for Mr W. C. Whitney, and the Hardwicke Stakes on Merry Gal for Mr W. Hall Walker, afterwards Lord Wavertree. The younger Reiff brother, Johnny, came over to England in 1899, when he won the last race at Royal Ascot: he had only six winners at Royal Ascot.

The charming but weak-charactered Danny Maher, who arrived in England in 1900 with a great reputation, which he quickly justified, was the American jockey who had the greatest success at Ascot. His first winner came in 1900 and before his death in 1914 he had ridden forty-six winners. He won four consecutive races in 1910, the Gold Cup on Bayardo, the St James's Palace Stakes on Lemberg and the first and second year of Biennial Stakes. In 1911 he won his eighth successive Ascot race on Sunder, owned by Mr Solly Joel and trained by C. Peck at Newmarket, one of the horses connected with his four-timer at Ascot in the previous year.

Among the most successful English jockeys was Mornington Cannon, the son of Tom Cannon, who took his unusual first name from a horse which won at Bath for his father on the day he was born. Although Morny was a jockey of the old classic school, he was very successful even after the American invasion, and won twenty-two races in the twentieth century at Ascot, a total of seventy-four Ascot races in all between 1889. His last win was on Lord Crewe's Polymelus, trained by Porter, in a Triennial in 1905.

Herbert Jones, who 'did' the temperamental Diamond Jubilee, became Edward VII's jockey because of his ability to get on with the horse. In 1899 he had ridden in forty-three races and won only two of them, but after his victory in the Two Thousand Guineas in 1900 he won many races, including twenty at Ascot.

Otto Madden was another European jockey who did well at Ascot.

Born in Germany in 1870, he was the son of the English jockey associated with the great Kincsem. Madden first won at Ascot when he was twenty-four years old in 1894, when he won the Wokingham on the Duke of Devonshire's Oatlands. In all, in spite of being warned off for a couple of seasons for keeping bad company, he won thirty races at Ascot. Afterwards he turned trainer. Otto Madden was exceptionally fond of his horses, and went on to the racecourse before breakfast, to select specially luscious clover and young grasses for his favourites.

Before the First World War Freddie Fox, Steve Donoghue and F. Bullock were among the youngsters who were winning races at Royal Ascot.

Many great horses were seen at Ascot in the early years of the twentieth century. Sceptre, by Persimmon out of Ornament, a sister to Ormonde, foaled in 1899, first ran at Ascot as a three-years-old. Her first start was in the Coronation Stakes of 1902. She was restive, and unseated her rider, Randall, at the start. When the race started, Randall allowed her to become tailed off; she made up ground rapidly but could only finish fourth. Randall never rode her again. Sceptre was pulled out on the following day, and duly won the St James's Palace Stakes, when she was ridden by F. Hardy.

When Sceptre reappeared at Ascot as a four-years-old, her owner Sievier had been overtaken by his debts. and had had to part with her to Mr (later Sir) William Bass for £25,000. She was sent to Alec Taylor at Manton where she received more consideration than had been her lot so far. She was gradually rebuilt physically, and her first race for the Manton stable was the Hardwicke Stakes in 1903, which she won. She ran as a five-years-old, three times at Ascot where sadly, she was beaten in all three races.

Sceptre is always linked with that other great racemare, Pretty Polly, foaled in Ireland in 1901, the daughter of Gallinule out of a moderate mare Admiration by Saraband. While Sceptre was a hard bay with a mousy muzzle, Pretty Polly was a big, powerful chestnut. Bred and owned by Major Eustace Loder of the 12th Lancers, Pretty Polly was trained at Clarehaven Lodge, Newmarket by Peter Purcell Gilpin, the only trainer of the time always referred to in *The Times* as 'Mister'. Her two-years-old career was glorious, but she did not run at Ascot. After winning the 1904 One Thousand Guineas and the Oaks, Pretty Polly's third race of her three-years-old season was in the Coronation Stakes at Royal Ascot. 'The fifth race on the card—if race it could be called—was the Coronation Stakes, and although the unbeaten Pretty Polly was opposed by seven other fillies, it was not with any expectation of beating her, but because there was a sum of £300 for the second. The task set Pretty Polly was not a light one, as she had to give from fourteen pounds to seventeen pounds to all her opponents, but she accomplished it without the semblance of an effort, and passed the post three lengths in front of Montem, who had won the New Stakes at Ascot last year.'

Pretty Polly was ridden by William Lane, who rode four winners that day, the others being Andover, trained by Braine, and Delaunay and Petit Bleu, both trained like Pretty Polly by Gilpin. Later that year William Lane was terribly injured in a fall at Lingfield and never rode in a race again.

Pretty Polly appeared for the last time on a racecourse in the Ascot Gold Cup of 1906. The mare was 'suffering the effects of a wart which had recently been lanced, and she was bathed in sweat while being walked round the paddock, where, of course, a mob of people came to see her'. In the race 'she suffered a very faint resistance to Bachelor's Button, who, to the horror of the many admirers of this remarkable filly, beat her quite comfortably by a length . . . Pretty Polly's defeat was such a blow to the great majority of the onlookers that not a cheer was raised for Bachelor's Button when he came back to scale, though he had run a gallant race. But Pretty Polly's defeat was regarded as something like the shattering of an idol, and Bachelor's Button was looked upon as the perpetrator of the deed.' Bachelor's Button, owned by Mr Solly Joel, trained by C. Peck and ridden by Danny Maher, had started at seven to one. He had won the Gold Vase in 1904 when ridden by Halsey, and again in 1905 when ridden by Danny Maher, when he also won the Hardwicke Stakes, so he was a pretty good horse in his own right.

There were some fiascos in the Edwardian Ascot races too. In 1902 there was an unusual mishap in the Wokingham when 'the machinery connected with the starting-gate went wrong, and only half the horses got away. Most of the favourites were left, and of the other half Mr Joel's His Lordship was an easy winner'. Mr Lionel Rothschild, owner of the favourite Valet, objected, but was overruled and the result stood. The stewards gave as their reason 'as the horses who had run their race would have had little chance in the re-run'.

There were incidents in two races on Cup day 1904. The All-Aged Stakes was described by *The Times* as

a complete fiasco . . . for only two came out to run for the All-Aged Stakes, and long odds were laid on Cossack, who had shown good speed in the Hunt Cup yesterday, his only opponent, Orchid, having deteriorated very much of late. The odds were fully justified and were very easily landed, but, to the disgust of those who thought they had won their money, it appeared that Cossack had carried the wrong weight. An objection was lodged by the owner of the second (Mr H. J. King) and, as it was found that Cossack should have carried four pounds more weight, there was no alternative but to disqualify him. The objector cannot be blamed for having stood upon his rights, but it is not creditable to the Jockey Club that there should not be a paid official to see that the horses are properly weighted, instead of this being left to the owner or trainer. In this case sympathy must be felt with Sir James Miller in his disappointment. The trainer had just suffered a severe domestic bereavement.

Nor did the Gold Cup itself follow its usual pattern.

The race was a peculiar one, for Throwaway was allowed to get a long lead, the jockeys of Zinfandel (Morny Cannon) and Sceptre (O. Madden) being convinced that he would come back to them, as the saying goes, and that they would be able to beat him for speed. But they delayed their efforts too long, and Throwaway was never caught, winning a length from Zinfandel. Sceptre was never dangerous, and the French horse (Monsieur J. de Bremond's Maximum II) was last throughout. No one can for a moment suppose that this was a true-run race, and victory may in fact be due to the admirable riding of W. Lane, who is in extraordinary form just now.

Throwaway started at twenty to one.

In 1908, during the running of the Hardwicke Stakes, just as the horses rounded the turn into the straight, a man rolled under the rails onto the course immediately in front of the leading horse Galvani, who jumped him safely, but strained himself so badly that he finished last and returned very lame to the paddock.

Young Frank Wootton took a nasty fall in 1909 when he was cut and bruised about the face in the fall of Mr S. B. Joel's Arranmore. Frank Wootton became a notable Ascot rider winning seven races at the 1912 meeting.

Ascot was a beautiful spectacle in those Edwardian days. Reports of fashion were becoming fuller and on Cup day 1909 *The Times* wrote:

Such fragile materials as muslin, laces, nets and soft silks were the only wear ... Yesterday it was undeniable that white—including dead white, ivory and ficelle—predominated in the dresses, while black achieved an extraordinary success in millinery. A delicate subtle mauve appeared in equally delicate materials ... Fine net or ninons, embroidered in filoselle

very handsomely worked in bold raised patterns and long coats were among
the successes of the day.

Eccentricities to be noticed in some of the fantastic tunics and in one
dress of willow-patterned blue and white silk with a wide sash of Chinese
blue girdling the waist and hips and tied in a bow at the back, but in front
giving a corselet effect. Hats were trimmed with feathers, ospreys, flowers
or merely a bow of lace, white, black or metal ... Attendance surpassed
that of all previous Cup days.

It was to be the last Edwardian Ascot.

The short reign of King Edward VII came to an end, after an illness of
only three days, on May 6th, 1910. The strength and depth of mourning
surprised those who were caught up in it. The death of Queen Victoria
had been the end of an era, stretching back beyond the memories of all
but the very oldest. The death of King Edward VII was severance from an
under-estimated, newly discovered, genial man, whom they discovered
they had loved and would miss with a sense of personal loss.

The Royal Ascot meeting took place on Tuesday, June 14th, 1910, five
weeks after the death of the King. The intensity of the mourning worn
was greater than that worn at the death of Queen Victoria. Again, and
perhaps with better justification, it was called 'Black Ascot'. 'Those who
were not present at Ascot can scarcely realise the gloom of the spectacle,'
wrote *The Times*. 'Year after year the brightly coloured dresses of the
ladies in the Royal Enclosure and in the paddock between the races give
extraordinary brilliance to the scene This year the deepest mourning is the
inflexible rule, and the sombreness of it all is in the most striking contrast
to the traditional Ascot.'

Edward VII was succeeded by his second and oldest surviving son, who
became King George V. The contrast was extreme between the worldly
father and the direct, sea-and-country-loving son, although each in his
way was a paternalistic autocrat: the plainness of George V's surroundings
was founded on a simple excellence. The new consort, Queen Mary, was
shy, conscientious and a lover of history and antiques, in contrast to the
fun-loving, pet-loving, friendly and sorely-tried Queen Alexandra.

King George V adored his father. He and Queen Mary determined to
change little of what Edward VII had done. But neither would choose the
part of leader of 'Society'. The outward form of Edwardian social
occasions continued, but the gusty enjoyment of pleasure for its own sake
had gone. However Ascot continued, outwardly little altered, until the
outbreak of the First World War, four years later, wrought a deeper and
more deadly change.

The races of 1910, run in the black frame of mourning, included 'Mr Fairie's' victory with Bayardo in the Gold Cup. 'Mr Fairie' was the pseudonym for Mr Alfred W. Cox. King Edward VII's Minoru, leased from Colonel Hall-Walker, had beaten Bayardo in the previous year's Derby, but Bayardo, by Bay Ronald out of Galicia, went on to win race after race. In the Gold Cup a large field of thirteen started, including the horribly named French horse Sea Sick II, which had won the French Derby in the previous year, and was considered by his connections to be virtually unbeatable. After Bayardo was restive at the post, 'apparently trying to pull Maher over his head', he ran a confident race.

> When Maher let Bayardo out, he passed the others simply at his leisure. When the turn into the straight was made the bearer of Mr Fairie's white, orange sleeves and cap was galloping comfortably in front and, sweeping on without a semblance of effort, won by four lengths ... Bayardo has done some extraordinary things in his time, but never before done anything like this. That there should have been a doubt of his staying now seems absurd. His space-devouring stride at the finish had in it not the faintest indication that he had galloped this long and tiring course.

A great reputation was — temporarily — lost at this same meeting. Americus Girl, by Americus out of Palotta, was greatly fancied for the King's Stand Stakes, the last race on the card. 'Americus Girl appeared to have won, and the spectators turned away, but those who glanced at the board were astonished to see she had been caught' by Mr H P. Nickalls' Spanish Prince, who won by a head. Americus Girl was to redeem her reputation at stud. The dam of the brilliant Lady Josephine, Americus Girl is the direct female ancestress, through Mumtaz Mahal, Mah Mahal, Mah Iran and Star of Iran of Petite Etoile (herself to be associated with an astonishing Ascot defeat) and is to be found in the pedigree of an impressive number of today's winners.

As a two-years-old, Craganour won the New Stakes by three lengths in 1912, before going on to pass the post first and be disqualified in the rough Derby of 1913. It was in this Derby, too, that Miss Emily Davison flung herself in front of the King's horse and sustained injuries which proved fatal. Fortunately neither Herbert Jones the jockey nor Anmer the King's horse were seriously hurt. But a carbon-copy incident followed at Royal Ascot.

A field of eight started for the Gold Cup, including the American-bred Tracery, winner of the St Leger, the Eclipse and the Champion Stakes, and the stayer Prince Palatine, winner of the previous year's Gold Cup.

'As the horses came to . . . perhaps seven furlongs from home, Tracery closed . . . and moving up very fast, drew away till two or three lengths clear. Prince Palatine behind was working up, but the attention of everybody was fixed on the leaders.'

At that moment a man with a suffragist flag in one hand and a revolver in the other, came out of a ditch on the outside of the course, and deliberately and collectedly walked out on to the course—the spectators thought he was an official. As Tracery came up on him he raised his arms and ran straight into the horse's path. 'He was struck in the chest by the animal's head, and flung with great violence to the ground. Tracery fell, and in doing so threw Whalley some yards away to the left, and that he was not seriously hurt (it will be remembered that he also had a bad fall at Epsom) is wonderful.' Prince Palatine jumped the fallen man. FitzRichard, in passing, struck him a violent blow on the head that fractured his skull. The other horses swung wide, and continued the race, which was won, almost unnoticed, for the second time by Prince Palatine.

The man had made no effort to fire his revolver, an old-fashioned six-chambered revolver, fully loaded, which was found on the grass, the police discharged the shots into the turf, which was heavily bloodstained from the man's severe injuries. He was quickly identified as Harold Hewitt of Hope End, Herefordshire, a zoologist, who had been to Miss Davison's funeral, and who had intended to commit suicide. He had left a note in which he wrote: 'I hope I shall not hurt any of the jockeys. Oh! The weariness of these races, and the crowds they attract. They bring out all that is worst in humanity.'

A happier incident in 1913 was the appearance at Ascot of the 'Spotted Wonder', the unbeaten The Tetrarch, whose portrait once hung in the entrance hall of the Royal Stand. Although 'The Tetrarch was not on the card for weights and colours, it was decided to bring him out'. He was swiftly backed down to odds-on and won 'the hollowest of victories'. But, as in the Woodcote Stakes at Epsom, an expert noted on the day that he several times changed his legs, and commented 'a thing we would rather not see done, but it appears in his case to mean nothing and it is hard to guess how much he had to spare'. Yet leg trouble prevented The Tetrarch from running as a three-years-old, so perhaps the writing was on the wall at Ascot.

A prolific Ascot winner at this time was Hornet's Beauty, owned by Sir W. Cooke, trained at Upavon by Peebles which, ridden by Herbert Jones, won the Trial Stakes in 1911, going on to win the Fern Hill Stakes and the King's Stand Stakes, when ridden by J. H. Martin. Hornet's Beauty did not win at Ascot in 1912. In 1913 Hornet's Beauty won two more Ascot races, the All-Aged at the somewhat prohibitive odds of nine to one on, and the King's Stand Stakes, again at odds-on. In 1914 the bay gelding was a six-years-old, and was still owned by Sir W. Cooke (although he was now trained by Elsey at Baumber). Hornet's Beauty again won the All-Aged, and in so doing gave Freddie Fox his first, but by no means his last, Ascot winner.

This 1913 Ascot saw the appearance of Americus Girl's daughter, Lady Josephine, in the Coventry Stakes on the opening day of the meeting, and ridden by Steve Donoghue 'at the starting-gate she was third from the tapes, however she was so fast that by the time fifty yards had been covered, she was clear . . . If it were not for the doubt of this filly being able to stay, a great future might be prognosticated for her. She comes, however, of a family of what are called "short runners".' Lady Josephine was owned by Mr W. M. Savill and trained at Netheravon by Fallon.

An innovation in *The Times* in 1914, which was not to survive the war, was a special correspondent down at the starting-gate, who gave copyright reports on the behaviour of each horse. For example, at the start of the Royal Hunt Cup he reported:

> There was a lengthy delay. Braxted [who finished second] who was on the extreme left with Santair and Aiglon, had to be held to the gate, and the two latter also refused to face the tapes properly—Aiglon had to be whipped. Blue Stone likewise gave a lot of trouble and Ambassador became very excited, and while at the post sustained a cut stifle. Bonbon Rose, Honeywood [third] Lie-a-Bed [who had a special attendant] [the winner] and Sands of Time joined in the disorder, twisting and turning, or hanging lengths back. Sands of Time was held near the tapes, and Cuthbert further lengthened the delay. Santair and Aiglon bumped each other badly at the start, and the latter was knocked back almost last with Flippant, who had been jostled and then half-whipped round.

Seven other horses were left!

It is tempting to describe, with hindsight, that period immediately before the First World War as utterly idyllic, but of course for those who lived at the time, without foreknowledge of the holocaust approaching, it was as full of problems as any other period, and to the Trustees of Ascot Grandstand those problems were particularly menacing.

Hardly had Edward VII died before the complaints of local residents were voiced regarding the subway under the racecourse which had recently been opened. The trouble concerned this and the erecting of a swing-gate across a right of way on the Heath. The chairman, Mr F. J.

Patton, explained that under the provisions of the Enclosure Act of 1813 the course and Heath belonged to the Crown, who let the land on lease to the Jockey Club, or to whoever was responsible for the racing at Ascot. The public had 'the right to race' and the right to use the path on which the gate was erected, but apart from this the public had no more to do with the royal Heath than they had with a private estate or with Windsor Park. The course authorities allowed people to walk about the Heath, but naturally objected to paths across the track, where the condition of the turf was of so much importance. The Council left it to the chairman to interview the Clerk of the Course to try to get the gate removed or opened, but decided they could do nothing about the subway.

A new hot-water apparatus was installed in 1912, which pleased the caterers, who reported 'for the first time there was no complaints on the shortage of hot water for tea.' (This was followed in 1912 by 'a new apparatus for washing plates and dishes'.) The water heater caused a fire. An account from an unknown newspaper dated May 20th, 1912, and pasted inside the Minute book, recounted:

> What might have been a very serious outbreak of fire occurred late on Monday night at the grandstand. As it was, the prompt use of up-to-date appliances kept on the premises for emergencies of this kind, and the energy displayed by the Ascot Fire Brigade, averted the danger which for a time threatened the range of buildings where the luncheons were served. It is believed that a pipe connected with the new hot water apparatus – then undergoing its test – brought about the mischief by its contact at some point or other with the wood-work.
>
> At all events, shortly before eleven o'clock, the alarming discovery was made that a corridor, extending along the east end of the large luncheon room, was in flames. Fully alive to the necessity of immediate action the caretaker Herd and his brother lost no time in getting hoses fixed and the gas engine at work, which is connected with a force pump.
>
> Other members of the grandstand staff, and the Secretary to the Trustees, joined in the fight. It was not of long duration. In less than three-quarters of an hour from the alarm the fire was not only mastered, but put out to the last spark. Happily there was no lack of water. From a tank underneath the building a supply equal to almost any demand was obtainable, and it is due to this provision and the excellent work put in by the staff of the grand-stand at the commencement that the flames were prevented from getting a hold on the main buildings.
>
> The corridor is used as a storing place for crockery and glass, while during the races plates, dishes and table cutlery are taken there from the luncheon room to be cleared. The structure itself was badly damaged and some of the contents – not to any great extent, however, were smashed up or burnt.

By the time the meeting came round the damage had been repaired.

The receipts at Ascot dropped after the death of Edward VII. It was only to be expected while the Court was in mourning, but they did not pick up, as expected, in Coronation year, 1911. The total grandstand takings of £35,530 1s 4d were made up from over £23,000 from the grandstand itself, £5,328 from the new five-shilling stand (of which more later) and £6,719 from the paddock. Badges were down by almost three thousand against 1909 to 21,979. (Eight people lost their badges, and fifteen left them at home.) The drop was caused, it was thought by 'the coal strike and labour unrest'. Disappointing returns in 1912, when even on Cup day not all the stalls were let, were blamed on 'the general unrest now going on in the country'. Takings dropped slightly to £34,027 13s 6d.

But all this was small beer compared with the row, long smouldering, which now blazed into the open between the Trustees of the grandstand and the Stewards of the Jockey Club. As early as February 23rd, 1903, Viscount Esher wrote, 'I have been very busy all day, with one thing and another, having finally to sit as arbitrator in a row about the Ascot stands.'

It came to a head over the five-shilling grandstand in what is now the Silver Ring Enclosure. This had been built in 1908 for the King's Representative, who had arranged to hand it over to the Trustees of the Grandstand. It is minuted by the Trustees that in 1910 the grandstand was acquired by the Grandstand Company from the King's Representative, together with 'the grounds and all the buildings connected' for the sum of £30,000. But all was far from plain sailing, and solicitors' letters were winging to and from between the Trustees of the Grandstand and the Jockey Club as early as April 1911, culminating in a court case in April 1913, brought by the Stewards of the Ascot Meeting, Viscount Churchill, the Honourable F. W. Lambton and Mr Eustace Loder against the Trustees of the Grandstand, Mr Charles Rivers Bulkeley, Mr Victor Van de Meyer and the Earl Fitzwilliam. The Stewards claimed that £30,000 should be handed over to them.

The Stewards' case put by Mr Upjohn KC, was 'whether under the provisions of the deed the Trustees were entitled to retain a sum of between £25,000 and £40,000 accumulated income in hand, to indemnify themselves against liabilities which were not very closely specified; and, secondly, if the plaintiffs were right and the defendants wrong, then the defendants seemed to him to claim that under a decree of 1854 they had some special discretion to retain one-third of the net income, though for what purpose was not stated'. When the last shares of the tontine were paid off in 1858 the one-third kept to reimburse subscribers was no longer needed. From that date until 1862 the whole sum cleared was paid over to the Stewards for prize- and cup-money. In 1863 the question of right to dispose of the final one-third in this manner had been queried, the matter taken to court, and the chancery court had decided that it must go on the same trusts as the other two-thirds. The King's Representative had, since 1902, exercised the duties of the Master of the Buckhounds, an office then abolished.

> The way in which the difficulty had arisen was owing to the erection of a five-shilling stand, which was considered necessary owing to the increased facilities for getting to Ascot. The stewards thought it was a necessity, and in 1908 a stand was erected at a cost of £30,000 but after the money had been paid over, the point was raised that the transaction could not be legally carried out by either party. The agreement for sale and purchase were accordingly cancelled, and Lord Churchill [wearing his hat as King's Representative—he was also of course ex officio a Trustee of the grandstand] repaid the £30,000, pointing out when he did so that that sum ought really to be paid to the stewards. The Trustees took a different view, and the present action was brought.

Colonel Gordon Carter, who as Clerk of the Course was an official of the Jockey Club, and as Secretary to the Trustees was an employee of the Trustees, was called on behalf of the Stewards. It was a measure of the man that he held the respect of both sides. He said the Trustees had £38,000 in hand. He liked to have a balance to hand of £5,000 to meet liabilities. He could not suggest any reason why £38,000 should be retained. Council for the Trustees, Mr Cave, was not in court, and cross-examination of Colonel Carter was postponed until the next day's hearing. Colonel Gordon Carter then explained that there were three bodies at the Ascot Race Meeting—namely the King's Representatives, who were Lord Churchill and Sir William Carrington; the Stewards; and the Grandstand Trustees. Lord Churchill was also the Senior Steward (so he wore all three Ascot hats). The duty of the Stewards was to see to everything connected with the racing; there was no property invested in them as stewards. The Trustees met as a rule in July, to settle up the accounts and they then voted a certain sum for the prizes at the next meeting. The racemeeting was held in June and the prizes payable fourteen days after the meeting. Formerly the Trustees paid the money for the prizes to the Master of the Buckhounds, but since the abolition of that office it was handed to the King's Representative about a week after the racemeeting. If there were no receipts from the grandstand and if the Trustees had no reserve fund it would be impossible for them to honour the vote of the previous July. The reserve fund began to be built up in 1869.

In 1910 the Trustees decided to purchase the new five-shilling stand from the King's Representatives and actually paid the sum of £30,000 to the vendors. There were difficulties in making the conveyance, and in the end the £30,000 were repaid, Lord Churchill borrowing the money from a bank for the purpose. Until that transaction there had been no objection made to the Trustees keeping a reserve fund either by the King's Representatives or by the stewards; the reserve was wanted for the purpose of paying off that debt. For the past three years the Trustees had voted £20,000, but in fact paid over £24,000 a year to the King's Representatives. If the grandstand were burnt down just before the race-meeting, the receipts would be destroyed and the promised £20,000 could not be paid unless they had a reserve fund.

In the Trustees' evidence, which was in the main the same as that of the plaintiffs, it emerged that if there were no Royal Procession, receipts fell considerably. They looked upon purchase of the five-shilling stand as an investment, 'far better than Consols'. Receipts were now lower, and expenses greater than they had been, and the reserve fund had almost all been accumulated before 1890.

Mr Justice Warrington, in his judgment, declared

the real question which he had to determine was whether, according to the true construction of the trust deed, and in the events which had happened, the three gentlemen who were the stewards for the racemeeting of 1912 were entitled to require payment by the Trustees of the sum in their hands. Whether anybody else could require payment was not the question which he had to determine. It was necessary to consider who the stewards were. They were three individuals, one of whom was the King's Representative . . . The other two were formerly the same persons as the stewards of Newmarket races, but now they were two persons nominated each year by His Majesty to be stewards of the races for that year. There was only one racemeeting held at Ascot each year, and the business of the stewards seemed to be to manage that meeting. They received from the Trustees some of the surplus receipts of the grandstand, and paid them over to the representatives of the Jockey Club, by whom the stakes were paid. Every year, in July, the Trustees passed a resolution, the effect of which was that the King's Representative knew that, unless the unforeseen happened, he would have the necessary money for the stakes and prizes in the next year.

Could the stewards of 1912, who were also the stewards of 1913, require the Trustees to pay over to them this sum of money which had accumulated between 1869 and 1890? In his lordship's opinion they could not. The stewards for the time being had nothing to say in anything except as to what remained of the balance of receipts over payment in the particular year after the Trustees had performed the duties imposed on them by the trust deed. These were not moneys which the stewards of 1912 could, under the direction contained in that part of the deed which related to the two-thirds of the surplus income, require the Trustees to pay them. The decree of Vice-Chancellor Wood, in 1864, gave the stewards no right to insist upon the Trustees paying the remaining one-third to them; all it said was that the Trustees were to be at liberty from time to time to pay the same to the stewards. His Lordship further thought that the trust deed gave the Trustees a discretion to keep in their hands such sums as they thought necessary. The exercise of that discretion could not be questioned, and the Trustees were to be the judges of what was necessary.

The action failed, the real ground being that the stewards for the time being, neither under the trust deed nor under the decree of 1864, had a right to come to the court and say that the trustees should pay over the reserve fund to them.

This would seem a total victory for the Trustees of the grandstand. But the Stewards of the Jockey Club were not done yet. In 1913 the Ascot Authority Bill was introduced into Parliament, to take over the functions of the Ascot Grandstand Trust. Mr Justice Warrington, in Chambers, gave permission for the disputed reserve fund of the grandstand trust to be used to provide funds to dispute the Bill, but it was all in vain, and the Ascot Authority Act passed into law. There were a few feeble protests in the press, notably a letter, signed 'Horseflesh', which was published in *The Sportsman*, which, after giving the background to the affair went on to say:

It is a well-settled rule that no private owners can, or ought to be, divested of their property unless for some public benefit and it seems remarkable that a Committee of the House of Lords should have allowed the Bill to pass when no evidence was produced of any public benefit likely to result from such a change, and indeed, the evidence was all the other way.

This evidence showed that the revenues derived from the grandstand and those derived from the stands etc leased to the King's Representatives were about equal, *viz* about £26,000 per annum, and it further showed that during the last three years the grandstand Trustees had given £72,000 in stakes whereas the King's Representative had given only £300 during the same period. The racing public might well ask what has happened to the money derived from the stands etc managed by the King's Representative; and may look with trepidation at a Bill which will give [to the King's Representatives] the whole of the revenues derived from the admission of the public to Ascot races.

The editor of *The Sportsman* added the comment: 'When the Bill was considered by a Select Committee of the House of Lords they recommended that a third Trustee should be nominated to sit with Lord Churchill and Sir W. Carrington, and also that a competent accountant should be appointed to assist them. Counsel for the promoters then said amendments would be made in the Bill in accordance with these recommendations, the third Trustee would be a member of the Jockey Club. If the facts are as stated above by our correspondent a further amendment might be sought for to the effect that the annual accounts be publicly audited.'

There was another comment, which is contained in a letter from one of the grandstand trustees, Mr Reginald W. Coventry, to Colonel Carter, dated July 9th, 1913, which is enclosed in the grandstand minutes.

... The accounts are quite satisfactory and are a further testimony of the great care and ability you have shown in the management of our affairs.

Whilst the fate of the Ascot Authority Bill is still in suspense I think it is unnecessary to comment upon the business referred to in the Agenda, there are however two matters to which I want to call the attention of the meeting [called for a date on which he could not attend]. The first is a most pleasant one, a desire, which I feel sure will be shared by my colleagues, to record in the minutes something to this effect:

That the Trustees of the grandstand wish to place on record their high appreciation of the services rendered by their Secretary, Col Gordon Carter, M.V.O., during the eight years in which he has held that office, and recognise that his devoted attention to the affairs of the Trust, and the skill, ability and tact he has displayed as Secretary have largely contributed to the success of the undertaking.

The second matter is not so pleasant, it is a suggestion to record in the Minutes:

That the Trustees consider that the conduct of Lord Churchill, in not giving his co-trustees notice of the intention to present a Bill in Parliament to abolish the Trust until after the Bill had been served upon them, was a most unfriendly act and one quite unworthy of his position both as the King's Representative and as a gentleman—and further that Lord Churchill is deserving of censure for placing in the preamble of the Bill (though it was withdrawn at the hearing) a statement which was tantamount to a lying suggestion that the Trustees had been guilty of fraud in respect of the purchase of the stand.

Soon the events following the declaration of war on August 4th, 1914, were to make these Ascot proceedings seem a very small storm in a very small tea-cup. But first there was one final, elegant Royal Ascot to come. The 1914 meeting was held in perfect hot weather and it was highly successful.

> In the enclosures, in front of the stands, it was very hot indeed. The small patches of shade under the trees in the paddock were oases in a desert, and people clustered there like swarming bees ... The subways were the one deliciously cool spot near the course.
>
> If this is necessary, as seems to be the custom, to give every event of the Season a nickname, this was emphatically a Parasol Ascot. Pink and blue, yellow, scarlet, mauve and apricot—with every intermediate shade and combination of tints—to look down upon the sunshades from an upper tier in one of the stands was like gazing down on a gorgeous flower garden where every flower was mushroom-shaped.

So ended pre-war Ascot.

CHAPTER EIGHT

From war to war

THE CONTRAST BETWEEN PEACE AND WAR HAS SELDOM BEEN MORE EXTREME than it was in 1914. The euphoria with which the unwitting Britons entered the war was soon displaced by bewilderment, uncertainty and a desire to win and get the thing over in which the national split personality showed itself clearly. There were those who felt that only by hardship and penance would we deserve victory; and there were those who believed we were fighting not only to win but for our way of life, and to give up that way of life was equivalent to defeat.

The battle raged in the letter columns of *The Times* and it was Ascot that was chosen as representative of all that was ephemeral and worthless on the one hand, and as the symbol of English elegance and excellence on the other. The controversy was sparked off by a brisk announcement in *The Times* of Monday February 14th, 1915, when 'Our Racing Correspondent' reported: 'Rumours have been current to the effect that the Ascot Meeting was to be abandoned this year, or held on some other course. I have the highest authority for stating that the meeting fixed for June 15th and the three following days will take place unless something totally unforeseen takes place. Lord Churchill is already beginning the customary preparations.'

The Times made its viewpoint clear from its first leader on March 4th, 1915:

We are convinced that any attempt to hold the great popular racing festivals, such as Epsom, and above all Ascot, will make a deplorably bad impression upon our neighbours, and lead to misconception in this country which we should try to prevent. We should like to see them [racemeetings] abandoned altogether for this year. The Ascot Meeting falls on a date when the war may be at its climax. Can it be seemly to hold it when millions of men including great numbers of our own people, will be at death-grips?

Mr Holland Rose, writing from Christ's College, Cambridge suggested:

If it was possible for the highwaymen of the north country to furnish squadrons of light horsemen for the wars of William III, it is conceivable that featherweight jockeys might render admirable service as scouts or messengers at the front. In that case these men and their mounts, instead of furnishing the excuse to large numbers of healthy young men to attend racemeetings, would be benefiting their country and stimulating skulkers to join the Army. The spectacle of large racemeetings and professional football matches is little short of a national disgrace.

Mr Henry Cust, editor of the *Pall Mall Gazette* and a prominent Conservative M.P., who was one of the founders of The Central Committee for National Patriotic Organisations, wrote from the House of Commons:

When many thousands of men have given their lives for their country, and while many more tens of thousands are following their high example, and will certainly be dying and suffering while the crowds cheer and lunch at Epsom, it is merely monstrous and indecent to celebrate the Great National Festival and Royal Ascot etc, with all their gay traditions and associations. Half England will be in mourning when these days come; all England will be on the rack of intense anxiety and national danger.

Lord Dunraven wrote: 'Ascot is a glorified garden-party with racing thrown in. It can be bracketed with Court Balls and functions of that character, and as these are postponed during the war, there seems no reason why Ascot should be retained.'

Colonel Henry Knollys, late Royal Artillery, thundered:

Is it unreasonable to hope that in 1915 the upper classes of men and women will forbear from assembling in their tens of thousands, say, at Ascot, peacocking in their plumes and prattling their puerilities, eating plentifully and drinking still more so, semi-intoxicated with the splendour and spangle of the gaudy scene, yelling with enthusiasm because one favourite has galloped a few inches in advance of the nose of another favourite, while thousands of our countrymen ... are enduring every description of pain, peril and privation and may indeed, at the exact coincidental moment, be moaning their agony or gasping out their lives to save their country from annihilation.

It is submitted that the indulgence this year of such racing pastime may be compared to attendance at a garden-party in the afternoon by those who have been present at the funeral of a parent in the morning.

The gallant Colonel did not need the excitement of racing for stimulus, his purple prose must have fulfilled the same function.

The Rev J. G. Cornish, vicar of Sunningdale Church near Ascot, wrote:

> The Fourth Berkshire Regiment is expected to go to the front. If racing takes place at Ascot, everyone will be spending money or making money or rushing about. But for months our interests have been much more wholesome. Golf and football have been nearly discarded. Nursing wounded men and taking care of Belgian refugees and seeing to the needs of soldiers' families have been the favourite occupations of the ladies. Many people like to come to church when they know that there will be prayers for our Navy and Army . . . why should we be thrown back into just the same rush for excitement and money which we had last year?

The Times published a second leader on March 13th, 1915, and in the same issue printed a letter from Lord Curzon of Kedleston, soon to join the coalition government under Asquith:

> EPSOM AND ASCOT . . . The sun that looks down upon their merry-making and the shouting of the throng would be looking down, not a hundred miles away, on the struggles, the perils, very likely upon the agony, of the flower of our race, pouring out her [sic] lives in order that we (and incidentally the English thoroughbred) may continue to live . . . are we to persevere in our two great yearly 'beanfeasts' against a background of awful tragedy and amid a world of tears?

The lovers of racing fought back. Lord Rosebery, who was born in 1847 and died in 1929, Prime Minister from 1894 to 1896, and who owned Ladas the Derby winner while in office, wrote:

> Many of our French allies will remember that the winner of the Derby was announced in General Orders during the Crimean War . . . Why, indeed, should we embark on the unprecedented course which you indicate, and condemn all our historical practice? Once before our country has been engaged in a 'life and death struggle' at least as strenuous and desperate as this: I mean against the French Revolution and Napoleon. All through that score of bloody years the Epsom and Ascot meetings were regularly held, nor indeed does it seem to have occurred to our forefathers that it was guilty to witness races when we were at war. I remember asking the late Lord Stradbroke which was the most interesting race he had ever witnessed for the Ascot Cup. He replied, that for 1815, which was run on June 8th, eight

days before Quatre Bras, when Napoleon and Wellington were confronting each other to contend for the championship of the world.

I am and desire to remain remote from controversy but am anxious to remind you of our history and tradition with regard to this question, and to ask you to pause before you condemn not merely Epsom and 'above all' Ascot, but also the principles and practice of ancestors not less chivalrous and humane than ourselves.

The Times racing correspondent, taking up the point of 'skulkers' said that at Gatwick races 'One noticeable fact was that a large portion of the material suitable for military service was already in khaki—approximately 200 men in uniform were present ... Among the 600 or 700 occupants of the Members and reserved enclosures there was not a score who were on the surface of an age and physique suitable for service.'

Lord Hamilton of Dalzell remembered:

In the Boer War it was at the close of the first day's march of Lord Roberts' Army from Johannesburg to Pretoria—I think at a place called Lewkop—and the troops were just settling down in their bivouacs. Suddenly we saw heliographs flashing and mounted messengers galloping to the various units their arrival being greeted by loud and prolonged cheering. When the message reached us it was found to be 'The Field Marshal Commander-in-Chief wishes it to be made known to all ranks that the Prince of Wales's horse Diamond Jubilee has won the Derby.'

The Hon Frederick Lambton pointed out: 'You are shocked that some people would wish to amuse themselves on four afternoons in June next at Ascot races; but I observe on the same broadsheet as your article a whole column of theatrical advertisements containing the names of thirty-four of the principal London theatres giving nightly and occasionally morning [matinee?] performances.' His brother, Admiral of the Fleet Sir Hedworth Meux, who had changed his surname by deed poll, fired a broadside:

The best horses in the world and the prettiest women are seen on the Royal Heath. We racing men go to Ascot to see the horses, non-racing men, such as Lord Curzon and Lord Robert Cecil and Mr Cust go to look at the women—and very good judges too. The incomparable beauty of English women is the real cause of the envy and hatred of their country that has been growing up for many years in Germany. Should peace not be in sight by June, I hope to hear that the usual fashionable crowds are conspicuous by their absence. But to stop Ascot races now in March would be absurd, for any racemeeting can be annulled at a few hours' notice—as, indeed,

frost often does during the steeplechasing season. Germany, in her mad and
illicit career on land and sea, is racing to perdition as surely as Smuggler
Bill did, and before Ascot may be crawling to a new and sadder Canossa.

A soldier in hospital, after saying he had no connection with horseracing,
continued, 'the amiable and generally unwarlike faddists continue to curse
racing, the betting, drink, bookies, jockeys and trainers, curse if curse you
must but please don't put curses in our mouths. We do so dislike being
exhibited by people we don't know as humbugs and prigs'. He signed his
letter 'A WOUNDED OFFICER WHO HOPES TO BE OUT OF BED IN TIME TO SEE
THE DERBY'.

The most thoughtful warning of the dangers of wartime racing came
from Mr Frederic Harrison of Bath (writing, it will be remembered, in
March 1915), 'War today, for the first time, is largely an affair of aeroplanes. The huge muster of some millions of men and women, with
booths, tents, cars and paddocks, is exactly known to the enemy – the spot,
the day, the hour, the nature of that vast encampment [at Epsom] are all
notorious and obvious. Imagine the scene if, as all eyes were strained to
the start, a fleet of Zeppelins and aeroplanes bore down and hurled a
store of bombs and fire bombs on the dense crowd.'

In the face of sustained criticism the Jockey Club held a meeting at
Derby House, Stratford Place, on March 16th, 1915, to consider the whole
question of wartime racing. Afterwards it was announced that if the
meeting at Ascot took place, the social element would be eliminated.
There was no intention of having tickets for the Royal Enclosure, no
luncheon tents would be permitted, and no special trains would be run.
The Stewards of the Ascot Meeting at once issued a statement that 'in view
of the altered conditions under which it is evident that the Ascot Meeting
would have to take place, as announced at the Jockey Club meeting this
morning, they are considering whether it would be practicable to hold
the meeting or not.'

On April 21st, 1915, it was announced that the Tuesday's racing would
be given up and the Royal Meeting last only three days. Five handicap
races would be abandoned. The Royal Enclosure was to be opened to the
public at a hefty admission charge, and the money received given to
charity.

Then, on May 7th, 1915, it was stated the meeting would be still further
pruned. On Wednesday the races would be the Ascot Derby, the Waterford Stakes, the Chesham Stakes, a third-leg Triennial and the Coventry
Stakes. On Thursday would be run the St James's Palace Stakes, the
Ribblesdale Stakes, the Rous Memorial Stakes, the Granville Stakes, the

New Stakes, the Gold Cup and the second leg of a Triennial. Friday's racing would consist of the second leg of a Triennial stakes, the Hardwicke Stakes, the Windsor Castle Stakes, the Alexandra Plate, the Prince of Wales's Stakes and the Bessborough Stakes.

All for nothing. A few days later Royal Ascot of 1915 was abandoned. A few races were transferred to Newmarket. The Gold Cup was run as the Newmarket Gold Cup over two miles and twenty-four yards of the Summer Course on Tuesday, July 27th, 1915, for a cup value £200 and £1,000 added money from the Ascot authority. The Windsor Stakes for three-years-old entered at Ascot was run over the mile and a half of the Suffolk Stakes course on the following day, with £1,000 added from the Ascot authority. On the Thursday the New Coventry Stakes for two-years-old entered at Ascot was run, again with £1,000 added by the Authority. There was no racing at Ascot for the duration of the war.

Ascot had already been adapted for wartime use. Field-Marshal Lord Roberts, former commander-in-chief of the British forces, had retired to Englemere House, Ascot, and become closely involved with local and especially local hospital affairs. The Field-Marshal went to France to visit the troops in November 1914, caught pneumonia, and died shortly after his return. His elder daughter Aileen succeeded him as Countess Roberts: a tireless worker for the Red Cross, she was instrumental in establishing a hospital for about fifty wounded soldiers in the Ascot grandstand, which she visited each day.

As a boy, David Dawnay, later General Sir David Dawnay, Clerk of the Course at Ascot from 1957 to 1969, lived with his mother Lady Susan Dawnay, with the Roberts at Englemere House, while his father, who had been on Lord Roberts' staff, was serving overseas. They were there when his father was killed in action on November 6th, 1914, and he left only to go to boarding school. Sir David clearly remembered the hospital in the grandstand, and the depot of hospital supplies in the Silver Ring Stand (as the five-shilling stand had become known), which was run by his mother, Lady Susan. The long bar was turned into a workroom for bandage parties, who worked at tables set out down the sides of the vast room.

Concerts used to be put on for the soldiers in the grandstand, and indeed he could remember being made to sing a song – he could not remember what it was – at one of them. The soldiers also used to organise 'races', between themselves, often on crutches, in Tattersall's ring and occasionally on the course.

The importance of the racecourse to the finances of Ascot town was underlined when the Ascot Authority appealed in August 1916 against a rates assessment, and it was stated that 'although the racecourse and stands at Ascot have not been used for racing for two years, the Ascot Authority is keeping up with the rates payments, which amount to *one-seventh* of the total collected'.

A pathetic sidelight on the effect of the war was behind a move for an injunction brought by Viscount Churchill against Mr Ebeneezer J. Whettnall in the High Court on Friday June 29th, 1917, and continued in April 1918. From 1900 to 1914 Mr Whettnall had issued vouchers for the Royal Enclosure in accordance with Viscount Churchill's instructions. He had access to the private registers containing the names and addresses of those admitted to the Royal Enclosure, which were kept at St James's Palace and York House. Ebeneezer Whettnall also worked as a secretary to a number of people in politics. but with the outbreak of war his salary for the Ascot work had ceased, he had four sons in the Army, and by 1917 he was in severe financial straits.

Lord Churchill was approached and wrote saying he would gladly give a small donation to a fund which Whettnall told him was being raised on his behalf. This gave Ebeneezer Whettnall an idea. He wrote a circular about himself and the alleged fund and sent it to 2,300 people on the register of the Ascot Royal Enclosure, together with a lithograph of Lord Churchill's letter, but without the knowledge of Lord Churchill.

The letter purporting to come from a Mr David Head, 'Hon Secretary of the Whettnall Fund', but in fact written by Whettnall, stated that 'Mr Whettnall, who has issued the vouchers for the Royal Enclosure at Ascot during the last fourteen years under the supervision of Viscount Churchill, is in great distress owing to financial losses during the war. Some of his friends have opened a fund to enable him to tide over affairs until times are better. And they think that those who have enjoyed the privilege of entering the Royal Enclosure would be glad to help him in these difficult days.

'As one of those who has participated in this advantage you are invited to subscribe to this fund ... Contributions are limited to £5.'

Viscount Churchill heard about the fund when he was in France. He was 'greatly vexed'. The injunction was granted, the documents which Mr Whettnall had borrowed were thereupon returned. The judge expressed 'the strongest sympathy' with Lord Churchill. 'He had written a generous letter which did not justify the interpretation which the recipient put upon it, still less the use he made of it. Lord Churchill did not go too far in characterising it as a great mistake and a grave indiscretion, but in justice to the defendant, he was bound to say that he did not think he used Lord Churchill's commendation with any dishonest intention.'

The First World War ended on the eleventh hour of the eleventh day of the eleventh month 1918: only a fortnight later it was announced that an Order in Council had been made: 'revoking the Defence of the Realm regulations which gave power to the Minister of Munitions to prohibit the holding of racemeetings and coursing where they were likely to impede or delay the production of war material.' The Order also rescinded previous instructions about the destruction of stray dogs, the regulation of public holidays, the holding of fairs and dog shows, the ringing of bells and striking of clocks, and the carrying and liberation of carrier pigeons.

After the appalling losses of the 1914–1918 war, the survivors began wearily to retrace the path to peace. Some events moved fast. On November 29th, 1918, *The Times* reported: 'Ascot house agents are already receiving enquiries as to what houses will be available for the race week ... The Air Force cinema, which stands on the Heath, and which is open to the public every evening, is to be moved to another site at an early date.'

The first post-war Ascot opened on Tuesday June 17th, 1919. *The Times* reported:

> Reconstruction is a word capable of two interpretations. Some who desire it mean the construction of a new world, differing as widely as possible from that which existed before the war; others are anxious to find – with a few reforms and ameliorations which seemed in any case on their way – the old world of 1913 revived.
>
> One thing that is very sensibly reconstructed is the method of travel to Ascot. The sale of railway tickets available for certain trains and platforms is a most convenient arrangement, saving much time and temper. For the rest, very little in the way of reconstruction is to be seen, and it may be questioned whether such would be welcomed. Lord Churchill is a competent administrator, and it is known he has devoted infinite pains to get things into order.
>
> If some people have a grievance in not receiving Royal Enclosure tickets ... the tickets issued were more than enough to fill the place to the utmost limits. The paddock and Tattersall's ring have been enlarged.

In 1919 for the first time the Royal Drive took place each day, instead of only on Tuesday and Thursday. On Cup day there was a downpour, and the ladies improvised overshoes from the straw covers of champagne bottles, to take them back from the luncheon tents to the shelter of the stands! Nevertheless it was a gay occasion – what was a downpour of rain compared with trench warfare? 'The dresses [gave] a general impression of lightness and flimsiness, predominately black and white, shading away into cream, dove-colour and grey, lit occasionally by grand splashes of blue, or by pink and yellow.' Specially noted were

> a wonderful sunshade decked with pink ostrich feathers . . . an almost equally remarkable hat with ostrich feathers of brightest yellow, a cloak of Lincoln green which Maid Marion might have worn . . . a black and white chessboard lady, a pink and white spotted lady, and a brown and white spotted lady, whose frocks appeared to the covetous male eye adapted for cutting up into entrancing foulard ties.
>   Nor did the men fail . . . Abyssinians in lovely turbans, Serbian officers — their imposing hats that look like a Bishop's mitre cut down — there were also plenty of red tabs which were really pretty things, and can be admired quite without bitterness by the demobilised.

This was a caustic comment on Staff officers. There was wry comment too, on the exclusiveness of 'the holders of the miniature shields of red and blue cardboard granting admission to the Royal Enclosure'.

Mr George Cornwallis-West in *Edwardian Hey-Days* recalled the unique atmosphere of the 1919 Royal Ascot.

> One of the last jobs I had as A.P.M. at Hounslow was to attend Ascot Races in 1919, when I received special instructions from the Eastern Command to make a note of the names of all general officers who appeared in plain clothes, as an order had been issued that uniform was to be worn. The first Generals I saw there were two old brother-officers, Sir William Pulteney and Sir Cecil Lowther, both in plain clothes. Sir Noel Birch and many others whom I knew were dressed in the same way. When, however, I saw that the general officer who had issued the order was also in plain clothes, I ceased to take any interest in the instruction, and proceeded to enjoy myself. My report to the Eastern Command was to the effect that as I had seen the G.O.C. himself in plain clothes I had taken it for granted that the order was either a mistake or had been cancelled.

By 1920 things were settling back to normal. The State Drives were once more confined to Tuesday and Thursday, and the King and Queen motored from Windsor Castle to within three miles of the course, where they transferred to the carriage. Ordinary motorists were advised that 'in these days of tarred roads the dust nuisance has been largely abated', but were warned to avoid the tramlines at Uxbridge.

House-parties had returned. Lord and Lady Desborough were at Taplow Court, Mrs Cardes at Silwood Park, Colonel and Mrs Hartick were entertaining at Little Paddocks, Monsieur Vagliano at The Grange, Lady Roberts was at Englemere, Mr and the Hon Mrs Percy Crutchley at Sunninghill Lodge, Major Claude Hay at Barton, Commander Melville Ward at Gilmuire, Lord Airedale at Swinley Hurst, while others staying in the neighbourhood included Lord Lonsdale, Major J. W. Taylor, Mr and Lady Barbara Smith, Sir Robert Jardine, Mr Walter Raphael and Sir Edward Boyle. An Ascot hotel proprietor remembers:

> The larger houses were let for the week at the most astronomical prices, and the tradesmen—butchers, fishmongers and bakers just charged what they liked. No items, just a round figure, might be £200 or £300 until someone disputed a bill, and there was a County Court case and the practice was afterwards dropped. I remember my mother being presented with a bill 'Race Week Bread—£50'—it was then a twopence halfpenny loaf! What changes—where those houses stood at Ascot there are now factories and flats and tenements, and the once-beautiful gardens all covered with 'bungaloid' growths. Ah well! They call it progress!

Most people, always excepting 'the Yellow Earl', the Earl of Lonsdale with his beautiful carriage, now came to the course by car. In 1920 'Rolls-Royces and the latest Sunbeams rubbed mudguards and hubs with real old "paraffin pots" which had been elegant twenty years ago. Motor omnibuses, obviously enjoying a holiday off the streets of London, compared notes with lorries which had certainly seen war service. And sandwiched in between them all were people on motor bicycles, ordinary cycles and in old and often decrepit-looking horse carriages. The roads were more congested and the travelling crowds more representative of all classes, than on an average Derby Day.' The traffic congestion on Cup day meant that cars were not successful as a method of reaching the Heath. Many people who started from London at eleven o'clock did not get there till nearly three o'clock, and then only by walking the last two or three miles.

However, *The Times* reported:

> The social cake was full of currants. Most striking is the changed dress of the multitude. In style and texture it is as ambitious as that of the leisured minority, and it is usually more highly coloured. 'Paris models', real or so-called, are worn by everyone, with varying degrees of success. There are the usual numbers of women who dress as well as the best dressed French-women. They are conspicuous for simplicity and finish—a few dress equally well in a style peculiarly English and well-bred. The rest have deserted their old gods for new, and the result is not quite what they dreamed it would be.

They have taken Paris models, lengthened the skirts, increased the trimmings, and strengthened the colours. The picturesque, the bold and a certain natural prudery struggle simultaneously for expression. Chaos is the result—grand-mother's shawl as a cloak, New Art embroidery on an already beaded dress, Bacchanalian fruits and spring flowers as a waistband on a flowered organdie, a hundred complications in one hat, and a mad riot of colour in everything.

The luncheon tents were back, a dozen of them, belonging respectively to the Guards, Cavalry, Royal Artillery, Highland Brigade (with N.C.O.s in full review order on the door), the Royal Army Service Corps, the Naval and Military, the Bachelors—they entertained 200 debutantes, the Wellington, tucked away as usual at the far end of the paddock, the Badminton, Automobile, Sports and Conservative clubs.

Ascot suffered its usual thunderstorm: Princess Mary (afterwards the Princess Royal, Countess of Harewood), who was visiting the paddock, had to take refuge with her lady-in-waiting and Lord Lonsdale in a horse-box.

At this time, just after the First World War, there was a gigantic betting boom, and strangely enough one of the most successful of the bookmakers was a woman. She was Mrs Helen Vernet, who was a member of the well-known Scottish family of Cunningham. She was born in 1877. Her father died when she was thirteen, and left her £8,000 which, as soon as she was old enough, she squandered in gambling. Her health, too, broke down and she suffered from tuberculosis.

She decided that it was better to take bets than to gamble. At first she took bets on her own account in the Members Enclosure at Ascot, and down by the parade-ring. The bookmakers objected, and Arthur Bendir, the head of Ladbrokes, suggested to her that she should represent the firm officially. She became one of the four Ladbroke representatives 'on the rails' and soon did the whole of the rails business herself, making not less than £20,000 a year for herself, and buying herself a partnership in the firm.

Mrs Vernet married twice, firstly a stockbroker named Spencer Thornton, and secondly Robert Vernet, a member of a famous Huguenot family. She was an extremely elegant woman, always dressed in the height of fashion, and she lived in the most lavish style. She was often seen driving a four-in-hand through Richmond Park or Hampton Court. Mrs Vernet represented Ladbrokes continuously until 1955. Many of her host of clients were women, but she always discouraged them from betting in large amounts.

In her later years she used to be pushed around the racecourse in a wheel-chair. When she died she left only a few thousand pounds.

Mrs Vernet was the first woman bookmaker on the course, and the only one of the early women bookmakers to stay the course.

The post-war boom in betting and race attendances began to fall off in 1921, when economy began to be the watchword.

In 1921 there was a train strike and few trains. Those who did travel by rail suffered great discomfort and there were 'incredible' numbers to a carriage. By road things were better, and traffic moved smoothly from London as far as Virginia Water. 'The right of the road was clear and occasionally along that side there passed the motor-cars of the really great, and the thousands of police sprang sharply to attention as they passed.' Traffic was directed from the airship R36, with *The Times* correspondent on board—his report was dropped by parachute 'from the air near Croydon'. It was afterwards reported that hens at Beckenham, frightened by the appearance of the aerial monster, had laid long eggs without shells!

Economy had begun to rear its dreary head and 'the innovation this year, of wearing the same dress on more than one day of the meeting, though much can be said in its favour, cannot claim brilliance as one of its arguments'. Dress was becoming more casual, flimsier. Nineteen twenty-four was 'very squash-hatty'. 'Ascot,' said *The Times* severely, 'is notoriously the best place in England to see beautiful women in beautiful clothes—and also less beautiful women in very odd clothes. I do not hold vaccination marks to be beautiful.'

Vulgarity was also appearing on the Ascot scene. In a Fourth Leader in 1925 *The Times* commented:

For Cup Day the wealthier ladies keep the smartest of their new gowns, the price of which some of them have been careful to let slip, in confidence to representatives of the Press. On Cup Day the less wealthy of their sisters hope to don dresses which though not so costly nor so well advertised, have been no less thoughtfully prepared and will be no less proudly worn ... One end of Society values [most] the privilege of the White Badge. Here the London season soars to its zenith.

The dislike of other people's pleasure, which has been an active force in English life for nearly three centuries, will always become vocal at such provocation as Ascot, that great public 'day out', can give.

Social changes have blurred distinction between social classes, formerly indicated by dress, now that money has become a more common standard of value, the old diversity is being replaced by a sameness in which imitation is the principal motive ... we cannot muster so picturesque or varied a crowd as that which Hogarth or even Wilkie had for model ... [Yet] perhaps the best way of ridding the mind of the misconception that all is

flat and dull is to go to Ascot, and there to see how, on both sides of the
course, the old spirit of pleasure is asserting itself, and how, in spite of all the
limits to expression, all sorts of people are happily behaving as if amusement
were a legitimate human function.

The effect of the war was to give women greater freedom in attitudes,
in employment and not least in fashion. Women actually changed their
shape. As the Honourable Mrs C. W. Forester confided to the readers of
The Daily Telegraph in an article about Ascot fashions, 'Corsets are so
slight that a woman aiming at good carriage must rely on herself for
success.'

Skirts rose immediately after the war, and were only two or three
inches below the knee in some cases at Ascot in 1920. The hemline was
narrow and the dresses were not easy to walk in. When there was a
shower of rain 'the skirts hobbled their wearers at the knees', producing
'a ludicrous stampede'.

In the following year hemlines were down and hair was up. 'Hair that
was cut short in wartime has grown again, waving and curling that was
neglected has been resumed; combs and ornaments were to be seen on all
sides, setting pretty hats at correct angles, keeping some of them, as large
as sunshades, firmly in place, despite a few brim collisions in the interest
of close conversation.' As for the hemlines, *The Battle of the Skirts* (headline) 'ended in advantage for the longer and toleration for the shorter
skirts . . . the longer skirt proved becoming to the figure of its wearers.
One says longer advisedly, because not the smallest inclination to return
to ground-touching hems is evident. The longest skirt seen at Ascot
touched the ankle, the majority did not reach it by one inch.' (*The Daily
Telegraph*.) Through the twenties the skirts crept up. Legs became important, and shoes and even stockings were fashion points. In 1927 *The
Daily Telegraph* reported 'thousands of pairs of feet in shoes of scarlet and
blue, green and most attractive of all, pewter, pewter or gun-metal too,
the prevailing fashion in stockings'.

Women not only wore different outfits on each day of Royal Ascot,
they brought to the course clothes to cover every vagary of the weather.
That year women displayed 'sleeveless frocks of patterned crêpe de
Chine, of beige lace or of flowered chiffon with huge crinoline hats'.
When the sun went in 'they were transformed and appeared in transparent
gossamer-like coats that floated behind them in the air, rainbow-like in
hue and (as it appeared) in texture'. When rain threatened 'they conjured
up rain-cloaks of orange and cucumber and terra-cotta, as they fled —
unnecessarily as it seemed — to the shelter of the trees'.

13

There were, of course, the usual occasional freaks, including 'the lady who wore what was believed to be an ermine cloak over what appeared to be a bathing dress.'

Meanwhile the men continued to wear the dark morning suits and top hats of pre-war days. Ascot was annually 'the zenith of the London season', and the epitome of male as well as female fashion. When Selfridges opened its new Orchard Street extension in 1922, it chose to advertise its new men's wear department with a display specially aimed at Ascot. A morning coat with waistcoat cost seven guineas. Trousers 'in very neat designs' ran from 30s to 47s 6d per pair. Silk hats were 45s each, 'or if you would prefer, the Grey Top Hat, which is sold at the same figure'. Ceylon day shirts cost 7s 6d each, and 'soft white shirts of cotton Repp, much in favour for smart occasions' cost 10s 9d. Calf leather shoes were 20s a pair, and white canvas spats were 7s 6d.

But even in men's fashion there were changes. 'Men were critical not only of the cut of other men's top hats . . . the bow tie was not in favour; buttonholes were being worn; and a few daring sparks discarded the pepper-and-salt trousers in favour of grey flannel.' There was worse to come. In the grandstand enclosure *The Daily Telegraph* reporter was shocked to note: 'Soft hats among the men outnumbered "toppers" and one even observed cloth caps. Moreover, one could overhear discussions in accents bred in the North country and the Midlands concerning the fortunes up to date of the flat racing season.'

There was an appalling thunderstorm on Royal Hunt Cup day in 1930. Mr John Hislop, the brilliant amateur rider who was then in the army, and who cycled in uniform from Aldershot, wrote in his autobiography *Far From A Gentleman*, 'When we got to Ascot the sky was the colour of charcoal and before long a storm of almost tropical violence broke out over the racecourse . . . after The MacNab had slopped through the mud to win the Royal Hunt Cup, the intensity of the rain making it appear that the runners were galloping through an interminable series of curtains made of glass beads, racing was abandoned.'

Everyone ran for shelter—a Club tent actually opened up to all-comers. The storm 'drove into shelter even the grass-coated foresters who guard the Royal Enclosure' (*The Times*). 'Only the police stood their ground . . . The storm never seemed to move. The rain came down straight. The intervals between the flashes were very short, sometimes the lightning and thunder were simultaneous.' Yet out in the paddock one man stood motionless 'his umbrella up, fascinated by the sight which, it is to be hoped, he will never see again, while the water ran over and into his shoes. He remained so motionless that it was feared that he had been struck by lightning.'

Meanwhile Mr Hislop had taken shelter in the tunnel which leads under the course. 'At first all went well, but as the rain continued the depth of water began to rise, and those in the middle, visualising being drowned, tried to get out, while those on the outside were trying to get in. For a few moments it seemed probable that a watery Black Hole of Calcutta was about to result, but thanks to the phlegmatic nature of the English character . . . disaster was avoided.'

Despite the intensity of the storm, for a considerable time nothing and nobody appeared to have been struck. 'Then came the most vivid flash of all, with a terrific crash of thunder, and a man standing in Tattersall's ring was seen to fall. The police were beside him at once, and an ambulance signalled for, but the signal was quickly cancelled and the man carried out.' The unfortunate man who was killed was a Mr Holbein, from Southport, who had been sheltering under a bookmaker's umbrella.

At last a slight breeze sprang up, and the storm moved on, leaving behind it a scene of desolation and ruin. There were large lakes of rain-water on the course, the two biggest being at the junction of the straight and round courses; and just beyond the winning-post. There were lakes in the paddock, which was almost all under water, on the lawns and what was described as 'a lagoon' by the archway leading from the paddock to the west car enclosure. In each, water was over ankle-deep. Chairs were brought out and a flimsy bridge built with planks across the paddock, but the chair legs sank unevenly in the mud and there were many falls. Another rickety bridge was built of little wooden boxes through the water which lay around the archway.

The effect upon the appearance of the beautifully dressed racegoers was unimaginable.

No male dress of Ascot order could be proof. To female dress of Ascot order it meant mere ruin. And that in the very year in which Ascot dresses were, as in ancient days, long. Some of them so as to trail on the ground . . . Women (some of them for the first time in their lives) impeded by long wet skirts that had to be huddled up in the hand, women drenched to the skin, women all but knee-deep in water, women left shoeless in the mud, women blown or pushed off their feet or slipping off the improvised bridges of chairs and boxes and falling full length into the lakes which once were grass. Women drove home 'half-naked and dressed in newspapers'

—John Hislop.

The Times again:

> Before a thought can be spared to their clothes, their friends will be anxious
> to learn this morning that the wearers of these ruined dainties are themselves
> none the worse for the shock and the chill. As for the trailing skirts, the
> delicate shoes, the big hats—all the emphatically feminine trappings which
> fashion has this year chosen for beauty's frame—it is monstrous hard luck
> . . . But the cloud may leave a silver lining . . . the considerable destruction
> of large hats and long skirts (however caused) is probably better for trade
> than a comparable destruction of small hats and of short skirts.

The ground staff worked all through the night, and miraculously it was
possible to race on the following day. The going was not surprisingly
very holding—the Gold Cup was won in five minutes five seconds, a
full forty seconds slower than the previous year, but it was even possible to
run off the races abandoned on Hunt Cup day. Overhead the sun shone.
The lawns were 'green, soft and pleasant to walk on'. Only a small pool
remained of the lake in the paddock, and a few boggy patches of the
flooding on the course. Colonel Sir Gordon Carter and his exhausted
assistants earned the congratulations heaped upon them.

Ascot appeared in an unfamiliar role in 1936 when it was the setting for
a film *Knight Without Armour* featuring the 1913 Ascot, in which Marlene
Dietrich and Robert Donat starred. A huge crowd of extras in 1913 Ascot
clothes were brought from London in buses. Their faces were plastered
with yellow make-up and the men, somewhat surprisingly, were carrying
shooting sticks! Marlene Dietrich arrived in black silk pyjamas and an
enormous fur coat. (She changed in a room in the grandstand into more
conventional Ascot garb.) Irene Vanburgh wore a huge pre-war hat with
a large brim and enormous bow, and swung a blue frilly parasol. Herbert
Lomas 'stalked villainously at her side with a forked beard'. Horses and
jockeys had been brought over from Epsom, race cards had been printed
with the correct data, bewhiskered stewards stood in the centre of the
paddock as the horses were paraded round before the yellow-faced
crowds.

'The only person I suspected of being slightly amused by this desecra-
tion of Royal Ascot was the aristocratic Sir Gordon Carter, the King's
Representative [*sic*] at the course for goodness-knows-how-many-years.
He met pyjamaed Marlene and walked with dignity to see the sound-film
being made in the beautiful enclosure. He remembers the Ascot of 1913
well' (*The Daily Sketch*).

King George V was not passionately interested in racing, although he liked to see his horses do well, and Queen Mary did not like racing at all, but when the King was well enough, they entertained at Windsor Castle for Royal Ascot. The Court was stiff, more so than it had been during the reign of King Edward VII and Queen Alexandra. Even at Windsor the Ladies of the Household, during the day, wore tailored clothes and at all times wore, or at least carried, gloves.

Even when the King and Queen dined alone without their Household, he wore tails and she wore evening dress with a tiara. Extremely formal dinners with guests were held at eight-thirty. Guests gathered in the Green Drawing Room, so called from its green damask walls and gilt chairs covered with green silk. The ladies assembled on one side of the room and the men on the other. The Royal Family waited in the corridor outside for the arrival of George V and Queen Mary. The King and his sons and senior members of the Household wore the Windsor uniform, only worn at Windsor Castle, consisting of a dark-blue evening dress with collar and cuffs of scarlet and gilt buttons, worn with knee-breeches. The other men wore black evening dress with knee-breeches. The ladies, of course, all wore full evening dress with tiaras. They wore long gloves. If they wished to remove their gloves during dinner, they were expected to remove their gloves completely, and not to bring their hands out through the unbuttoned wrist, which Queen Mary considered vulgar.

The table was laid with the Grand Service of silver-gilt, made for George IV, decorated with boar, stag and fox hunting scenes. String music was played by a band from one of the Regiments of Guards, from behind a gauze wall, painted to look solid. At the end of the meal, the long side-cloths were rolled back by the footmen, leaving the undercloth spotless for dessert. When the ladies withdrew, each faced the King and dropped him a deep curtsey.

After dinner, Queen Mary sat on a settee in the drawing-room, and those guests with whom she wished to talk were brought up individually. The other ladies chatted somewhat stiffly among themselves. When the men returned from the dining-room, they talked with the women for only a short time, before following the King to a further room where they smoked their cigars. After Lady Elizabeth Bowes-Lyon married the Duke of York she introduced the singing of folk and popular songs, herself sitting down at the piano and playing the accompaniment, as she had so often done at Glamis. In the later years of the reign bridge or mahjong were sometimes played.

The Prince of Wales had established himself at Fort Belvedere, where he entertained his friends in far less formal surroundings, coming to the Castle only when summoned.

The Duke and Duchess of York, delighted with their grace-and-favour country home of the Royal Lodge, the Windsor retreat of George IV, used to entertain their close friends there for Ascot. A member of the Duke's Household who was fond of racing told the author, 'I was Extra Equerry when they moved into the Royal Lodge. They used, most kindly, to put me in waiting for the Ascot week when I stayed with them there. It was the most charming, comfortable and simple house you can imagine. I can honestly say that never in my whole life have I seen a family so happy.'

At the Royal Lodge guests came down for breakfast at nine a.m., and afterwards they all went riding. The Duke's hacks and the Princesses' ponies were stabled at Cumberland Lodge. They lunched at the Royal Lodge, and then took part in the Royal Drive down the course. After racing they got back to the Royal Lodge about four thirty p.m., and if the weather was fine, the Duchess of York gave orders for tea to be served in the sunken garden. Dinner was always at eight thirty p.m.

At Ascot each year between the wars brought small improvements towards the standard of perfection sought by Viscount Churchill and Sir Gordon Carter. In 1924 and 1925 the lawns in front of the Royal Enclosure and grandstand were regraded to give them a better slope, and the turf relaid. The Silver Stand (entrance now cost 6s) was enlarged, and a bar one hundred feet long was put into the cheap stand in 1925. The house in the High Street which had belonged to Dr Paterson was pulled down to make a better approach to the grandstand.

In 1926 a new Iron Stand to accommodate 250 was built on the Royal Enclosure lawn, and the Enclosure buildings were lengthened to provide more room for members and owners. Disused stables were acquired and pulled down to allow a new road to be made from the main road to the Silver Stand.

In 1926 and 1927 a new water system for the course was installed, which could discharge two million gallons of water through five thousand nozzles. (The reservoir inside the course was built in 1936.) It was inspected before the 1927 meeting by King George V, who prodded the turf with his walking stick. One wonders if the condition of the course might have improved more rapidly if the large flock of sheep, said to number 300 to 400, were removed elsewhere. It was the custom to send one sheep to be butchered each Monday. The meat was hung in the subway which led under the public road into the Royal Enclosure. On Friday Sir Gordon Carter requisitioned what he required, and the remainder of the meat was sold at one shilling per pound to the employees.

Ascot fell in with the times in 1928 when a cocktail bar and soda fountain were installed in the grandstand. It was noted that some 3,000 people took paddock tickets only, and two more luncheon rooms were provided for them. The parade ring was improved and an additional number board was put up. In 1929 the grandstand lawn was extended to 300 yards in length, with room for 20,000 people. An avenue of lime trees was planted in the centre of the Silver Ring lawn.

After initial trouble in 1929, the Totalisator was in use in 1930 and worked well, although the turnover, a mere £44,803, was considered disappointing. The giant Tote, said to be the largest in the world, was by 1932 employing a staff of 500, with 360 pay and sell windows in operation. That year the Tote took over half a million pounds in the four days, a record for any British racecourse.

Cars had now almost completely taken over from carriages: an estimated 20,000 cars were parked within a mile of the course on Gold Cup day. Racehorses too travelled by road. The special railway siding for racehorses was almost deserted, and a special parking lot for a hundred horseboxes was provided at the junction of the London/Reading and Guildford/Windsor roads.

In 1935 Professor A. B. Richardson's luncheon room was built on to the back of the Royal Pavilion. The flowers were—and are—a feature of Royal Ascot. Pink and mauve carnations were massed in the Royal Stand, while on the balcony was 'a tasteful grouping of standard bays, golden privet, geraniums, antirrhinums, clarkia, hydrangeas, lilies and ivy'. (Queen Mary, in fact, obsessively hated ivy.) A vast rhododendron bed blazed with colour in the centre of the Royal Enclosure, and the balconies of the dining-room were interlaced with pink rambler roses. In 1938 there were changes in the Royal Stand where 'the former (flower-massed) balcony has given way to a graceful structure in Portland stone with a curved glass screen which can be raised or lowered by the pressing of a button. Steps lead down on either side to the Royal Enclosure, and there is a shapely cantilever roof covered in copper.' The old iron rails were replaced by simpler rails.

At the time of the 1929 meeting George V was still far from well after his serious illness in late 1928, indeed his abscess was still unhealed when he attended the Thanksgiving Service in Westminster Abbey to celebrate his 'recovery' on July 7th, 1929. He was at Windsor but unable to come to Ascot. Again in 1935, the year of his Silver Jubilee, he was unable to attend the races, but went instead to Sandringham to rest, while Queen Mary entertained at Windsor Castle and drove to the course. The death of the King's beloved sister Princess Victoria in December 1935 was a heavy blow, which seemed to take from him the will to live. On January 20th,

1936, King George V died at Sandringham, deeply mourned as 'the Father of his Peoples'.

George V's eldest son succeeded him as King Edward VIII. As Prince of Wales he had long been the idol of the country, but his interests and character appeared to those around him to be changing. At his accession there was considerable apprehension among traditionalists at Court and on the Royal Estate as to what the future might have in store. One feels very sorry for the Prince of Wales, a man of high courage of the nervous, introspective kind, who had been denied all chances to prove himself among his own war-decorated generation. Even in peacetime he was denied the outlet of point-to-point riding, because he suffered a number of falls. How different from the present Prince of Wales, a pilot, a parachutist, a diver, or his great-niece Princess Anne, who is permitted to compete over ferocious event courses.

Be that as it may, Edward VIII sought out flattering, witty companions and after fulfilling his continuing exacting public duties, turned to pleasures which differed greatly from the quiet, formal and somewhat dull home life of his parents. They were a reserved family: little was said. But it was certain that the new reign would be very different. At Sandringham and Balmoral ruthless and sweeping economies were immediately instituted. Ascot waited in trepidation. On the day before Ascot opened in 1936, the young King, wearing the service uniform of the Welsh Guards —he had come straight from Aldershot—minutely inspected the course, the buildings, even the small stable in which his horses were quartered— they would run in the black and white colours of Lord Derby. The King gave no indication of any future plans, but the feeling of apprehension was not allayed.

In other spheres the new King was alive to the needs of the day.

Edward VIII had earlier shown his understanding of the problems of industry when he made known in February at the British Industries Fair that he would *not* expect the general public to wear mourning at Ascot in June, giving time for the clothing trade to plan for the fashionable race crowds.

The Abdication crisis exploded at the end of November. On Friday December 11th, 1936, King Edward VIII abdicated and was reluctantly succeeded by his brother the Duke of York, who became King George VI. The motto of the day was 'Back to King George V's time'. It cannot be denied that those at Ascot breathed a sigh of relief.

There was an unseemly brawl in the weighing room after the Gold Cup of 1937 won by Precipitation, which resulted in jockey Tommy Burns

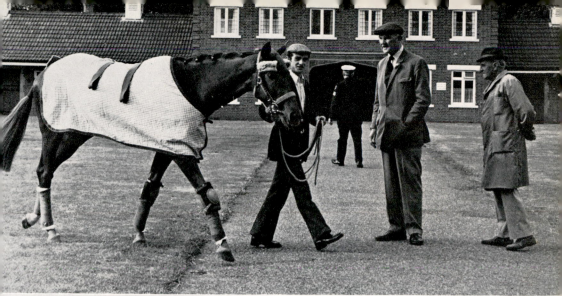

Brigadier Henry Green, deputy director general of Racecourse Security and the late Harry Metcalfe, stable manager, in the palatial but inconveniently remote Windsor Forest Stud, admiring Admetus, owned by Sir Michael Sobell and trained in France by J. Cunnington jnr, winner of the Prince of Wales Stakes at Royal Ascot in 1974.

Plucking grass for the horses: early morning, Royal Ascot, 1974.

Unique among racecourses, Ascot has a special stable for the Sovereign built for Queen Victoria's horses, and never before photographed. This picture shows the Queen's home-bred Carlton House, by Pall Mall out of the Alycidon mare Alesia, after winning the Fen-wolf Stakes: Saturday, June 22nd 1974.

The indefatigable Mr Douglas Butt, superintending clerk, giving an instruction to Mr Peter Garraway, assistant bailiff.

A first photo of the Ascot Office, in the room which was originally the Queen's boudoir in St James's Palace, where Miss Anne Ainscough and her assistants prepare the voucher lists for the Royal Ascot Enclosure.

Chefs with walkie talkies consult in the kitchens of the Ascot Grandstand: Outside, the shellfish ladies put flowers in their straw hats and do a roaring trade.

Catering for Royal Ascot is the biggest non-permanent catering activity in the country.

An impressive assembly of bowler-hatted gatemen.

An entrance to the Royal
Ascot Enclosure.

Wearing the traditional forest green velvet coats of the Yeomen Prickers, gatemen Tom Humphries and John Summers with the Munnings bronze of Ascot favourite Brown Jack. This is exhibited before the two longest flat races, the Queen Alexandra Stakes which Brown Jack won six times, and the race named after him which is run at the July meeting.

The number board man (Paddy McMahon) hoists the numbers of the placed horses into the frame.

Cyril Acers, a member of the groundstaff sweeps the already immaculate winners' enclosure.

Running (rail) repairs under the eye of Mr Hugh Mounsey, who retired in 1974 after many years as bailiff. The rail had been broken when Overtown had charged it and unseated his rider on the way to the post in the Norfolk Stakes 1974.

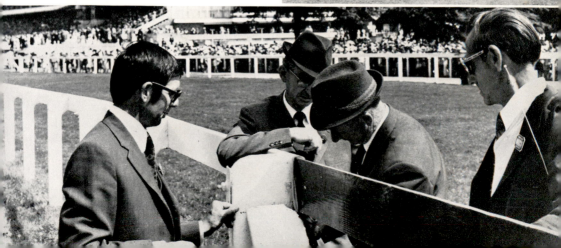

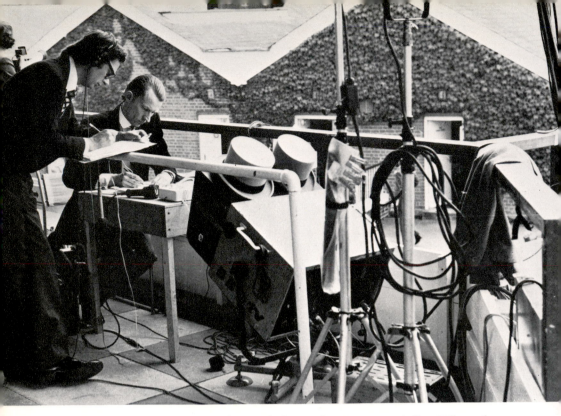

Telling the world: with top hats parked out of camera range, Julian Wilson plans a television interview.

The racing Press crowds round the trainer (Doug Smith) for news of the race and plans for the future.

suing trainer Jack Jarvis for 'slander and assault'. Tommy Burns, who was a forceful jockey, was riding Raeburn (which broke down and never raced again), and Eph Smith was riding Fearless Fox, trained by Jarvis. Burns did not appear to give Smith overmuch room on the turn, and Fearless Fox returned with 'definite white marks on his ribs' (*The Times*). Mr Jarvis was said to have called Burns 'most offensive names and made aggressive signs with an umbrella'. Burns complained to the stewards of the Jockey Club, who fined Mr Jarvis £50, and Tommy Burns went to court, suing Mr Jarvis for 'slander and assault'. The famous, but non-racing Sir Patrick Hastings appeared for Tommy Burns and said in court, 'It may be that Smith, with the enthusiasm of youth, had in mind the apocryphal story of Fred Archer going round Tattenham Corner with his legs over the rail.'

Mr Justice Hawke interjected drily, 'One leg.'

Sir Patrick, 'I stand corrected, one leg at Tattenham Corner and the other over the rail when he was going the other way.'

The charge was withdrawn and 'substantial damages' were paid.

King George VI and Queen Elizabeth attended Ascot in their coronation year, 1937, and drove each day in state down the course, and again entertained for Ascot at Windsor Castle in 1938.

Although the Depression had touched Ascot remarkably little (the number of luncheon tents halved, and in place of a queue for boxes, a few were available), open signs of poverty contrasted with the established wealth at Ascot, especially on the approaches to the course. In 1938 Sir Charles Hyde complained:

> On the roads outside the racecourse conditions are disgraceful. From an early hour bands of so-called ex-soldiers play on the roads, and trainers tell us the noise causes considerable trouble with their horses in the stables. Unpleasant gangs hire blind and maimed men at so much per day to stand in the road, with the permission of the police, and they reap a rich harvest by putting their collecting boxes through the windows of motor-cars and begging from those proceeding on foot. They obstruct the traffic and are often insulting ... Foreign visitors to Ascot have asked us 'Are your ex-soldiers starving?'

The racing correspondent of *The Times* reported:

> On enquiry from the Berkshire County Constabulary, though begging is prohibited at Ascot there is, in the sight of the law, a distinction between begging and collecting; and disabled men collecting on behalf of a street band are regarded as giving something, to wit, music ... Some at least of

this ostentatious display of misery seems unnecessary. There is no evident need for a limbless ex-serviceman, if his disability is accepted by the Ministry of Pensions, to parade the streets without an artificial limb, since that appliance is supplied and maintained for him by the Ministry ... The war-blinded are entitled to a full pension, with the appropriate allowance, to support his wife and children and to meet the cost of a guide. Civilian blind receive from their local authority maintenance allowances which ... in London amount to £1 7s 6d a week.

The King and Queen were in Canada when the war clouds were gathering in June 1939. They embarked at Halifax in the *Empress of Britain*, on their way home, on Gold Cup day. The Duke and Duchess of Gloucester acted as host and hostess in the Royal Stand, but 'Ascot without the King and Queen is not Ascot at all,' wrote a *Times* reporter, 'like being asked to dinner and being told on arrival that the host and hostess have gone elsewhere and would one make oneself at home, and ask for what one wants?'

Everywhere anxiety and apprehension flourished. Unlike the First World War, which dropped from a clear sky, war appeared as inevitable as it was dreaded. Still, there were the Silly Season controversies to make reality bearable. Should men's top hats be worn or not during the races? The subject was raised by a brave man—figuratively and actually— General Hornby, v.c., who suggested in a letter to *The Times* that the younger men should remove their hats to allow the ladies to see. 'Most of them seem to forget that the hats they wear, whether black or white, are absolutely opaque, and they are asked to remove hats, not to stick their elbows out, nor carry a folded paper in their hands.' This inspired a light-hearted *Times* leader: 'It may be said that only someone with the v.c., like General Hornby, would have dared make the suggestion. For the proposal almost impudently flouts an established tradition of every social function—namely, that it is the women's hats that are always in the way of the serious spectator.'

The last day of the last Ascot racemeeting before the war, 'was "a real Black Friday" of a meeting which never came alive. Just when the meeting was about to be finished, the rain ceased and the sun came out and for the first time the weather was like a real Ascot. But it was too late, for the end came with mackintoshes still being worn, umbrellas being carried, and those hideous over-boots still being worn by many of the lady visitors. To make matters worse another outsider won the King's Stand Stakes.'

In the twenty-one years of Royal Ascot between the wars there had been much fine racing. When the first post-World War One meeting of

1919 attracted its huge crowds, the greatest racing triumphs came to the shipping magnate Lord Glanely, who was to die in a Second World War air-raid. Lord Glanely won seven races including a dead-heat. All seven horses were trained by Frank Barling, father of trainer Geoffrey Barling, and five were ridden by A. Smith and two by F. Slade. The races were the Prince of Wales Stakes (Dominion), the Churchill Stakes (He—a walk-over), the Visitors' Plate (Sky rocket, dead-heated with the Duke of Portland's Sir Berkeley), the Granville Stakes (Juliet), the St James's Palace Stakes won with his Derby winner Grand Parade, the Windsor Castle Stakes (Bright Folly) and the Wokingham (Scatwell).

The gambler Jimmy White won the Hunt Cup when his 'splendid chestnut' Irish Elegance carried a record nine stone eleven pounds, with F. Templeman wearing the famous white, pale blue and khaki hooped colours, ahead of Lord Jersey's Arion, carrying seven stone thirteen pounds.

Three fillies fell in the Coronation Stakes, when Carslake's mount Mons Star struck into the heels of the filly ahead, and Hulme and Freddie Fox also fell but fortunately with no serious injuries. Hulme won the Gold Cup, riding By Jingo, so he had compensation. After the Gold Cup was run, Steve Donoghue was taken along to the Royal Box and 'in the presence of the King, Queen and Princess May' presented with a gold-mounted whip to commemorate a win for the King on Viceroy at Epsom.

Diadem, owned by Lord D'Abernon and trained at Newmarket by the Honourable George Lambton, was an Ascot specialist in the early post-war years. Lambton called Diadem 'the sweetest and most gallant little mare that ever was seen on a racecourse'. Her first win was in the Coventry Stakes, the substitute race run at Newmarket. She won the One Thousand Guineas and ran in the substitute Derby and Oaks. In 1919 Diadem won the Rous Memorial over seven furlongs and the sprint King's Stand Stakes, repeating the double in 1920 when she also won the All-Aged Stakes. As a seven-years-old she tried to win the Rous Memorial Stakes for the third time running, but the ground at Ascot was very hard in 1921, and she was beaten by Sir H. Bird's Monarch, pulling up very sore. It was her last race. George Lambton tells in his superb *Men and Horses I Have Known* how his wife lost her lucky Diadem brooch, which she always wore when the filly ran, on her way to the paddock, an omen she considered so unlucky that she did not tell her husband until after the race. 'Diadem's favourite jockey was Donoghue,' wrote her trainer, 'who with his beautiful hands and his tender treatment of a horse, combined with his marvellous dash and nerve, has always been a pleasure to watch.'

The Queen Mary Stakes was a new race introduced in 1921, a sweep-stakes with 1,000 sovereigns added for two-years-old fillies, run over five furlongs. The first winner was Mr W. E. Whiberay's Wild Mint, trained by H. Cottrill and ridden by J. Shatwell, and the value to the winner was £2,680, making it the fourth most valuable race of the meeting, exceeded only by the Gold Cup (£3,690), the Coronation Stakes (£3,600) and the Hardwicke Stakes (£2,821).

There was a popular win in the Gold Cup of 1923 by Happy Man, owned by Mr F. Hardy, trained at Russley by Captain Hogg and ridden by Vic Smyth. Happy Man was considered an unlucky loser in 1921. He had been badly injured in the Chester Cup, and it was only thanks to the fine work of his veterinary surgeon that he was able to race again. Second was the seven-years-old Silvrian, trained by George Lambton. Tommy Weston had the ride at the request of Lord Derby, even though he had to carry two stone deadweight, which, it was thought, caused Silvrian to lose by a short head, when he came again with great gameness after being headed. The stable jockey E. Gardner had resigned after he had been criticised for his riding of Lord Derby's Pharos in the Derby, and Tommy Weston's riding in the Gold Cup (which was approved) led to him getting many fine rides for Lord Derby.

There was more behind-the-scenes jockey friction in the Queen Mary Stakes and the St James's Palace Stakes on the opening day of the 1924 meeting. Each was won by horses owned by Lord Woolavington and trained by Fred Darling, the Beckhampton perfectionist and ridden by Archibald — most important was the St James's Palace Stakes, which he won on Tom Pinch. 'Archibald had been "jocked off" Tom Pinch in the Derby [in which the horse, ridden by H. Beasley, was unplaced], as it was thought the colt did not go well for him. He made practically all the running and won easily. Tom Pinch has never run so kindly for anyone as he did for Archibald yesterday — keep him to a mile and he will often win.'

On the last day of the meeting Frank Bullock, riding Stavropol was knocked over and rolled on in the High-Weight Stakes. Badly bruised and shaken he was brought back in an ambulance which, it was said, had been a very long time in appearing. In 1926 there was another bad accident, when Mr J. A. de Rothschild's mare Vionnet was brought down and broke her back in the Ascot Stakes. Her rider, Sirett 'was rendered unconscious and still unconscious last night, and in King Edward's Hospital, Windsor, where his condition is very critical'.

There was plenty for the connoisseur in 1926. Book Law by Buchan out of Popingaol a beautifully bred and very strong bay filly owned by

Lord Astor and trained at Manton by Alec Taylor, won the Queen Mary
Stakes. 'R. Jones rode her most admirably. I cannot pay higher praise than
to say Bullock could not have ridden an inexperienced high-class two-
years-old filly with finer judgment or greater kindness.' Book Law,
narrowly defeated in the One Thousand Guineas, went on to win the
St Leger very easily.

The Gold Cup was won by Solario, which had won the Ascot Derby in
the previous year, 'making mincemeat' (Roger Mortimer) of Manna,
but which had finished only fourth in the Derby itself, after being caught
up in the tape and left some lengths. Solario led throughout the race until
'half-way up the straight Priori II drew up to and actually headed Solario.
For an awful silent moment there were visions of Solario's defeat. Shaken
up by Childs and shown the whip (not used) Solario sailed away. He is a
great colt, certainly the greatest I have seen,' wrote the experienced
Times racing correspondent, adding, 'Childs is the best of all modern
Jockeys over a distance of ground.' The owner, Sir J. Rutherford, who had
refused many offers for the colt, led him in himself 'to the clapping of
many hands and the raising of innumerable hats'. Joe Childs wrote in his
autobiography, 'I will always remember the deafening cheers as Solario
was led in from the winning post to the unsaddling enclosure. Royal
Ascot is always a memorable meeting and Gold Cup day is one of the
most notable in the history of the Turf.' On the following day
King George V sent for Childs and congratulated him on Solario's
win.

In 1927 a passenger ship was specially chartered to bring over the
French runners for Ascot by Monsieur Jacques Wittouck. Thirteen
humans accompanied the horses, including the owner, his trainer Carter
and three French jockeys Allemande, Vatard and Bartholomew. But the
only French-owned horses which won at Ascot were trained in England:
they were Monsieur M. Boussac's Asterus, winner of the Churchill
Stakes and Alexandra Plate and Monsieur E. de St Alary's Finglas, trained
by Gilpin, ten to one winner of the Royal Hunt Cup. The main bid for
French supremacy was in the Gold Cup. 'Five horses in the Gold Cup were
bred in France, and another is out of a French mare and with a French
owner. The only pure-bred English horse from an English-based stallion
is Foxlaw, and he is owned by a South African (Sir Abe Bailey) and
ridden by an Australian (Brownie Carslake).' Monsieur Jacques Wittouck
ran Bois Josselyn ridden by Allemande, and he also ran Altay, ridden by
G. Vatard. This was the first year in Britain that the rule had been dropped,
which had said that a stable which had two runners in a race, should
declare to win with one.

The French outsider Altay seemed to have everything beaten until Carslake brought Foxlaw in a late run on the outside.

> So little distance to go, so much ground to make up. Suddenly Foxlaw, aided and abetted by Carslake, began to reduce the gap. The silence in which, at first, his effort was made became a growing murmur, which swelled into a roar of encouragement as the intervening gap was gradually reduced. Jockey and horse, moving as one, caught the Frenchman, gallant beyond words, and after a struggle which seemed interminable in length, but in reality was only a second, they forged ahead to such a volley of cheering as is seldom heard on a racecourse. In the end Foxlaw won by two lengths. The brave Foxlaw was out on his feet, stopped himself and took some time to recover. But eventually he walked in quite cheerfully.

The immortal Brown Jack made his first appearance in 1928 on the course with which he will for ever be linked. This brown gelding by Jackdaw out of Querquidella was foaled in 1924, and bought as a three-years-old for Sir Harold Wernher by trainer Aubrey Hastings. After his death he was trained by Ivor Anthony. Brown Jack won the Champion Hurdle at Cheltenham as a four-years-old, ridden by L. B. Rees.

It was then decided to turn Brown Jack's attention to the Flat, when he struck up his famous partnership with Steve Donoghue. Brown Jack won a race at Ascot for each of seven years. He followed his 1928 win in the Ascot Stakes by winning six successive Queen Alexandra Stakes. He also won the Goodwood Cup and the Ebor Handicap, and in all his twenty-three victories earned over £23,000. 'I find it hard to write of Brown Jack as though he were an ordinary horse, or even a horse at all,' wrote Steve Donoghue in his autobiography. 'If you try to think of a perfect gentleman with a few strange and particular little habits of his own, that is Brown Jack. He was the most delightfully mannered old gentleman you could wish to meet. He was also the gamest, most intelligent, and generous horse that ever looked through a bridle.

When Brown Jack won his first race at Ascot he was just a very good, game young horse, and no special notice was taken of him. His first star billing came in the very heavy Ascot of 1930, after racing had been interrupted by the famous thunderstorm. On the Friday Brown Jack received special attention for the first time in some of the reports. 'A deserved ovation for Brown Jack as lastly – after failing, as last year, in the Ascot Stakes, in which he was very unlucky, he won the Queen Alexandra Stakes.' In 1932, when Brown Jack won his fourth consecutive Queen Alexandra Stakes, 'soon after entering the straight Brown Jack and his usual jockey Donoghue decided that it was time to go home, and pulling with ease up to Delete, this gallant pair went on to win with ease, from Arctic Star, with Delete third.' In 1933, his fifth consecutive win was reported as 'Donoghue up, Brown Jack cantered to the front and there he remained, cantering to the end of the race, no matter how hard his opponents tried to get to him. He was cheered the whole way up the straight.'

In 1934 Brown Jack won his sixth successive Alexandra Stakes. When the bell rang, and Brown Jack and Mr J. V. Rank's Solatium, six years younger and receiving much weight, entered the straight, the two horses were well clear of the other runners. 'Solatium, on the rails, hung on most gallantly to Brown Jack. Indeed he hung on so long that the suspense to me became almost unbearable,' wrote *The Times* racing correspondent. 'Solatium belongs to a great friend of mine but how I hoped that his horse would fall back beaten, so that Brown Jack should win. And then slowly but surely Brown Jack and Donoghue began to draw away; at first by inches and then by feet, and then, quite close to the winning post, they were clear.'

Steve Donoghue had lost his whip in the race, and had to talk the horse home 'I am certain the old rogue was laughing at me for having dropped my whip, and I know that he enjoyed giving me that fright. Just as he had done every time before, he pricked his ears as he approached the post and did his comic little dance—he always did this when he won—as he passed it.'

'Never have such scenes been witnessed,' wrote *The Times*. 'Everyone flocked from the Royal Enclosure; they rushed from the lawns and Tattersall's Ring, they arrived through the famous tunnel breathless in the paddock . . . And when he reached the gates of his enclosure, which he was entering for the sixth time after winning this race, he stopped and looked around. None could make him walk in until he was certain that everyone who wanted to see him go in was present.' Steve Donoghue recalled 'Never will I forget the roar of that crowd as long as I live, Ascot or no Ascot they went mad . . . All my six Derbys faded before the reception that was awaiting Jack and myself as we set out to return to weigh-in. I don't think I was ever so happy in my life.'

His trainer, Ivor Anthony, was waiting for Brown Jack in the un-saddling enclosure, standing quietly and shyly, stroking his chin. So great was the tension he had not been able to watch the race, but had sat alone behind the stands until the cheers told him Brown Jack had won. That was Brown Jack's last race: he lived on in happy and honoured retirement until 1948.

Priory Park, which won the Hunt Cup in 1928, the year of Brown Jack's first Ascot win, was another horse with an unusual record. He was the first horse to win the Hunt Cup (ridden by Brownie Carslake, carrying eight stone twelve pounds), the Lincolnshire Handicap, the Stewards' Cup and the City and Suburban. He was owned by Mr J. B. Joel and trained at Foxhill by C. Peck.

There was an unusual accident in the Ascot Stakes in 1929, in which Mount Hawke fell 'and threw his small jockey (C. Brown) into the crowd, where he landed on a spectator. Neither was hurt. There was sympathy from the crowds for the jockey, but none for the spectator, who was mistaken for a wrongdoer under arrest.'

In 1929 the Ascot Gold Cup attracted enormous crowds, as Mrs J. D. Hertz's Reigh Count, the best stayer in America, had been sent over. Reigh Count had already won the Coronation Cup at Epsom. Ranged against him were the French Palais Royal II, owned by Monsieur Wittouck, which had been second in the St Leger, and another French horse, Cacao, which had won the French St Leger. Paddock judges considered Palais Royal II had run up very light, but that Mr R. Reid Walker's Invershin, trained at Stanton by G. Digby, was beautifully muscled up and turned out. Reigh Count was 'a greyhound'. In the event the English horse won fairly easily from the American Reigh Count and the French Palais Royal II. So Invershin brought off a second successive Gold Cup win, the first horse to do so since Prince Palatine in 1912 and 1913.

Gordon Richards' first Ascot win was in 1925. He won three races in 1931, including the Hunt Cup on Grand Salute for Lord Glanely. He rode the fancied Singapore in the Gold Cup. Although the early pace did not suit him – Gordon Richards thought he should have had a pacemaker – he was in the lead half way up the straight when Joe Childs on Trimdon came up on his outside. Singapore had been hanging off the rails and Gordon had his whip in his left hand. 'Joe drew up alongside, hard at work too, and somehow our whips got caught and his was knocked out of his hand. We then got very close and finished locked together as we passed the post. The judge said Trimdon had won by a short head.' Gordon Richards' opinion that he would have won the race on objection was echoed by *The Times*: 'Both horses ran out their races to the bitter end, and both jockeys rode as fine a race as it is possible to see. I do not think I have ever seen Richards ride a better finish, and he was certainly an unlucky loser, for Childs and Trimdon forced him on to the rails . . . he came in with his right boot covered with paint from the rails.' Gordon Richards commented: 'I don't know whether we would have got the race or not, but I do know that I was every bit as irritated with Joe Childs as he was with me.'

Strangely enough Joe Childs makes no mention of the incident in his autobiography, although he mentions briefly his Ascot successes in 1932, when he won the Gold Cup for the second time on Trimdon, the Rous Memorial Stakes on Heronslea, and the Ribblesdale on Rose en Soleil—three successive races. He took even more pleasure from his win on the Friday in the Hardwicke Stakes, on the King's three-years-old Limelight. The King's horses had been running disappointingly. 'I knew that Limelight was a real good horse when in the right mood, but unfortunately one never knew with such a temperamental animal how he would act . . . when something had occurred to upset him, he would work himself up into such a temper that it was a difficult matter to get him even to the post. As so often happens on these occasions, Limelight was not on his best behaviour. It was not that he was in a real bad temper but he was nervous and fidgety at the start, and I had to do everything I know to calm him down, so that he would give of his best . . . Much to my relief I got away to a pretty good start and was well placed when we came into the straight. Limelight was going beautifully, but there were two horses heading me, Nitsichin ridden by Bernard Carslake and Donna Sol with E. Smith up, who did not intend to give in.' Limelight just got up, and the win gave great pleasure to the King.

In the 1933 meeting when Tavern charged the tapes in the Prince of Wales' Stakes, Steve Donoghue was hurt in the back by the tapes, and trodden on and injured in the face by the horse.

A shadow was cast over the meeting by a tragedy on the same day. Mr Fred Leader had trained the favourite, Gainslaw, to win the Ascot Gold Vase. After the meeting he and his wife were being driven back to Newmarket when their car ran into the back of a stationary lorry near Stevenage: both were killed instantly.

In the following year Viscount Churchill died. Only the Duke of Norfolk in more recent times has had a greater influence on Ascot. An upright, rigid perfectionist, Viscount Churchill was held in awe and unqualified respect by all who worked for him. The running of Ascot was split into two. Lord Hamilton of Dalzell became the King's Representative, and controlled the conduct of the meeting, while Lord Granard was appointed to a new post as His Majesty's Comptroller at Ascot, and controlled entrance to the Royal Enclosure. In 1935 Lord Granard was also appointed by the King, the second of the three Trustees who administer, under the Ascot Authority Act of 1913, the revenue and property of the trust under the King's authority. The third Trustee was

14

Lord Wigram who had been King George V's Private Secretary and was Keeper of Windsor Castle.

The atmosphere at Ascot changed almost overnight. In contrast to the authoritarian Lord Churchill came the gentle Lord Hamilton, as conscientious and hard-working as his predecessor, but sweet-natured and considerate. Those who worked with and for him were devoted to Lord Hamilton. At this time he was a sick man, who had only one lung. It was necessary for him to work in a room kept at an even temperature, and he used to have to go to Cornwall to avoid the worst of the winter weather.

Lord Hamilton was a man who was not content to take things as they had been accepted, but who looked for himself. He discovered, for example, that when the rails on the inside of the straight course were interrupted where the two courses joined, when they were resumed again for the final straight, they were not, and never had been, in a straight line. New rails which *were* in a straight line were substituted, making riding the straight course much easier. 'How it is that nobody ever thought of the new rails on the far side of the straight course until Lord Hamilton of Dalzell did so, will always remain a mystery,' commented *The Times*. The new running rail began some yards beyond the judge's box, and was carried back, in line with the New Mile rails, at an ever-widening angle until it came to the junction of the courses. This involved a new angle to the bend from the round course into the straight, and although it was feared this turn might prove too sharp, it 'rode' well.

Lord Hamilton installed the comprehensive watering system, with hydrants every 150 yards which was backed by the Ascot Authority's own reservoir, which holds three and a half million gallons of water, and which, since 1949, has been linked with the Sunninghill Reservoir. He drew up far-reaching plans for the reconstruction of the grandstands, but these were frustrated by the outbreak of the Second World War in 1939.

He also removed the omnibuses which had in recent years been allowed inside the course, as they are at Epsom. But at Epsom the ground on the far side of the course is higher than that at the finish, while at Ascot the ground slopes away to Swinley Bottom. The tall buses had interfered with the view from the lawns. A minor change was made in 1938 in the time for luncheon. The first race time was put back to one-thirty p.m., with an hour for luncheon following. The third race became the most important of the day, with the start at three-ten p.m. instead of, as formerly two-thirty p.m. Lord Hamilton remained King's Representative throughout the war, retiring in 1945. He died in 1952.

Lord Granard as His Majesty's Comptroller at Ascot, not only controlled the issue of vouchers to the Royal Enclosure but also chose the
Cups for the racemeeting. At that time the Cups were chosen as the result
of design competitions. In 1939 he judged the merits of 168 designs
submitted for the Gold Cup, the King's Gold Vase and the Hunt Cup,
each of which had to incorporate the Royal Arms. The winning entry for
the Gold Cup was designed by R. H. Hill, a recent winner of the Goldsmiths Company's travelling scholarship, that for the Gold Vase was
by R. G. Baxendale, headmaster of a Birmingham School of Art, and that
for the Hunt Cup by J. L. Auld, who also designed a dish presented
to the City of New York. The winning designs were exhibited in the
Goldsmiths' Hall. The added money and stakes in 1939 amounted to
£67,870.

So peace ran out, and the country faced another war.

In February 1940 the Ascot Royal meeting was cancelled. In April
however — just as 'the phoney war' was coming to a bitter end — it was
announced that a two-day substitute meeting would be held at Newmarket, where the Gold Cup and the Wokingham Handicap would be
run on June 21st, and the Royal Hunt Cup and Ascot Stakes on the
following day. Incidentally racehorse owners were complaining bitterly
that it cost £3 a week to keep a racehorse! But on June 19th, 1940, the
stewards of the Jockey Club announced that all racing in Britain was
cancelled until further notice. The next racemeeting in Britain did not
take place until Saturday, September 14th, 1940, at Ripon, and when
Newmarket resumed with four days of racing in November, there was
no room on the card for the four Ascot races.

In 1940 Ascot Heath was inspected to find out if it were suitable for
cultivation, but was found unsuitable.

In 1941 some of the Ascot races were run at Newmarket. On July
2nd, 1941, the Coventry Stakes for two-years-old was won for the King
by Big Game, trained by Fred Darling and ridden by Harry Wragg.
Bred in the National Stud in 1939 and leased to the King, Big Game was
by Bahram out of Myrobella, the brilliantly fast filly which was a great
favourite of Gordon Richards. Big Game won all but one of his nine
races: unfortunately his one defeat was in the substitute Derby. The New
St James's Palace Stakes for three-years-olds over one mile was won by
Orthodox, owned by Mr James Rank, trained by Noel Cannon and
ridden by Doug Smith, the Gold Cup was won by Sir H. Cunliffe-
Owen's Finis, trained by Ossie Bell and ridden by Harry Wragg; the
Queen Mary Stakes completed a double for the King when the brilliant,
erratic filly Sun Chariot won by a head from Perfect Peace.

In 1942 the substitute Ascot races were run at Newmarket on June 30th and July 1st. The Coventry Stakes was won by the Aga Khan's Nasrullah, trained by Frank Butters and ridden by Gordon Richards. The Queen Mary Stakes was won by Samovar, ridden by Michael Beary, owned by Lord Wyfold and trained by 'Atty' Persse. The Gold Cup went to the winner of the previous year's Newmarket Derby, Owen Tudor, owned by Mrs (now Lady) Macdonald-Buchanan, trained by Fred Darling and ridden by Gordon Richards.

There was a strange state of affairs from 1943. Racing re-commenced at Ascot, but the traditional Ascot races, moved to Newmarket, continued to be run there until the end of the war.

Wartime racing in England was zoned. Races at Newmarket were limited to horses trained on the Heath there, with the exception of eight important races which were open to all-comers, and which included the substitute Gold Cup, the Queen Mary Stakes and the Coventry Stakes from Ascot. Horses trained south of the Trent, except those trained at Newmarket, could race at Ascot, Salisbury and Windsor. Horses trained north of the Trent could only race at Stockton and Pontefract. In the season there were nine days' racing at Ascot, twelve days at Newmarket, eleven at Pontefract, eight at Salisbury, ten at Stockton and eight at Windsor. Meanwhile racing continued on ten courses in the neutral Republic of Ireland.

The races at Ascot were for prizes ranging from £197 to £890, and nearly all were given the names of neighbouring towns and villages. Both at Newmarket and Ascot 'the Cambridgeshire' and 'the Cesarewitch' were run, while the north, though missing out on an autumn double, put on a substitute November Handicap at Pontefract. The wartime races on Ascot racecourse were run not by the Ascot Authority, but by the Jockey Club.

Following the death of Sir Gordon Carter in November 1941, there was a new Clerk of the Course at Ascot. Colonel Sir Arthur Erskine, G.C.V.O., D.S.O., was appointed Clerk of the Course in December 1941. He too was a gentle man, and to those accustomed to the brusque Sir Gordon, was easy to deal with, but he was in poor health. He had been ill in bed at the time of the Abdication, but had got up to attend to urgent matters, and had contracted rheumatic fever.

Wartime racing was naturally not on the usual Ascot scale. Most of the stands remained closed, and several tons of iron railings had been removed in answer to the national appeal for scrap metal. The first wartime meeting at Ascot was held on Saturday, May 16th, 1943. 'Thousands reached the course on bicycles, in farm carts and on foot. If in any part of this country there is a racemeeting, no matter how difficult the authorities may make it to reach it, the general public will still reach it,' commented *The Times*. King George VI and Queen Elizabeth were present, their first visit to Ascot since 1938 and their first visit to a racemeeting since the outbreak of war.

'It was indeed a day of "First Times",' wrote *The Times*. 'The first time that thousands of people have been in the Royal Enclosure at Ascot, the first time that a girl in jodhpurs has been seen in that enclosure, the first time that R. Hobbs has saddled a flat race winner, the first time that Carey has ridden a winner over the course, the first time that Lord Porchester has had a winner of any kind, and the first time that the general public have known how comfortable a racemeeting can be. The demand for the general improvement of racecourses has had a great advertisement.'

Getting home was the crunch.

With such limited opportunities to race, there were some unusual runners in modest races. On June 14th, 1943, in the Finchamstead Plate over two miles, worth £495 to the winner there was a useful lead to the outcome of the Derby, which was run at Newmarket on June 19th, 1943! 'Among the runners was Bravona, who has recently been galloped with Straight Deal.' Bravona, ridden by Carey and carrying one pound overweight had finished second to Royal Academy. 'Bravona was baulked of an opening in the straight . . . I understand that Straight Deal is a very long way in front of Bravona at home, and that Miss Paget's colt must have a great chance on Saturday'. At Newmarket Straight Deal duly won. The New Derby Stakes was followed by the Coventry Stakes, which provided an unusual double for owner Miss Dorothy Paget, trainer Walter Nightingall and jockey Tommy Carey. On the previous day the Queen Mary Stakes was run on the same card as the New Oaks Stakes and the substitute for the Ascot race was won by Mrs B. Lavington's Fair Female, trained by Harvey Leader and ridden by F. Lane. The substitute Gold Cup was run on July 7th and won by Ujiji, owned by Mr A. E. Allnatt, trained by J. Lawson and ridden by Gordon Richards.

At Ascot there was a truly remarkable riding feat during this revival year of 1943, but it received little attention because of the war. Tommy Carey rode five consecutive winners at Ascot on Saturday, August 28th, 1943 and then rode the winner of the first race at the following Ascot meeting on Saturday September 11th, 1943.

Tommy Carey's record was achieved as follows:

Owner	Horse	Trainer	Type of Race	Price	Prize money	Name of Race
Saturday, August 28th, 1943						
		Walter				White
Miss Dorothy Paget	Straight Deal	Nightingall	12F 3y	6/5 Fav	£504	Waltham Stks
Sir M. McAlpine	First Edition	V. Smyth	7F H'cap	9/2 Fav	£560	Shurlock Row Hdcp.
Miss Dorothy Paget	Lady Maderty	W. Nightingall	5F 2y F	1/4 Fav	£504	Dunsden Plate
Mr J. B. Walker	Acceleration	P. Nunneley	12F 3y	100/8	£251	Taplow Stks
Miss Dorothy Paget	Easter Bonnet	W. Nightingall	5F 2y	8/1	£373	Woodley Stks
Saturday, September 11th, 1943						
Miss Dorothy Paget	Yashmak	W. Nightingall	5F 2y	20/1	£251	Riseley Plate

At this September meeting Carey rode three winners, though not consecutively, and there *was* a tribute to his riding in *The Times* linked to the win of Filator, owned by Lady Cunliffe-Owen, trained by Ossie Bell in the Farley Hill Handicap over the Ascot Gold Cup distance of two and a half miles.

> The feature of the race was perhaps not the fact that Filator won with ease, but the masterly exhibition of race-riding given by his jockey. There have been few if any better judges of pace than Carey in recent years. He does not seem to care what the other riders are doing. If they go what he considers too fast he is content to be behind; if, on the other hand, he considers that they are not going fast enough then he goes on in front. At the end of a mile and a quarter on Saturday he did not consider the pace was fast enough, so he at once sent Filator into the lead, and the genuine staying gelding stayed there until the race was over. He makes his own pace, either in front, in the middle of the field or it may even be last. Much of his marked success as a race rider is due to this most valuable gift.

Tommy Carey had eighteen winners at Ascot in 1943, and forty-four throughout the country during the season, finishing second in the championship table to Gordon Richards, who had sixty-five winners, including ten at Ascot.

Incidentally 1943 may be classed as the beginning of the new, all-the-year-round Ascot. It was the busiest season Ascot had so far seen in its 232 years of history, with racemeetings in every month from May to October inclusive, and a total of sixty-seven races.

The last meeting of the season saw Sugar Palm win his sixth race in a season of very limited opportunity, when he took the Warren Row Stakes over five furlongs for his owner Major A. Bonsor, his trainer F. Hartigan and his jockey—the ubiquitous Tommy Carey.

Ascot had ten race-days, with immensely long cards, some of twelve races, in 1944. This was the period of the flying bombs. On June 21st, 1944, it was announced: 'A succession of short blasts on the warning bell will indicate that there is [sic] flying bombs in the vicinity. One prolonged blast will indicate that the bomb is about to crash and that the public are advised to adopt the prone position . . .'

The attendances were fantastic. In 1944 *The Times* commented, 'The vast crowd surged on Ascot by every means known to man before the advent of the internal combustion engine.' The Tote took £110,714 6s on Saturday May 13th, 1944.

There was a nasty accident in the paddock at the June meeting. Elysium, a two-years-old first time out, owned by Jack Hylton and trained by Vic Smyth 'reared up when Beary mounted him, and fell backwards on his jockey, just as Happy Holiday had done on Elliott at the last Ascot meeting. Beary managed to extract himself unhurt, but the colt, apparently dazed by his fall, slowly cantered up to the rails of the parade-ring and fell over them. It was like a slow-motion film of a steeplechaser falling at Becher's Brook. Elysium must have jarred himself horribly, and there was no question after that of him being started in the race.' Elysium did not appear on the racecourse again until August, but it is pleasing to note that he started in six races, won three and was second in three in his second season, and that two of his wins were at Ascot.

There was tremendous enthusiasm over the result of the tenth and final race on June 28th, although there was nothing outstanding about the one-mile race itself, the second part of the modest Hurst Stakes, in which the winner, Bois de Rose, started at 100 to 8. The reason was the immense popularity of Steve Donoghue, who owned and trained the winner, which was ridden by his son Pat, an officer on leave from the R.A.F. In a dashing finish Bois de Rose got up to beat Vermouth, ridden by Michael Beary, by a head.

But the July meeting had to be cancelled, on account of the danger from flying bombs.

In 1944 the duel at Ascot between the jockeys Richards and Carey resulted in a narrow win by Gordon Richards, who rode sixteen winners to Tommy Carey's fourteen—and they were split by the brilliant Michael Beary, with fifteen winners at Ascot.

Even before the opening of the 1945 flat race season, and before the end of the war, it was planned to return the principal Ascot races, which had been kept in being at Newmarket, to their own racecourse. In the event one wartime racemeeting was held at Ascot in 1945, when a ten-race card brought a big crowd to Ascot on Easter Monday.

CHAPTER NINE

Moving with the times

ON A DAY OF 'FIRSTS', PRINCESS ELIZABETH, THEN AN OFFICER IN THE
Auxiliary Territorial Army, first went racing, at Ascot on Monday, May
21st, 1945. This was the first racemeeting at Ascot after VE Day. With her
parents, King George VI and Queen Elizabeth, she arrived just before the
fourth race in the eight-race programme, which was the first running of
the Gordon Carter Stakes. This seven furlong race, commemorating the
late Clerk of the Course, was the first worth over £1,000 to the winner at
Ascot since pre-war days, and was won by Mustang, owned by Mrs P.
Hill, trained by Fred Darling and ridden by Gordon Richards.

Princess Elizabeth was an immediate and enthusiastic recruit to racing.
When her parents left, she begged to stay on. She therefore saw the first
winner of an Ascot race trained by a woman, when Mrs Florence Nagle's
Sun Up won the second division of the Bisham Handicap, the last race
on the card. Although Mrs Nagle trained Sun Up, the horse was officially
trained by her head lad R. Brown, a polite fiction which covered the
identity of women trainers, who were then prohibited under Jockey
Club rules.

This was the beginning of Princess Elizabeth's involvement with horseracing, which has continued through her reign as Queen Elizabeth II.
Over the years she has become an expert on horseracing, especially in the
field of breeding. Racing gives the Queen relaxation and continual
interest; she enjoys everything to do with it—planning the breeding of
her mares, watching the development of the young stock, even the apt
naming of her racehorses—always a feature, news from her racing
manager and trainers of the horses in training, her visits to her trainers'
stables, when she watches the early morning gallops, going to the paddock
on the racecourse to see her own and famous horses, and the races
themselves. How fortunate this genuine love of racing has been for
Ascot.

Meanwhile Ascot gradually returned to normal. The first two of the important Royal Ascot races which had been in wartime exile at Newmarket came home at the one-day meeting held on Saturday, June 16th, 1945. The Aga Khan won them both, the Coventry Stakes with Khaled ridden by Gordon Richards and the Queen Mary Stakes with Rivaz, with Charlie Elliott up. On Saturday, July 7th—a wonderful day of fourteen hours continual sunshine, before a relaxed, happy crowd of 50,000—the Royal Hunt Cup returned to Ascot and was won by Colonel J. H. Whitney's Battle Hymn, trained by Cecil Boyd-Rochfort and ridden by P. Maher.

The Gold Cup followed immediately, for which ten horses started. Tehran, owned by the Aga Khan and ridden as usual by Gordon Richards, was odds on favourite. The race renewed the running fight between Tehran and Lord Rosebery's Ocean Swell, trained by Jack Jarvis and ridden in the race by Eph Smith. In 1944 Ocean Swell had beaten Tehran in the substitute Derby by a neck, while Tehran beat Ocean Swell into third place in the St Leger. The horses renewed their rivalry as four-years-old colts in the Thorney Stakes at Newmarket on May 9th. There were only three runners, Dilawarji acting as pacemaker for Tehran. Gordon Richards recalled in his autobiography:

Going into the dip, I pulled out and passed the pacemaker and Tehran did this in effortless style. But then Eph Smith on Ocean Swell drew right up to me, and frankly it must have looked a million to one Ocean Swell going right away to win. Not from gallant Tehran, however. He just kept on pulling out a little extra, and he stayed on to win by a neck ... But this race cost us the Gold Cup. That very astute trainer of Ocean Swell, Mr Jack Jarvis had learned a big lesson from that Newmarket race. So he got together with his jockey, Eph Smith, and he made a plan ...

When we got to Ascot, Tehran seemed grand on the morning of the race. Although the ground at Ascot was on the firm side, I thought Tehran's wonderful fighting qualities would pull him through ... Harry Wragg on Borealis made the pace at first—imagine Harry Wragg making the pace!—and then Dilawarji took it up. Tehran was going beautifully. In fact, he was going so well that I let him go into the lead running into the straight. Then I sat there, waiting for Ocean Swell to challenge. But Mr Jack Jarvis had made his plans too well. As he entered the straight, Eph Smith took Ocean Swell right across the course to the stands-side, far away from me. I saw him too late. Tehran thought he had nothing to pull out the usual extra against. I tried to get over to Ocean Swell but Eph had now got first run on me, and I could not get near him.

Ocean Swell was the first Derby winner since Persimmon to win the Gold Cup at Ascot.

The Britannia Stakes returned at the next meeting, on Saturday, August 4th, 1945, and was won by Joan's Star, ridden, like four other winners, including Rising Light for the King, that afternoon, by Gordon Richards. The modest, well-liked Gordon Richards, with his unorthodox style, marvellous balance and great will to win, was a most successful rider at Ascot, as elsewhere. His first winning ride at Ascot was on Tuesday, June 16th, 1925 — the year in which he first became champion jockey — on Lord Glanely's Sunderland in the Trial Stakes, and he had ridden forty-two Ascot winners by the outbreak of war. When Ascot was a zoned wartime racecourse, Gordon Richards added a further forty Ascot winners to his score, and after the war he had a further ninety-six winners at Ascot, ending with a win on The Queen's Landau, trained by Noel Murless, in the Rous Memorial Stakes on Friday, June 18th, 1954. In all Gordon Richards rode 178 Ascot winners. He won the Gold Cup in 1934 on Felicitation (beating Hyperion) and in 1952 on Aquino II, and he won the King George VI and Queen Elizabeth Stakes on Pinza.

Important changes in the administration of Ascot were made in November 1945. The King appointed the Duke of Norfolk, hereditary Earl Marshal, to be his Representative at Ascot. The King's Representative was also given control over admission to the Royal Enclosure and election to the Iron Stand, while the post of Comptroller to the Ascot Authority ceased to exist. The Duke of Norfolk, Lord Hamilton of Dalzell and Sir Ulick Alexander were appointed Trustees of the Ascot Authority.

The Duke of Norfolk was an organiser of genius. He was responsible for stage-managing such splendid ceremonies as the wedding of Princess Elizabeth to the Duke of Edinburgh in 1947, the Coronation of Queen Elizabeth II in 1953 and the funeral of Sir Winston Churchill in 1965. At Ascot he found a field worthy of his skill. A complete re-think of the whole racing pattern at Ascot was necessary, as it would be an anachronism to continue to operate Ascot, as hitherto, as a four-day a year function.

The Duke of Norfolk was assisted by Major Crocker Bulteel, who was appointed Clerk of the Course in January 1946, on the retirement of Colonel Sir Arthur Erskine. Major Crocker Bulteel was an outstanding racing administrator. A member of a family closely involved in racing — his father owned Manifesto when he won the Grand National of 1897, and Manifesto was turned out in a field at Ascot for the last years of his life. Major Bulteel had been a handicapper, and later Clerk of the Course at Liverpool and Hurst Park. Courteous and popular, he had much to do with bringing Ascot meetings up to date, and was primarily responsible for the institution of the King George VI and Queen Elizabeth Stakes, originally introduced to mark the Festival of Britain, which swiftly became the most important race in the Ascot calendar.

The first post-war Royal Ascot took place in 1946, in the prevailing atmosphere of austerity. Only refreshment buffets were available. In the Royal Enclosure ladies wore day dresses with hats, men service dress or lounge suits. (There was a humorous fourth leader in *The Times* concerning a man who had rung up the newspaper, complaining 'because he *only* has a top hat and morning coat respectable'.)

The King and Queen drove down the course only on Gold Cup day, and the postillions wore blue and gold liveries in place of the customary scarlet. *The Times* reported:

Royal Ascot has been restored to the calendar of social events, but, like much else in our new peacetime, its grandeur is greatly diminished ... Neither the Royal Enclosure nor the paddock had any startling note of fashion to catch the eye, nor was there any procession of elegantly dressed people to the Heath, across the course, because the Heath had none of its marquees for the sumptuous luncheons and teas of bygone days.

One particularly cheerless special constable, whose job it was to see that people did not stand on the seats, pointed out that before the war people's manners were enough to prevent them doing so ... The refreshment pavilion and the lesser buffets ... suffered severely from the prevailing austerity. Even so, there were strawberries and ice-cream for half-a-crown and champagne for sixty shillings a bottle, while on the course a peach could be bought from a tray for five shillings.

Far-reaching plans to change Ascot from a once-a-year to an all-the-year-round course, at the request of King George VI were occupying the Ascot Authority. But first urgent maintenance work had to be undertaken. The place was smartened up with unrationed cream and green paint in 1948, and in 1951 the Golden Gates were regilded for the first time since the death of Edward VII. The parade ring was enlarged and rails put up round the saddling boxes. A new type of sprinkler was installed, and also a photo-finish camera. At last, after two centuries of complaints, carriages and luncheon tents were forbidden in the centre of the course, which could no longer be crossed at will, except by the tunnel. But the Iron Stand had to be closed, as the bolts holding together the upper storey were nearly rusted through—some of the rusted bolts were displayed as proof in the Clerk of the Course's office. Rebuilding of the course began in 1948, the right-hand rails of the old straight course becoming the left-hand rails of the new course, thus freeing more room between the stands and the rails. The Old Mile was being altered, so that runners entered the straight at a safer angle.

Racing was enjoying its customary after-war boom. French horses, which had been more generously fed in occupied France than in Britain, at first carried all before them at Ascot. French horses filled the first three places in the 1946 Ascot Gold Cup, won by Monsieur Marcel Boussac's Caracalla II ridden by Charlie Elliott. The Jersey Stakes was taken by Madame J. Lieux's Sayani; and the Hardwicke Stakes went to Priam II and the Queen Alexandra Stakes to Marysas II, both owned by Monsieur Boussac.

An unusual visitor to Ascot was the Eclipse Stakes, in 1946, as Sandown Park had yet to re-open. Run over a mile and a quarter, it was won by Lord Derby's Gulf Stream, trained by W. Earl and ridden by Harry Wragg.

In 1947 the French again took the Gold Cup across the Channel, won by Monsieur F. R. Schmitt's Souverain, ridden by M. Lollieroll; the Hardwicke Stakes with Monsieur Boussac's Nirgal, and the Queen Alexandra Stakes with Mr H. Barnard-Hankey's Monsieur L'Amiral. The next year was just as bad. Madame P. Thomas-Morel won the Queen Anne Stakes with Selina, while Monsieur Boussac took the Gold Vase with Estoc from Vulgan, the Queen Mary Stakes with Coronation V and the Gold Cup with Arbar, odds-on favourite. The five-years-old Vulgan—his future as a sire of jumpers still undreamt-of—then carried off the Queen Alexandra Stakes for Monsieur H. Coriat. At the July meeting the Queen Elizabeth Stakes went to the Italian horse Tenerani, owned and trained by Signor Tesio and ridden by E. Camici. Although forecasts of doom for the English thoroughbred rent the air, fortunes change swiftly in racing, as in life. At the 1949 royal meeting only one race went to a French horse (the Queen Alexandra Stakes, won by Alindrake), although Monsieur Boussac took minor races at the September and October Ascot meetings. Again in 1950 there was only one French victory at Royal Ascot, when Baron G. de Waldner's Fastlad won the Gold Vase. Pan II won the Gold Cup for France in 1951, but by the end of George VI's reign, the number of French wins had dropped to an 'acceptable' level.

Patriotism received a fillip in September 1949 when Mr Winston Churchill's game Colonist II destroyed his opponents to win the Ribblesdale Stakes by eight lengths. Cheering broke out as the horses entered the last furlong 'by the time Colonist II reached the winning-post the view halloos and full-throated applause were reminiscent of the finish of the Grand National or the Gold Cup at Cheltenham. Mr Churchill was quickly down from his seat in the stands, but the crowd had already run to the winner's enclosure and were there to cheer again as he shook hands with his trainer Walter Nightingall and jockey T. Hawcroft.'

Excitement of another kind marked the race for the King Edward VII Stakes in 1950, which the brilliant and disappointing Prince Simon failed to win, as he had failed to win the Two Thousand Guineas by a short head and the Derby by a head. Harry Carr was bitterly disappointed: 'Prince Simon ran deplorably and finished unplaced in a scrabbling, messy race ... There was no sparkle in him, and though his lovely sweeping action was there, I got the impression that he was shod with heavy steel shoes instead of the feather-weight racing plates.' Returning disconsolate and dejected, Harry Carr 'came face to face with Her Majesty the Queen Mother, then Queen of England. She was talking with the late King, Captain Boyd-Rochfort and the late Captain Charles Moore, manager of the royal horses. I touched my cap and bowed, and to this day I remember what Her Majesty said to me, "You are an unlucky boy. Never mind, your luck will change soon" ... I went into the weighing-room a great deal happier man.'

On the last day of that topsy-turvy meeting Abernant, reckoned 'the fastest horse in the world' failed to give fourteen pounds to Tangle in the King's Stand Stakes and was beaten half a length, after starting at eleven to four on. Indeed in the twenty-four races of the 1950 royal meeting only four favourites obliged, and there were two twenty to one winners, two at 100 to 6, one at 100 to 7, one at 100 to 8 and three at ten to one.

When the Royal meeting of 1951 came round, King George VI was ill at Windsor Castle. Influenza had left behind a condition diagnosed as pneumonitis, which was soon to advance into a worse condition, and necessitated an operation for lung resection in September. The Queen and the Princesses attended Ascot as usual, driving in procession up the course, although the Queen left the races early each day.

So the King was not present when the King George VI and Queen Elizabeth Festival of Britain Stakes, as it was cumbrously titled, was run on Saturday, July 21st, 1951. It was worth £25,322 to the winner, and was the most valuable prize ever run for up to that time in Britain. The Derby that year was worth £19,386. This race, the concept of Major Crocker Bulteel, has developed into the King George VI and Queen Elizabeth Diamond Stakes, a truly international race of great importance, for three-years-old and upwards, entire horses and fillies, run over the mile and a half of the Swinley Course on the Saturday of the Ascot July meeting.

It was made up from the King George VI Stakes instituted in 1946, for three-years-old over two miles which had been run in October, and the Queen Elizabeth Stakes, first run over a mile and a half at the July meeting of 1948, when Tenerani won from Black Tarquin. In 1975 the race was worth £81,910 to the winning owner, when the total prize money for the race was £121,000. It is at present sponsored by De Beers Consolidated Mines Ltd to the sweet tune of £44,000 p.a., plus large contributions from the Horserace Betting Levy Board and the Ascot Authority.

This first race attracted a field of nineteen runners. The favourite was Arctic Prince, recent winner of the Derby, in which he had also been ridden by Charlie Spares. In the paddock the horse looked hard and fit. Tantième, the second favourite, had arrived from France just before the race, and looked a little spare, although he was on his toes in the paddock. The temperamental Zucchero was ridden by young Lester Piggott. The redoubtable Colonist II owned by Mr Winston Churchill was in the field, as was Mossborough and Belle of All – 'that splendid filly', according to her jockey Gordon Richards, who had won the One Thousand Guineas and the Coronation Stakes on her.

At the start Supreme Court backed off once or twice but they got off 'with even Zucchero' in line. Mossborough led into the straight, followed by Colonist II, when E. C. Elliott made a perfectly timed run on Supreme Court to win by three-quarters of a length from Zucchero and Tantième in record time for the Ascot mile and a half of 2′ 29⅝″. The owner was Mrs Tom Lilley, the trainer E. Williams from Kingsclere. The riders of the first and second (E. C. Elliott and Lester Piggott) were praised because 'they had rightly refused to go the early, furious pace'.

The last Ascot meeting of 1951, on Saturday, October 13th, was the first to be televised. It was planned to begin the television programme with the Cumberland Lodge Stakes at three p.m. But the King was beginning to recover from his extremely serious operation, which had taken place on September 22nd. Good Shot, a colt the King leased from the National Stud was thought to have a good chance in the Tankerville Nursery Stakes at two thirty p.m. Would it be possible to show this earlier race on television, so that the King might see it? The BBC swiftly arranged to open the programme earlier. The television announcer on the day, Miss Mary Malcolm, told the writer how dearly she would have liked (but did not dare) to open with a spontaneous message of good wishes to the King. All went well. 'Gordon Richards did his part. He flew out of the gate and rode one of his cleverest finishes to win with Good Shot by half a length.' (*The Times*) Before the next racemeeting at Ascot, King George VI had died, and his elder daughter had succeeded to the Throne as Queen Elizabeth II. The King, who had been so little prepared when he was hustled into the Throne on the abdication of his brother, had everywhere won affection and respect. Queen Elizabeth II followed by wish and inclination in the footsteps of her father and at Ascot there was no change in forward thinking and planning.

The big race was retitled the King George VI and Queen Elizabeth Stakes and was first run under its new name on July 19th, 1952. The race was won by Tulyar, owned by the Aga Khan, bringing the horse's winning stakes to £60,596, and so beating the long-standing record of £57,455 amassed by Isinglass, winner of the 1893 Derby. Little Tulyar was placid and indolent. When he appeared in the parade ring at Ascot, with his Derby triumph behind him, the spectators saw 'a small colt come reluctantly from his box, dragging idly behind his attendant – he fooled no one this time'.

The start was complicated by Mat de Cocagne, a horse with an unruly reputation.

The starter and jockeys knew what to expect from Mat de Cocagne (ridden by C. Maire) at the gate, and they all gave him a wide berth. This one-time champion has a reputation for unpleasant aggressiveness at both ends. Another unnatural and much resented accomplishment is that he can go backwards at much the speed he can go forwards. When the horses went up for the first time, Mat de Cocagne was behind, and the starter in fairness to him had to surrender an otherwise perfect break to give him another chance. There was a few minutes' delay then while Mat de Cocagne was being persuaded to turn round. Suddenly he exercised one of his reverse dashes straight at the waiting group of horses. The field scattered as if a tiger had come among them – all except the reformed Zucchero, who was standing patiently with his trainer at his head. W. Payne junior sidestepped like a matador, but Zucchero received a full-blooded kick just below the shoulder. Like many another who has turned back to the path of virtue, there must have been a momentary doubt in Zucchero's mind whether the bad old outlook had not been the right one.

The race was won by Tulyar, ridden by Charlie Smirke (putting up two pounds overweight) after 'a copybook race'.

At the end of the season Queen Elizabeth II chose her Trustees for Ascot. The Duke of Norfolk remained the Senior Trustee 'charged by the private Act of Parliament of 1913 with managing the Ascot Crown properties, including the racecourse and everything pertaining to it'. Lord Tryon, Keeper of the Privy Purse, was appointed trustee, replacing Sir

Ulick Alexander, and Lord Lewes was appointed in place of the late Lord Hamilton of Dalzell.

The Queen had her first Royal Ascot winner when Choir Boy won the Royal Hunt Cup, the first horse ridden for her by Doug Smith, at the long odds of 100 to 6. But in the King George VI and Queen Elizabeth Stakes the Queen's Aureole was beaten three lengths by Pinza, repeating the Derby placings. The temperamental Aureole's chances had not been improved when he was kicked in the ribs as he left the paddock, after which he 'seemed disinterested'.

The year 1954 was packed with incident, some good, some not so good. The ground was very wet, and although the Royal Drive took place on the Tuesday, the carriages entered the course at the four-furlong post to avoid the uphill pull over the first two furlongs of the straight mile.

It is the custom of the Royal house-party to take part in an impromptu race on the course one morning during the royal meeting, generally Gold Cup morning. This year, as they galloped up the course, the Queen had to duck to avoid a telephone cable sagging between the stand and the notice-board on the inside of the course. It was so low that it had to be held up to allow some members of the party to pass under it.

A timing device was installed at the royal meeting, similar to (but much larger than) that used in London taxis. It consisted of a radio set and batteries weighing about seventy pounds, and was mounted on a small truck and connected to the starting gate, which automatically flashed a signal to the winning post as the gate went up, the impulse starting a clock linked to the photo finish camera. Like the photo finish camera, it was developed by the Race Finish Recording Company. The Queen won the Rous Memorial Stakes with Landau, and the Hardwicke Stakes with Aureole. 'Karali (J. Boullenger) crashed the tapes and fell, but accomplishing the same manoeuvre safely at the second try, led for eight furlongs. Aureole lay close up, Janitor far back. Aureole was four lengths up turning into the straight, but Janitor came with a devastating run and drew level fifty yards from the post. Aureole is nearly blind in the offside eye, caused when cast in his box, but Janitor was on his good side, he saw him, refused to be passed, lengthened his stride and just held on by a short head'.

The sensation of the meeting took place in the King Edward VII Stakes, in which the eighteen-years-old Lester Piggott was riding Never Say Die on which he had won the Derby. 'The King Edward VII Stakes caused the watching crowd to gasp. As the horses came round the turn into the straight Rashleigh (ridden by Sir Gordon Richards who had returned after injury) and Garter received bumps that nearly put them on the floor. Never Say Die with Lester Piggott up, had been pocketed on the inside of these two.' Lester Piggott was suspended for the rest of the meeting and later the stewards of the Jockey Club withdrew his licence, and decreed 'that before an application for renewal of licence would be entertained, he should attach himself to a licensed trainer other than his father for a period of at least six months'. Lester Piggott then worked as a stable lad for Jack Jarvis who wrote: 'The stewards of the Jockey Club thought it would do him good to be away from home for a bit, and his father asked me to take him. This I gladly did, and he "did his two" and rode out for me.' Mr Jarvis was pleased with the way the young jockey took his suspension, and was instrumental in getting his licence back before the end of the season.

Those so disturbed by the brilliant young tearaway could hardly have foreseen the elder statesman that Lester Piggott would become, nor perhaps the calm, industrious way in which he worked in stables. Lester Piggott has been an outstanding rider at Ascot, as elsewhere. His first Ascot win was in the Buckingham Palace Stakes on Tancred, trained by Ken Cundell, on September 21st, 1950. His first Royal Ascot win was on the 100 to 6 shot Malka's Boy, trained by Walter Nightingall in the Wokingham on June 20th, 1952. After the royal meeting of 1975 Lester Piggott had taken his score of Ascot winners past the 200 mark. He had ridden seventy-four at the Royal meeting, and a total of 200 Ascot winners besides the winners of eleven Ascot races which had been moved to Newbury, Newmarket or Kempton Park because of rebuilding or waterlogging.

He has ridden the winners of six Gold Cups (Zarathustra, Gladness, Pandofell, Twilight Alley, Fighting Charlie and Sagaro), five winners of the New Stakes (now the Norfolk Stakes), four winners apiece of the Hardwicke and King's Stand Stakes, and was the winner of the Royal Hunt Cup three times. His most successful race at Royal Ascot has been the six-furlong Cork and Orrery Stakes, which he has won seven times. His best Ascot race is the Princess Margaret Stakes for two-years-old fillies, run at the July meeting, which he has won on eight occasions. Students of form may be interested that he has done noticeably *less* well on the opening day of the meeting. His best Royal Ascots were in 1965 and 1975 when he rode eight winners apiece, and his best year at Ascot was 1966 when he had twenty-three winners.

In Ascot's prestige King George VI and Queen Elizabeth Stakes, he has won on three fillies and two colts—Meadow Court (1965), Aunt Edith (1966), Park Top (1969), Nijinsky (1970) and Dahlia (1974).

To return to 1954, the King George VI and Queen Elizabeth Stakes
15

was won by Aureole. Aureole was, to put it mildly, temperamental. He behaved appallingly on the Heath. But, after being treated by Dr Charles Brook, a neurologist, Aureole became somewhat more placid. Mr Bill Curling, in his biography of Sir Cecil Boyd-Rochfort recounted: 'Brook came down from London twice a week to Freemason Lodge. He would go into Aureole's box, and would put his left hand on Aureole's shoulder and his right on his girth, and resting his head on the colt's shoulder, would stand quietly alone with him for perhaps twenty minutes while Aureole continued to eat his hay, surprisingly making no fuss.'

Harry Carr had 'made' Aureole, but in the Cumberland Lodge Stakes in October 1953 he could not do the weight and Eph Smith won on him. The Queen's racing manager, Captain Moore thought he went best for Eph Smith, while Sir Cecil would have liked his stable jockey to continue to ride him. In the end Eph Smith got the rides, and Mr H. J. Joel, who had first retainer on him, released him to ride Aureole in all his races, and in work when possible.

Going to the start in the King George VI and Queen Elizabeth a man in the crowd suddenly put up his umbrella. 'Aureole stopped suddenly in his canter, ducked and precipitated his jockey to the ground. *But* Aureole did not gallop off, snatched a mouthful of grass, and allowed himself to be caught.' Aureole 'showed temper' at the start, and got off second last in a field of seventeen, left by six lengths. Eph Smith made ground rapidly on the leaders, as Aureole did not like to be left behind. At the turn into the straight Aureole began to storm up to Savoyard II, the leader. Roger Poincelet on Madame Suzy Volterra's Vamos challenged bravely, but Aureole again accelerated and held on by three-quarters of a length. Aureole finished in a storm of cheering. The Queen actually *ran* to the unsaddling enclosure to see her winner come in.

The racecourse at Ascot has been transformed in recent years. There have been four major developments. The course has been altered by re-making the round course, re-shaping the bends and re-grading the bottom of the course near Swinley Bottom and making an entire new straight course (carried out in 1954/55). Work on the Round Course was begun in 1947, and the improved round course was brought into use in 1955. The new grandstand, named the Queen Elizabeth II Stand was first used in 1961. The new Royal Enclosure stand was built for the meeting of 1964, and the new steeplechase and hurdle tracks were first used in 1965.

The effect has been to change Ascot from a four-days-a-year social and racing gathering to a Grade 1 racecourse with upwards of twenty days' racing a year, and with the course and its buildings also used for a multiplicity of other purposes. The twenty years following the end of World War II were the busiest and had the most far-reaching effect that Ascot has ever known.

The first stages of the four-prong plan involved the course. The ideas for improving the course originated as far back as 1895 with Lord Ribblesdale, then Master of the Buckhounds, who had perceived that the angle of the existing course in relation to the angle of the stands was wrong. As it was impossible to do much about changing the angle of the stands, even if they were rebuilt, because they backed onto the main road, in order to improve the viewing angle, it would be necessary to alter the angle of the straight course to the stands. Lord Ribblesdale drew up plans, but his term of office terminated and they were not put into effect.

In the 1930s Lord Hamilton of Dalzell independently prepared very similar plans, but the Second World War intervened. When the Duke of Norfolk succeeded Lord Hamilton (who remained a Trustee) as the King's Representative he brought forward the plan again, and it was approved by King George VI in 1946.

The main reasons for providing a new course were:

To provide more space in the Enclosures as viewing and circulating areas.

To provide a better view of the racing for the public by laying out the course to better advantage and by regrading the enclosure.

To improve racing by building a new straight mile and by forming new bends curved to an even radius and properly graded and super-elevated.

The first part of the new plan was carried out in 1947 by Sunleys Ltd, when the Old Mile was widened between the starting gate and the Swinley Bottom, which provided a better alignment of the course.

The reconstruction of the new straight mile was approved by the Queen and announced by the Duke of Norfolk after the 1954 Royal meeting, to start at the end of the season and be completed in time for the 1955 meeting. The land between Fireball Hill and Winkfield Road, which was required for the changes, was leased by the Ascot Authority from the Crown Commissioners for a period of ninety-nine years. The little wood near the Old Mile course, which was cut down to make the new straight course, had been known locally as 'Blackman's Wood' after a coloured man once found dead there; it had been a popular venue for three-card men and gamblers.

On the round course, which is roughly triangular, all three main bends, the Paddock bend, the Swinley Bottom bend and the Run-in bend, were reconstructed by George Wimpey and Co. The hillock in the centre of

the course, which had masked Swinley Bottom from the lawns in front
of the stand, was removed. The earth was used to raise the ground at the
Swinley Bottom turn, and to make the bend easier. As some distance was
lost on the turn into the straight, this was made up at the Swinley Bottom
turn so that the length of the races on the round course remains the same
as it was before the alterations.

The construction of the new straight course from Fireball Hill to the
Winning Post was a considerable undertaking. A little valley ran to the
east of Fireball Hill. It was decided to build an embankment over it, of
earth taken from high ground between Winkfield Road and Sunninghill
Lodge, to carry the new straight mile. Now that this has been completed,
the rise and fall on the New Mile course is sixty-nine feet, which is ten
feet less than the rise and fall on the Old Straight Mile course. The chance
was taken to form a new Coach Parking area on the north side of the New
Straight Mile, giving a parking area of more than ten acres. The new
alignment increased the angle between the course and the stands, and at
last the spectators in the boxes could see the horses on the Royal Hunt
Cup course before they had crossed the road.

Also for the first time, the Ascot Straight Mile was really a full mile in
length, in place of the former seven furlongs and 155 yards. The Jersey
Stakes, which had hitherto been run over the Hunt Cup course has
thereafter been run over seven furlongs on the New Straight course.

The change meant that the traditional Golden Gates, which were
erected in 1878/79 and which incorporate the Prince of Wales's arms no
longer formed the entrance to the Straight Mile for the Royal Procession.
Modern twin lodges, based on those at Eridge Park, the home of the
Marquess of Abergavenny, were built to flank plainer Golden Gates at
the head of the New Straight Mile, while the old lodges and the old gates
still remain in their accustomed position. From the stands today the Old
Straight Mile can be seen to the right of the present straight course and
helicopters can be seen landing on it at today's top meetings.

The change created far more room in front of the stands, where the
lawns had become intolerably crowded. The area of the Royal Enclosure
was nearly doubled from 3,165 square yards to 6,071 square yards, and the
area of lawns in front of the grandstand was similarly increased. The area
of the Silver Ring lawns was trebled. In all, 70,000 turves had to be laid on
the new lawns.

The reconstruction involved all sorts of minor work. A new access road
was constructed from Sunninghill Park to the Winkfield Road: the old
road was closed and turfed to avoid an extra tan crossing. The reservoir on
Ascot Heath was connected by pipeline and pump house with the lake at

Sunninghill Park, so that the water supply for the course became entirely independent of public water supplies. New and larger number boards, each sixty feet long were erected, as they were now much further from the stands; these are lowered into pits during racing, so that they do not interfere with viewing. A sunken path was made from the grandstand to the paddock area, which passes in front of, but at a lower level than the Royal Enclosure, to take some of the pressure off the tunnel under the Royal Enclosure at the back of the stands.

With the greater area of the Royal Enclosure, new regulations for its use were brought into effect before the 1955 royal meeting. Now there were two forms of Royal Enclosure. The main and enlarged enclosure was renamed the Royal Ascot Enclosure, and applications for admission had to be made, as before, to the Queen's Representative at St James's Palace. But the laws restricting the admission of divorced persons no longer applied.

A tiny, titular lawn was set aside in front of the Royal Stand, to which admission is by the Queen's invitation: to this the Court rules governing the admission of divorced persons still applies. 'It is a good moment to affect a compromise,' commented *The Times*.

Today entrance to the Royal Ascot Enclosure is by voucher, which is exchanged for a badge either at St James's Palace, where the Ascot Office has been situated since the beginning of the century, or on the racecourse. The granting of a voucher is at the discretion of the Queen's Representative who usually requires that new applicants should be sponsored by someone who has been granted vouchers during recent years, and whose name is therefore 'on the list'. Once a voucher has been granted a request for renewal in any year will usually be granted without further formalities, providing, of course, that space permits and that the request is not too late. The voucher may be exchanged for a badge admitting on all four days of the royal meeting, or it may be exchanged on a daily basis. There are junior vouchers for those under twenty-five. Those under seventeen years of age are not admitted to the Enclosure.

Exceptionally rainy weather delayed construction of the new course for three weeks in the autumn of 1954, and there was something of a rush to get it ready in time. The royal meeting was planned for June 14th–17th, 1955, but in the event, on account of a railway strike, it was postponed until July 12th–15th, 1955.

On Gold Cup day 1955, on the altered date of Thursday, July 14th, there was a devastating Ascot thunderstorm. Just after four o'clock, when the King George VI Stakes had just been won by Prince Barle ridden by Manny Mercer, a violent storm broke out. 'A vivid flash of lightning travelled the length of the straight opposite the Royal Box, appeared to contact the wire fencing surrounding the bookmakers' enclosures on the far side, and scores of people near the fencing were struck to the ground,' wrote *The Sporting Life*. 'It was a wicked flash of lightning, which struck into the closely packed crowd and scattered them like a pack of cards,' said Mr A. J. Harvey, a gateman close by. One young woman, Mrs Barbara Batt from Reading was killed on the spot, and Mr Leonard Tingle of Sheffield died in hospital next day. The injured, including an A.A. patrol man who was struck while patrolling the road outside the racecourse, were taken to King Edward VII Hospital in Windsor. The Duke of Norfolk at once informed the Queen, who was on an official tour abroad, and she sent a message of sympathy to the bereaved.

After an interval of an hour one more race (the Ribblesdale Stakes, won by Ark Royal ridden by Doug Smith), was run, but the rest of the card was postponed; the Bessborough Stakes to the Friday and the Rous Memorial Stakes to the Saturday.

Ascot suffered a heavy blow in the early months of 1956 when Sir John Crocker Bulteel had a heart attack at his home at Ascot and, although his condition was not at first thought to be serious, he died two days later on February 18th, 1956, at the age of sixty-five. Under his care the number of racedays at Ascot rose from four to twelve a year. He carried out the construction of the new course, and he was the first racecourse manager to permit television, which he believed would attract more people to racing. He was acknowledged as the outstanding racing administrator of the period. After his sudden death Major J. D. Watts, who was Clerk of the Course at Epsom, was appointed to officiate at all the 1956 Ascot meetings.

In the autumn of 1957, Major General David Dawnay was appointed Clerk of the Course. He told the writer that he first heard of the possible appointment when he was serving as Commander of the 56th Armoured Division on Salisbury Plain, when he was telephoned by Sir Anthony Head, then Home Secretary. He was interviewed by the Duke of Norfolk and later taken before the Queen—it was at Ascot on the day Ribot won the King George and Queen Elizabeth Stakes. 'I was attracted,' he said; 'It was obviously a job of exceptional interest, not only because of the horses, but because there was land and all sorts of buildings to look after, requiring all-round organisation. One met such interesting people of all sorts. Ascot is the Mecca of racing. At that time I was going to retire to Ireland, where I had a house waiting for me. It was a big decision.'

It was now time to renovate the antiquated stands. 'The Duke of Norfolk was the real, moving figure in the reconstruction', said General

David Dawnay. 'We decided to build the grandstand before the Royal Enclosure stand on the principle of democracy. The object was to accommodate as many people as possible under cover, bearing in mind the all-round view. That meant that the cantilever principle had to be adopted. At the same time a cantilever stand *lessens* the number under complete cover. The stands were built at the best viewing angle possible, relative to the new course. It is interesting that in the old days when the women wore big hats, and the angle was worse, we had no complaints at all about the angle – but when the angle was improved *then* the Press began to complain, when it was better than it had ever been before.'

The main plans for the new grandstand were announced by the Duke of Norfolk just after the royal meeting of 1959. The whole of the grandstand and the boxes were rebuilt between July 1960 and May 1961 at a cost of one million pounds. The new grandstand, called the Queen Elizabeth II Grandstand, is 560 feet long and 74 feet high, and contains 280 boxes, each with its private luncheon room. Plans had been finalised during the winter of 1959–1960 with the builders, the Wimpey Organisation. The Queen, accompanied by the Duke of Norfolk and Lord Tryon, spent an hour and a half inspecting the models and plans at the builders' headquarters in December 1959.

The September meeting was transferred to Newbury, the October meeting to Kempton Park.

Work on the site started immediately after the July meeting. First, the turf was stripped from two acres of the well-tended grandstand lawns – a heartbreaking sight for the bailiff and groundsmen! The course itself was protected by a bridge. With Ascot's usual luck with weather, the autumn and winter were the wettest on record. At the peak period of construction about 550 men were at work. There were a dozen cranes on the site, including three tower cranes, besides innumerable lorries and dump trucks. Off the site 1,300 tons of steel were prefabricated before construction was begun, there were 3,000 floor units, 1,600 pre-cast steps, stairs and panels, and 1,500 fluted concrete units for balcony fronts.

The new stand was shown to the Press on May 14th, 1961 and Mr Peter Bromley gave his impressions on BBC radio.

The Duke of Norfolk described the idea of the new Queen Elizabeth II Grandstand as an adventure – I would call it a brilliantly successful adventure. The boldness of the plan was staggering; immediately the July meeting was over, to remove the Old Stand and replace it with a modern concrete cantilever stand, 100 yards long, to hold 10,000, and have the whole thing finished in time to be used for this year's royal meeting. Well, the constructors,

Messrs George Wimpey, have done it, and in only forty-four weeks. Several times during the winter and spring I went down to the site, and it seems incredible that out of that sea of mud and concrete and to my eye chaos, has risen this modern, spacious and practical stand.

The old clock and chimes from the former grandstand are incorporated in a new tower 122 feet high, and topped with a weathervane of a horse in the royal colours. There are three tiers of 280 boxes, let at prices in 1961 from £300 to £400 p.a. (and in 1975 from £360 to £630 p.a.). On the steps there is room for 8,000 spectators, and higher up there are 1,000 numbered, tip-up seats which are let for the big meetings. The Grandstand with its underfloor heating, lifts and escalators was a revelation in comfort and convenience to the British racegoer.

A new Royal Enclosure stand followed four years later. In July 1963 the Duke of Norfolk announced the new stand would again be built by Wimpey, to plans by their Chief Architect Mr Eric V. Collins A.R.I.B.A. The new stand increased accommodation from 3,500 to 8,000. It cost one and a quarter million pounds, making a total of two and a quarter million pounds for the two stands. The contractors estimated in January 1975 that then it would cost at least three times the original price to erect. A number of smaller structures were absorbed into the new building. It had been intended to keep the viewing part of the Royal Box, but it was found this would interfere with the view of racing from the tiers on either side, so, with the Queen's permission, the Royal Box was entirely rebuilt. It is now four feet six inches higher from the ground than the old Royal Box, but in the same position relative to the winning post. The portico to the Royal Box was rebuilt almost to the same design, using the old materials where possible. At the bottom of the staircase in the old Royal Box there was a newel post with a wooden star inlaid into the cap: rumour had it that the Queen liked to touch the star 'for luck', and a similar star is built into the new staircase.

The Royal Household, previously accommodated in the Royal Box, were given separate viewing facilities, the Jockey Club stand disappeared as a separate entity and members are accommodated on the lower balcony. The Iron Stand disappeared as a separate building, but has a reserved part of the stand adjacent to the Tattersall's rails. Under the stand is a new, comfortable weighing room, complete with sauna for the jockey who is overweight. The Duke of Norfolk presented the two recumbent lions that guard the entrance to the weighing room.

Again, only careful preparation and vigorous efforts enabled the Ascot Enclosure Grandstand to be used at the royal meeting in 1964, which opened on Tuesday, June 16th, with a luncheon to celebrate the re-building. The racecourse looked well, the new buildings were generally approved, even the lawns were in remarkably good shape in spite of the wet spring and turmoil of building during which they looked, in the Duke of Norfolk's words 'like No Man's Land in 1918'.

But Ascot was not to reap its reward. The Tuesday and Wednesday cards were carried through with no particular difficulty, although the ground was described as 'dead'. Then on Wednesday evening the rain began to fall, increasing steadily until, at two-thirty on Cup afternoon, it was 'falling with a whistling jungle-note'. Racing was put back. The new stands were crowded with well-dressed, damp men and women. A vivid account of Ascot's plight was given by an American, the late Mr David Alexander in *The Thoroughbred Record*, the well-known American racing journal, of September 1964.

I have long suspected that the British are the last truly civilised people left on earth and this theory was proved beyond all reasonable doubt on Thursday, June 18th. . . . For the first time since the royal meeting was established the entire card of six races and the Ascot Gold Cup were abandoned because of weather conditions. Rain at Royal Ascot, especially on Gold Cup Day, can do more damage than rain at almost any place else on earth. The entire four days of royal week are a fashion parade for both ladies and gentlemen, but the ladies retain their maddest Ascot bonnets and their most expensive Paris gowns and the gentlemen wear their best brushed grey toppers on the afternoon the Gold Cup is decided.

Nothing can look quite so dishevelled as a chiffon gown and tulle bonnet or a tailcoat and grey topper when they are soaking wet, and even the gentry who frequent the Royal Enclosure and arrive by Rolls Royce got soaking wet between the parking lots and the stands when it rains at Royal Ascot . . .

My wife accompanied me, and for this reason I was in the reserved section of the Queen Elizabeth Stand instead of the Press Box. Elegantly attired ladies and gentlemen sat dripping steadily, like trees in a rain forest, all round us. No one complained at all. They were, in fact, cheery to the point of being chipper. At two o'clock it was announced that the Royal Procession had been cancelled. One lady said, 'All I really care about is the procession, but I'm glad they've cancelled it. The Queen is subject to colds'.

A few moments later it was announced that the first race would be post-poned fifteen minutes while the stewards inspected the course. A Land Rover drove out onto the course. Stewards emerged from it in lashing rain, and this afforded a sight indeed. There in front of us on the puddled greensward were the Duke of Norfolk, K.G., K.C.V.O., the Earl of Derby, M.C., the Earl of Halifax and Brigadier the Lord Tryon K.C.B., K.C.V.O., D.S.O., all tail-coated, boutonnièred and top-hatted and all stamping their feet like irritated roosters to test the turf . . . At seventeen minutes past three there was a curious announcement over the loudspeaker. 'The stewards are satisfied', it began, and there was an audible sigh of relief among the dripping customers, but then the announcement continued, 'after inspecting the course that racing is not possible today'. . . . A lady near me, her gown as wet as wash on a line, had focused her binoculars on the Royal Box. 'What a beastly shame', she said, 'the Queen does look so lovely today too'. A gentleman who had been shaking water from the brim of his topper for the last hour remarked, 'I say, I'm rather glad, you know! Let's all go to the bar. It's a splendid day for getting squiffed, isn't it?' Another gentleman of such mature years that one wondered how he managed to totter over the woodland path to the course said, 'Only thing to do, I suppose. Must think of the horses first, mustn't we?'

The biggest problem of all was getting out of Royal Ascot. The rain was pouring harder than ever now and there was no shelter. The thousands had to exit in single file, since each one was handed his emergency ticket by the gateman. It took me something over a half-hour to advance about ten yards up an alleyway. You then walk over an uncovered woodland path to the tiny Ascot race station. Here there were thousands waiting for the infrequent locals, which were the only trains available, since the race specials were not due for an hour or so. But I must say that the British Railways, which are by no means the best loved of England's institutions, rose to the occasion magnificently. They managed extra trains, and I even found the first-class-only limited that had taken me down. It was early for tea by British standards, but they served it in the buffet with jam and crumpets, and that historic restorative was enough to revive the spirits of even weaker souls like myself . . .

The monument to British patience and muddling through that was afforded by the press of humanity waiting to exit from the narrow gates was incredible to me. One lady apologised to a stranger after she had virtually removed his eyeball with the rib of her brolly. 'Not at all, Madam. No bother at all', the gentleman said, rubbing his inflamed eye. There was no shoving, no pushing, no anger, a great deal of joking. At Waterloo Station in London, the soaked chiffons and wilting toppers queued up in an endless line again for taxis, and no one tried to get ahead or to flag down a cab before his turn.

There must be something after all in this business of living in unheated dwellings all winter, eating food that is boiled to the consistency of pablum, using tea and hot water bottles as sovereign remedies for all diseases, and winning battles on the playing fields of Eton. Had the same thing happened at any race track in America, the stands would have been demolished completely by the rioting crowds and the entire Board of Stewards would have been hanged by their necks from the width pole. The British simply managed to enjoy the fiasco.

On the Friday racing had again to be cancelled. The Queen solved the problem of what to do with her large party of house-guests by taking them, in a procession of eight Rolls Royces and Daimlers, accompanied by the Duke of Edinburgh driving his green Lagonda and the Earl of Snowdon driving a green Mini, to Ascot where they lunched in the Royal Box and roamed round the buildings, including the weighing room, where they tried out each others' weight on the scales, and the Press Room, where the Duke of Edinburgh answered a casual telephone call.

All around them hundreds of workmen were mopping up after Thursday's floods. The damage to the newly-laid track was considerable. Mr Clive Graham reported, 'Little pot-holes suddenly appeared between the three and four furlong marks, the size of trees uprooted to make room for the New Straight Mile.' In some ways this was a new and undesirable development for Ascot. In previous storms there had been great damage, even death, but racing had been possible again after a very short time. *The Times* expressed a generally held view in a nutshell in its heading 'ACHILLES HEEL OF ASCOT: EXTENSIVE DRAINAGE NEEDED.' Like many others before and since, the Ascot authorities learnt the dangers of any interference, however well-intentioned, with natural drainage.

Immediately the Duke of Norfolk began to plan how the drainage of the course could be improved. He called on a Dutch firm to advise on the drainage difficulties, which were being increased by the current construction of a steeplechasing course, which greatly increased the area of track requiring drainage. Together with the Dutch drainage experts a comprehensive scheme was worked out, which involved laying twenty-three *miles* of drains (to which a further five miles were added later) at a depth of around thirty inches. This has proved the answer to the main problem, although the Ascot thunderstorm remains a threat. Statistically, the quantity of rain causing the abandonment was an impressive 0·65 inches of rain which fell during Wednesday/Thursday night, followed by 0·73 inches of rain, which fell on Ascot on Gold Cup day in the seven hours up to four p.m. The cancellation of the meeting was covered by insurance, and eventually the Ascot Authority was reimbursed to the extent of £45,000.

In the repercussions which followed the cancellation of the Thursday and Friday of Royal Ascot and the Saturday Heath meeting, a minor vandalism passed almost unnoticed. On Hunt Cup day the staff going on duty found Hull Rag week slogans daubed along the front of the Royal Box, at the Gold Cup start, on the paddock buildings, and on the grass at the winning post. The students had used yellow distemper, which fortunately washed off easily. A telegram of apology was sent from the Rag committee to the Queen.

Hand in hand with the new stands were plans for increased use of the track. Even with dolling out, twenty days' racing a year is about the maximum that one section of grass track will take. It was proposed to increase the use of Ascot by building a steeplechase and a hurdle course, so that racing could take place all year round, without further wear and tear to the flat racecourse. The first idea came from a Christmas card drawn by Sir John Bulteel's daughter, which fancifully showed horses jumping at Ascot. In December 1960 the Queen authorised an investigation to see if racing under National Hunt rules could be practicable at Ascot, and a definite plan to build a new jumping course was announced in October 1962. Work began in the following month, and racing started during the 1964/65 jumping season. The new tracks were built inside the existing flat course. The turf came from Hurst Park racecourse, which had recently succumbed to the pressure for building land. In all twenty acres of turf were moved from Hurst Park to Ascot. The turf was cut into foot-wide swathes at Hurst Park, rolled up like so many carpets and taken by lorry to Ascot, where they were re-laid on the same day. The work progressed at the rate of a furlong a day.

The work was under the constant supervision of Mr Hugh Mounsey, c.v.o., b.sc. (Agric.) bailiff at Ascot from 1935 to 1974, whose father had been farm manager to Lord Lonsdale at Lowther Castle. He told me, 'I have seen the course grow from a four-day meeting to twenty-two days' racing a year, and I have had to grow with it. When I came to Ascot, my work was mostly with sheep and cattle. It was all right to have sheep on the course when you were confined to four days a year; it did the course a lot of good, and you had to re-seed only after the sheep were taken off, as they made paths across the course. Sir Gordon Carter used to call the course "a turkey carpet", but it is in much better condition today — it has to be, it has to stand up to a lot more work. We used to water the course with fire hoses, now it is "pop-up" sprinklers, and it is cut by a seven-unit gang mower, which can complete the job in six hours.

'The racecourse now is made of imported soil. Work on making the new track began at Swinley Bottom when the dip was filled in and we took the top off a hill to extend the course in 1947. Routine work on the course consists chiefly in renovations after racing; making the ground good. We always put on a seed mixture after racing, mostly rye-grass — S 23 Rye Grass is as good a mixture as any for Ascot, I find. It germinates quickly and grows within a month. Seeding is done in July to December, and again in June and July.'

General Dawnay, a great hunting man and chasing enthusiast, concerned himself enthusiastically with the new steeplechase and hurdle courses, which were ready for inspection in April 1965. The steeplechase track is one mile five furlongs and twelve yards in circumference, and the hurdles course one mile five furlongs and one hundred and forty one yards. The flat course has a circuit of one mile six furlongs and thirty four yards. There are ten fences on the chase course, and it then incorporated the first water-jump with a safety sill below the water on the landing side. The water jump is now further modified, in accordance with the modern thinking led by Lord Oaksey, into a much safer shallow watersplash. Buff-coloured bars on the take off side of the fences, to give a better ground-line for the horses, were used at Ascot for the first time in southern England. The six hurdles are constructed with six bars in place of the more usual five bars. The rail dividing the tracks is made of a French plastic which is both safer and easier to maintain. A road was built inside the course, to carry doctors, ambulances, veterinary surgeons and horseboxes quickly to any incident: this is also used by a vehicle carrying a television camera to give a close-up view of the fences. All possible safety factors were introduced into the new course by the late Brigadier Tony Teacher, the Inspector of National Hunt courses, who was advised by a panel of jump jockeys. In winter, for jumping meetings, a special parade ring is opened in front of the Queen Elizabeth II Grandstand, the paddock parade ring is closed, and a temporary line of saddling boxes erected close by. The Silver Ring remains closed, and the Queen Elizabeth Grandstand is divided between Tattersalls' and Silver Ring patrons. Ascot's new era of racing opened with an annual programme of four days' jumping, seven days of mixed flat and jumping, and ten days of exclusively flat racing, a total of twenty-one days, later increased by two extra one-day fixtures.

Stewards who officiate at the small winter meetings are not all members of the Jockey Club although they must all be very experienced racing men. It is important in winter months that they live or stay close to the racecourse as a decision as to whether racing is possible on any day may have to be made in the early hours of the morning after an inspection of the course.

At the same time as these basic changes were taking place, many minor changes and improvements were accomplished. The work of maintaining, improving and polishing Ascot never ceases. The Heath enclosures, which are in the same position as the hallowed carriage enclosures of early Ascot, were opened in 1950, and provided with betting facilities, bars, tea tents and toilets at a cost of two shillings. The Silver Ring has been greatly improved. In 1954, to mark the Queen's Accession, a fine pair of wrought iron gates were erected at the back of the Royal Stand. They were made by Mr James Rathbone of Kingham in Oxfordshire, an outstanding master-smith, from designs based on the Duke of Norfolk's gates at Arundel Castle. New luncheon rooms in the Georgian style were built on either side of the gateway and opened in 1955. In 1956/57 substantial improvements were made in the paddock. A new hostel for 140 stablemen and stablegirls was built at the Windsor Forest Stud, and stabling increased there in 1957/58, and at the same time the Police Barracks were modernised and their offices centralised in the same building as the Magistrates Court. In 1955 a children's playground was opened, at the instigation of the Duke of Norfolk, who had noted the constant stream of announcements about lost children at another meeting, and on the advice of Sir Billy Butlin. Since 1970 racemeetings other than Royal Ascot are described simply as Ascot meetings. not as Ascot Heath meetings. The coach parks were moved much nearer to the course to cut down walking, and restaurants and bars were laid out with the modern tendency towards shorter and less formal meals in mind. It is planned to move the stables and hostel much nearer to the course. Ascot is constantly evolving. Apart from racing, the stands are used for a multiplicity of activities, including receptions, exhibitions, dances, and dog shows, while there is an indoor golf school in winter in the Silver Ring stand. The ground inside the racecourse is used for an eighteen-hole golf course, and a cricket pitch. The improvement of Ascot is a never-ending task.

In 1969 Major General Sir David Dawnay, K.C.V.O., C.B., who had served a further period after reaching retirement age, retired and was succeeded as Clerk of the Course and Secretary to the Ascot Authority by his assistant for the previous five years, Captain the Hon. Nicholas Beaumont, M.V.O., who works unsparingly to improve Ascot in every way. He has travelled widely to see the way in which racecourses are run in other parts of the world.

An era came to an end with the retirement in 1972 of the 16th Duke of Norfolk (who died in 1974), who had held office since 1945, and who, ably assisted by General Dawnay, had brought Ascot into the modern age, transforming a four-day meeting into a grade one racecourse, taking its full part in the racing world. *The Sporting Life*, in its tribute to the Duke, wrote: 'In spite of the large sums spent on improvements, the Duke maintained prize-money at a high level and with the former clerk of the course Sir John Crocker Bulteel saw the King George VI and Queen Elizabeth Stakes established as a major international race. When the Duke took over in 1946, prize-money at the royal meeting was £39,950. In

1972 the total was £157,500. Another interesting comparison is the 1946 total of prize-money for ten days' racing which was £71,450. In 1972 the twenty-three days' racing offered £422,250 prize-money.'

When the Duke retired, the Queen wished to name a race at Royal Ascot in his honour. It was decided to rename the historic New Stakes, first run in 1843, the Norfolk Stakes. It is run on Gold Cup day and retains the same conditions as in recent years, namely a five furlong race for two-years-old, with £4,000 added money. Before this could be arranged the Doncaster Race Company had to be approached and to agree to drop their Norfolk Stakes, run during the St Leger meeting. The northern race was renamed The Flying Childers Stakes, after the famous, unbeaten racehorse foaled in 1715. At what was to be the Duke of Norfolk's last royal meeting, he was delighted to win the Ascot Gold Cup with Ragstone.

The Ascot Authority has been blessed with a hard-working, efficient and devoted team. Administration has been in the vigorous and organised control of Mr Douglas Butt, M.V.O., late of the Scots Guards, since December 1945. Mr Tom Edwards has long been Clerk of Works, while Mr Gordon Hiscock took over from Mr Hugh Mounsey C.V.O., as Bailiff in 1974. The permanent staff at Ascot consists of around fifty persons under the control of the Clerk of the Course, who is also manager. The permanent labour force includes clerks, the tradesmen — carpenters, plumbers and painters in the Clerk of the Works Department, and a force of some thirty groundsmen, gardeners and maintenance workers.

At Royal Ascot around 650 men and women are added to the staff, quite apart from the armies of catering staff. Gatemen, car-park attendants, racecard sellers, lift attendants etc., they are styled as 'casual' employees but in fact most of them have done proud and regular duty at Ascot for many years. It is quite a sight to see the parade of well-brushed, sober-suited, bowler-hatted gatemen on the mornings before racing. There are eighty uniformed police on duty, as well as forty plain-clothes officers and a further hundred policemen on traffic duties.

The area of the racecourse is 150 acres, of which fifty acres form the track. There are four main stands and innumerable other buildings, including a nursery where plants and flowers are raised for the meeting. The horses are at present stabled at the Windsor Forest Stud a mile and a half from the course, which has room for 182 horses, and where the Ascot Horse Sales are also held. The stables were in the care of the late Harry Metcalfe from 1949 to 1975. The present stable manager is Mr Leonard Lightbrown.

On the social side, Miss Anne Ainscough M.V.O. and her staff of girls diligently look after the applications for vouchers to the Royal Ascot Enclosure from the quiet offices of the Ascot Office (formerly the Queen's Boudoir) in St James's Palace. There are regulations regarding dress laid down for the members of the Royal Ascot Enclosure each year. In 1968 lounge suits for men were permitted as an experiment, but few made use of the concession and the rule reverted to morning dress or uniform for men in the following year, with day dress with hats for ladies. In 1970 ladies were permitted to wear trouser suits. On the days of the royal meeting two offices are opened at Ascot, where an augmented staff of thirty-five issues badges in place of vouchers.

Side by side with the beautifully dressed members of the aristocracy, the diplomatic world and Society there have always been, right from the first Ascot of all in 1711, when Miss Forester attended Queen Anne in her man's riding garb, outbursts of ebullient eccentricity of dress, mostly in the grandstand and paddock areas, but also in the Royal Enclosure. The extroverts who don this extraordinary garb hold a kind of horrifying fascination even for the elderly gentlemen who tut-tut most loudly, and they play their part in the unique spectacle of Royal Ascot. In recent years the most egocentric and the most original has undoubtedly been Mrs Gertrude Shilling, with her amazing and often amusing confections. Many of her unbelievable hats are the result of ingenious inspiration and construction, such as her giant gold tea cup on Gold Cup day, her ballot box on the day after a General Election, her outsize jockey's cap—she arrived 'riding' on a hobby-horse. Less innocuous and more distasteful are the commercially inspired attempts to shock for the sake of publicity, which seem to increase from year to year. 'The perennial Ascot'— an enormous straw cartwheel, against which the women bent forward as though facing a gale—is not so prominent as it once was—but perhaps the Ascot hat to end all Ascot hats was one that never entered either the hallowed Enclosure nor the grandstand and paddock. It was worn by a baby elephant from Windsor Safari Park which paraded up and down the road outside the racecourse, bearing a monstrous *titfer* of paper flowers and fruit until sent on her way by a humourless constable.

Enormous sums are bet on the outcome of the races at Royal Ascot. Harry Carr told in his autobiography of the pressure the jockeys felt there, especially in the days before starting stalls: 'At no meeting in the season is the betting more fast and furious than at Ascot, and often one of my brother jockeys has said to me as we cantered together down to the start "I hope to God my fellow wins. The owner has £10,000 on him." Small wonder if nerves get frayed and there are a good many verbal slanging matches, as jockeys wheel and manoeuvre their mounts up to the gate to get into position for a quick break in a five-furlong race, for a couple of lengths lost can mean the loss of many thousands of pounds.'

The universally respected Mr Geoffrey Hamlyn, who became a *Sporting Life* price reporter in 1933, and was chief Starting Price reporter for *The Sporting Life* from 1957 until he retired in 1975, and who knows more than any other person about the betting scene during that period, has most kindly written for this book an account of betting at Royal Ascot in his experience:

Royal Ascot has always provided the heaviest betting week of the season, though more than once in recent years it has been rivalled by the National Hunt meeting at Cheltenham.

Even in these hard times the leading firms (some of whom have two pitches on the rails) have told me that their turnover has been well in excess of six figures for the four days. Although this does not compare with the five years or so after the war, when bookmakers of the calibre of the late William Hill were taking more than £20,000 a race, it is still very satisfactory.

I am often asked which were the biggest gamblers I have seen at my forty odd royal meetings. One or two stand out in bold relief. In 1947, there were two major gambles on the same race, the Queen Alexandra Stakes. Reynard Volant, trained by Jack Jarvis, was an odds-on chance, largely through the activities of the late Hughie Rowan, the heaviest professional backer at that time. Reynard Volant had won the Ascot Stakes three days previously, and also the previous year. But he had reckoned without the French horse, Monsieur L'Amiral, who had won the Cesarewitch the previous Autumn at 33–1. The layers could not have been very impressed by that performance, as he was introduced into the betting for the Alexandra Stakes at 100–8. I can remember clearly the furore that then ensued, though it is nearly thirty years ago. Monsieur L'Amiral was quickly laid at £1,000–£80 and £1,000–£100 innumerable times, and finally tumbled down to 7–2. It took a great deal of money to shift a horse at Royal Ascot nine points at that time. It must also be remembered that while this was going on, Rowan was laying thousands of pounds' worth of odds on Reynard Volant. The latter ran gamely, but was beaten a length by the French horse.

More recently, John Banks landed a nice little coup in the Hunt Cup of 1969 with Kamundu. Banks managed to strike a few bets of £1,000–£80 about his seven-years-old and continued to back the horse at all rates down to 7–1.

In 1973, Leslie Spencer, William Hill's representative on the rails, laid a client £1,000–£80 twenty times each way, Penny Halfpenny in the Chesham Stakes. The bookmaker was rescued by a 33–1 chance, Live Arrow, but the other one finished second, and netted his backer more than £4,000 for the place money.

It is always true to say that the worse the economic plight of the country, the heavier is the gambling. It was so just after the war, and it is so again today.

In 1965 the Lester Piggott magic caused havoc with the layers' books. Ladbrokes, who do enormous business at Royal Ascot, recall, in *The Ladbroke Story* by Richard Kaye, the trouble the firm had with accumulators—generally considered 'a mug's bet' at Royal Ascot.

On Wednesday Lester Piggott won the Royal Hunt Cup on Casabianca at the handy price of 100 to 9. On Thursday, Gold Cup day, mixed doubles, trebles and accumulators on Piggott's five mounts were the order of the day. The champion's first mount was in the second race, and, justifiably made favourite, won at 7–4 on.

His next mount was Fighting Charlie in the Ascot Gold Cup. Fighting Charlie at this time would hardly be rated up to Classic standard. A month before he had been beaten by Grey of Falloden, admittedly a top class staying handicapper, but not a Classic type, who gave him 7 lb. and 1½ lengths' beating. However, Fighting Charlie won the Gold Cup, holding off the French challenge of Waldmeister, ridden by the French champion jockey Yves St Martin, thereby giving great delight to the patriots but casting a slight chill on the bookmaking fraternity, as his Starting Price was 6–1 against ... Lester Piggott rode the last two winners, Swift Harmony in the Chesham Stakes, and Brave Knight in the King George V Stakes ... both of the winners starting at 6–1 against. Mixed doubles and trebles on his mounts showed a handsome profit.

In the race after the Gold Cup, the King Edward VII Stakes, he [Piggott] had ridden Bally Russe, which started at 9–2 against. Bally Russe was leading with a furlong and a half to go, when Convamore, ridden by Joe Mercer, took up the running and held on under pressure to win by a neck. Afterwards there was a Stewards' Enquiry as it appeared that Convamore had interfered with Bally Russe, but the result was allowed to stand.

Had Bally Russe won, by the time of the last race there would have been utter confusion in the ring, as the sums of covering money sent down from the Starting Price offices would have been colossal. As it was, bookmakers could hardly look on the day with any remote feeling of satisfaction, to say the least.

If Bally Russe had won, or had been allowed to take the race after the Enquiry, the pay-out on the day by Ladbrokes would have been in the region of a million pounds. This does not necessarily mean that we would have lost £1,000,000—but the blow would have been bad enough to have hurt.

As it was, the estimate was that Piggott cost Ladbrokes round about £350,000 during that Ascot of 1965, even though he rode four losers on the Friday, after winning the first race at 4–1 against.

The royal meeting at Ascot presents a considerable challenge to the Horserace Totalisator Board. The staff for the meeting are brought in from as far away as Scotland. During the 1970s at each meeting there have been around 600 windows manned—632 in 1972—and the staff employed has been over 1,000, although economies have recently been effected, and the staff was reduced to 864 Tote employees in 1974.

The Tote's biggest Royal Ascot meeting was in 1966, when the total turnover for the five days, including the Heath meeting on Saturday, June 18th, was £1,907,157 3s. This was the meeting at which the Jackpot was inaugurated, and the Tote's biggest single day at Ascot was on Cup day of that year, when the takings for the day totalled £476,233 11s.

Catering at Ascot, particularly at Royal Ascot, is an enormous and complex operation. Everyone wants only the best. It is divided between two firms, Ring & Brymer (Birch's) Ltd in the Royal Ascot Enclosure, and Letheby and Christopher, who cater for the restaurants in the grandstand area, the Silver Ring and last but certainly not least, in the 280 boxes. A normal Ascot week order for Letheby and Christopher includes 6,000 lbs of best Scotch smoked salmon, 10,000 gulls eggs, 2,400 lobsters, 7,500 lbs of finest strawberries, 500 gallons of double cream, 10,000 bottles of vintage champagne and 10,000 specially tubed cigars. Around 2,000 catering staff are employed.

In the Royal Ascot enclosure and paddock alone, the domains of Ring & Brymer (Birch's) Ltd, there are three large luncheon and tea rooms, thirteen bars, seven snack bars and tea and coffee lounges, a Pimm's bar, the Jockey Club Rooms, the Queen's Representative's Rooms, the Officials' Room, the Press Room, the Owners' Bar and the last of the private luncheon tents, White's, which is erected at the far end of the paddock. The supplies for the Royal Ascot enclosure and paddock include 100 turkeys, 600 apiece of chickens and ducks, a further 2,000 lbs of Scotch salmon, 1,000 lbs of lobsters and 2,500 lbs of strawberries.

The innovations continue, at a faster rate than ever before at Ascot, but introduced so carefully that the atmosphere is virtually unchanged. When Hurst Park racecourse closed down, it was not only the Turf that moved to Ascot: the important Victoria Cup, a handicap for four-years-old and upwards over seven furlongs, was transferred to Ascot, where it is run in April. Its first 'Ascot' running was actually at Newbury, where that meeting was held in 1964 while rebuilding went on at Ascot, so the same important race was run on three different racecourses in three successive years. It is now sponsored as the Top Rank Club Victoria Cup. At the same time, most appropriately, the Crocker Bulteel Stakes were trans-ferred from Hurst Park to Ascot, and the Pall Mall, the White Rose, the

Great Harry and the Paradise Stakes, also moved from the defunct racecourse to Ascot.

Miss Crocker Bulteel's Christmas card fantasy became reality when the steeplechase course was opened on Friday, April 30th, 1965. The first race was the Inaugural Hurdle, won by the favourite Sir Giles, trained by Fulke Walwyn and ridden by Willie Robinson. The first chase, the Kennel Gate steeplechase, was won by Another Scot, ridden by Tim Norman, who, in spite of hitting the last fence, overtook Grand Admiral, ridden by amateur Brough Scott on the flat. No horse fell, although one unseated his rider. 'Good fences—and the course takes some getting', commented Tim Norman after the race.

The first sponsored race at Ascot was the Kirk and Kirk Handicap Steeplechase, run on November 19th, 1965, and won by Rupununi, owned by Mrs P. Dunne Cullinan, trained by Arthur Thomas at Warwick, and ridden by H. Beasley. The following day saw a complete day's sport sponsored by Black & White Whisky, when race names commemorated such famous racehorses connected with the late chairman Lord Woolavington and his daughter Lady Macdonald Buchanan as Hurry On and Coronach. The principal event, the Black & White Gold Cup for novice chasers was won by Flyingbolt, stable companion of Arkle.

Although no race at Royal Ascot is permitted to be sponsored, at other meetings, the prestige of Ascot has attracted many excellent sponsors, who have raised the value of the prizes and attracted the great horses to meet in competition. The legendary Arkle won his last race at Ascot in the second running of the S.G.B. chase in Ascot's first-ever December meeting in 1965: he was injured in the King George VI steeplechase at Kempton Park later in the same month. The Whitbread Trial chase, run in February, and the Heinz chase for novice horses run over two and a half miles in April, are other important jumping races already established at Ascot.

The first sponsored race on the flat was Ascot's first charity day, run on September 29th, 1967 in aid of St John Ambulance who, together with the British Red Cross, do such sterling work on the racecourse. Each race was handsomely sponsored with between £2,000 and £10,000 added to the stakes. Since then one day's racing each September has been set aside for a charity racemeeting, and among the charities which have benefited have been Cancer Research and the British Heart Foundation. Unfortunately the Stable Lads Welfare Fund which should have benefited in 1974 was out of luck with the weather, which caused the first-ever cancellation of a September meeting at Ascot.

Sponsorship of the King George VI and Queen Elizabeth Stakes was approved by the Queen in 1972, and in the following year the race was boosted into the first £100,000 race under Jockey Club rules when the internationally famous diamond company De Beers Consolidated Mines Ltd, increased its contribution from £20,000 to £44,000, while the Horserace Betting Levy Board added £27,000 and the Ascot Authority £29,000 to the stakes. In 1975 the title of the race was changed to the King George VI and Queen Elizabeth Diamond Stakes, while the important day's racing continues to be known as Diamond Day.

It was on Diamond day in 1973 that Ascot saw its first official ladies' race—although there have been many informal races by the Queen's house-party, including the Queen, Princess Margaret, Princess Anne and Princess Alexandra. The Jockey Club had decided to permit a dozen ladies' races under rules in 1972. This was increased to twenty ladies' races in 1973, when the Cullinan Diamond Stakes, sponsored like the big race by De Beers, attracted a field of twenty-nine runners, and was won by Miss Caroline Blackwell, riding her father's Hurdy-Gurdy trained by Bruce Hobbs: it was her first race.

The stage is set by forethought, but what happens each year, at each meeting and in each race is unpredictable up to the fall of the flag. Un-doubtedly, however, the King George VI and Queen Elizabeth Stakes at the July meeting, which brings together top mile and a half horses of different ages is always a race of outstanding interest.

The title of Racehorse of the Year, awarded by the Racecourse Association on the votes of leading racing journalists, has gone to the winner of the King George VI and Queen Elizabeth Stakes in seven of its first ten awards. The great Ribot, in the course of his unconquered run of sixteen races, won the King George VI and Queen Elizabeth Stakes in 1956. In the following year, Crepello, winner of the Two Thousand Guineas and the Derby, seemed to have the race at his mercy, but a torrential downpour changed the going, and he was withdrawn, and the French filled the first four places.

In its comparatively short life the race has been won by three outstanding fillies—Aunt Edith, owned by Lt-Col J. Hornung, trained by Noel Murless and ridden by Lester Piggott in 1966, Park Top, owned by a jubilant Duke of Devonshire, trained by Bernard van Cutsem and ridden by Lester Piggott in 1969, and twice by the brilliant filly Dahlia, owned by Mr Nelson Bunker Hunt, and ridden as a three-years-old by Bill Pyers in 1973, and by the ubiquitous Lester Piggott in 1974. A lovely filly which just failed to attain the same objective was the sweet-moving Petite Etoile which, again ridden by Lester Piggott, failed by half a length to overtake

Aggressor. In the following year Petite Etoile won the Rous Memorial Stakes at Royal Ascot.

Gladness, trained by the great Vincent O'Brien was in 1958 the first mare since Quashed in 1936 to win the Ascot Gold Cup, and is still (including 1975) the most recent of her sex to triumph in this two and a half mile test of stamina. The first filly to win the Gold Cup had been Janette, by King Bladud out of Drug, owned by Mr Fulwar Craven, in 1811, and then only on the disqualification of Smallbones. The famous Beeswing won the Gold Cup in 1842. In all a dozen mares have won the Gold Cup.

A trainer with a great record at Ascot is Noel Murless. He won the King George VI and Queen Elizabeth Stakes in three successive years from 1966 to 1968, with Aunt Edith, Busted and Royal Palace respectively. In all, from Noel Murless's first Ascot winner in 1947 until 1975 inclusive he has trained the winners of 117 races at Ascot, plus five Ascot races run elsewhere. Of these, fifty-five wins have been at Royal Ascot, where he has won every race except the Queen Mary Stakes, the Ascot Stakes and the Queen Alexandra Stakes. He has won the King Edward VII Stakes and the Hardwicke Stakes six times apiece, and when the Rous Memorial Stakes was run at the royal meeting, he won it no fewer than eight times. He has also won the Royal Lodge Stakes, run in the autumn, seven times at Ascot and once, when Ascot was closed, at Newbury.

Another trainer who had an excellent record at Royal Ascot was Sir Cecil Boyd-Rochfort, who won forty-five Royal Ascot races, including the Ascot Gold Cup on three occasions with Precipitation, Flares and Zarathustra, and he also won the King George VI and Queen Elizabeth Stakes twice, with Aureole and Alcide.

Vincent O'Brien, the brilliant Irish trainer of Derby, Grand National, Cheltenham Gold Cup and Champion Hurdle winners, added to his laurels at Royal Ascot in 1975 when he achieved the remarkable training feat of winning six races from seven runners at the royal meeting, together with a further winner, his only other runner, at the Saturday Ascot meeting.

There was a tragic accident at Ascot on September 26th, 1959 which resulted in the death of Emmanuel ('Manny') Mercer, who was among the leading riders of his day, and had ridden 125 winners in the previous season. He was riding a filly Priddy Fair to the start when the filly slipped and fell in front of the stands. It seemed a simple enough fall, but as the filly struggled to her feet she kicked him on the head, and he sustained terrible injuries from which he died at once. His brother Joe had just ridden a double. The last race was abandoned, 'hats came off and with many expressions of deep regret and sympathy, the people quietly dispersed'. Priddy Fair never raced again, her owner Sir Foster Robinson sent her at once to stud.

In June 1972 Joe Mercer rode at Ascot although still shaken after a flying accident on the previous Sunday when the light aircraft in which he and four others were flying to a race in Belgium, shortly after taking off from Newbury racecourse, stalled, crashed on high tension wires and burst into flames. It was only the courage and instantaneous action of Joe Mercer who dragged his three fellow-passengers clear, that saved their lives. The pilot was killed. At Ascot the Queen and the Duke of Edinburgh crossed the paddock before Joe Mercer mounted Brigadier Gerard to ask him how he was. After Joe won the Prince of Wales Stakes a doctor had to be called as he collapsed temporarily with exhaustion and strain. In July he again partnered Brigadier Gerard in the King George VI and Queen Elizabeth Stakes. That was a golden era in British racing, when chance threw up two of the best horses to have raced in Britain this century (or ever), Mill Reef and Brigadier Gerard – and that following the vintage years of Sir Ivor and Nijinsky. Whether Mill Reef or Brigadier Gerard was the better horse will be argued for many years: each horse had his supporters as fervent as the Liverpool 'Kop'. Each in his turn won the King George VI and Queen Elizabeth Stakes. Everyone who puts pen to paper in the racing world has described those victories, none more authoritatively than the accounts in *Racehorses of 1971* and *Racehorses of 1972*, from which these passages are taken:

Mill Reef faced an Irish Derby winner in Irish Ball; an Italian Derby winner in Ortis; a Derby third in Stintino; a St Leger third in Politico and an Irish Derby third in Guillemot. Of the remainder two were pacemakers, Bright Beam and Loud; Acclimatization had finished a good fourth to Ramsin in the Grand Prix de Saint-Cloud, and Nor had finished fourth to Nijinsky in the Irish Sweeps Derby. Mill Reef, though overshadowed by some of his larger rivals in the paddock, slaughtered the opposition. As in the Derby the writing was on the wall a long way from home for Mill Reef's adversaries; Mill Reef was still on the bridle in third place to Ortis and Politico coming into the straight and he moved to the front so smoothly when shaken up two furlongs out that the race was obviously his, barring accidents. He showed clear of his field a furlong out, drew further and further ahead, and beat Ortis by six lengths. At the line he was still galloping on strongly and resolutely, giving absolutely no impression of weakening or losing his action. Those who had held that Mill Reef barely stayed the mile and a half at Epsom, and won the Derby simply because he was so much superior to his opponents, were made to look very silly at Ascot.

Next year, with the added sparkle of the diamond money, it was the turn of Brigadier Gerard. The tragic accident to Mill Reef (although after breaking his near foreleg he was successfully saved for stud), prevented the horses meeting as four-years-old. Brigadier Gerard continued with a triumphant four-years-old career. He won the Prince of Wales Stakes at Royal Ascot and returned for the King George VI and Queen Elizabeth Stakes, which was over a mile and a half, a testing quarter of a mile further than he had run before. According to *Racehorses of 1972*:

'Ride him on the assumption that he stays', was the instruction given to Joe Mercer before the King George VI and Queen Elizabeth Stakes. The field was a strong one. Five of the nine runners had won Classics. As well as Brigadier Gerard, there was Riverman, winner of the French Two Thousand Guineas, Steel Pulse, winner of the Irish Sweeps Derby, Gay Lussac, winner of the Italian Derby and unbeaten in seven races, and Parnell, winner of the Irish St Leger and already established as one of the two best extreme-distance horses in Europe. At the finish the Classic winners filled the first five places. ... on the final turn Brigadier Gerard was in second place, about two lengths behind Parnell ... Once into the short straight the race resolved itself into a battle between Brigadier Gerard and Parnell. Brigadier Gerard took a little time to work up to his top pace but two furlongs out he drew alongside Parnell on that horse's outside. Brigadier Gerard immediately started hanging to the right and Mercer had to crack him with the whip to pull him off Parnell. Balanced again, Brigadier Gerard shot past Parnell but almost immediately, with barely a length between the two, Brigadier Gerard appeared to veer sharply across towards the rails. Parnell's jockey stood up in his stirrups and switched his mount to challenge on Brigadier Gerard's outside. With Parnell losing momentum, Brigadier Gerard was able to establish a two-length advantage with a couple of hundred yards to run. The margin at the line was a length and a half, a gap that was shrinking visibly in the last thirty yards.

The stewards held an enquiry into whether Brigadier Gerard had taken Parnell's ground. It was thirteen minutes before the announcement was made that the placings would remain unaltered.

In the 1975 King George VI and Queen Elizabeth Diamond Stakes Grundy, winner of that year's Epsom Derby and Irish Sweeps Derby, met Bustino, winner of the 1974 St Leger in what many have described as the greatest horserace they have ever seen. 'In a perfect setting—Ascot on a flawless summer day, a race that caught us by the throat ... leaving all who saw it full of wonder, gratitude and pride,' wrote John Oaksey in *Horse and Hound*.

When the pacemakers fell away and the horses came to the home turn

Bustino, ridden by Joe Mercer, had drawn three lengths clear of Grundy ridden by Pat Eddery. The rest, including Dahlia, winner of the race in the two previous years, and Star Appeal, soon to win the Arc de Triomphe, were outpaced.

> Once straightened out for home Patrick Eddery drew his whip . . . Bustino's stride had never wavered but in less than a furlong the lead was swallowed up. To poor Joe Mercer Grundy's blond mane and white-slashed face must have been the least welcome sight in the world, and needless to say it never broke the rhythmic thrust and drive on which his supremely stylish finish is based . . . As he called for a counter-punch and got it, the two horses battled together head to head . . . it was poor Bustino who finally reached the bottom of even his reserves. Tongue out, dog tired he staggered briefly towards his rival — and then, as Joe Mercer straightened him, ground on indomitably.

Grundy won by half a length: the course record was smashed by an unbelievable 2·46 seconds.

Possibly the unluckiest horse ever to race at Royal Ascot was Rock Roi, first home in the Ascot Gold Cup of 1971 and 1972, and disqualified on both occasions. He was a thoroughly genuine stayer and won (and kept) the Goodwood and Doncaster Cups. Another truly unlucky race was the opener for the 1974 Royal Ascot, when the first three horses past the post in the Queen Anne Stakes, Confusion, Gloss and Royal Prerogative, who finished in that order, were *all* disqualified and the horses that finished fourth, fifth, sixth and seventh ended up in the frame.

But the happy memories of Ascot far outweigh those of trauma and dispute. Each succeeding generation on the Ascot turf has his or her memories . . . the author's include the pale faces of small apprentices riding out for the last race on the card . . . the Duke of Norfolk in tweeds and a cap, driving out in a red *moke* to see that all is well on his course on the morning of a royal meeting . . . the bank of colourful hats round the winners' enclosure as the pageantry of the Royal Drive passes before them . . . eminent trainers milling round the crowded parade-ring for just a glimpse of a Nijinsky or a Dahlia . . . the sound of the bell ringing as the horses turn into the straight . . . and the man with the broom sweeping the last leaf from the immaculate grass.

Here at Ascot, one feels linked with history and with one's forebears, not on a battlefield where terror and death have reigned, but in a pleasant place where men and women have cheered and won, and lost and cursed, met their friends and admired fine horses ever since Queen Anne created Ascot Racecourse away back in 1711.

Royal Ascot Races

The form of the Royal Ascot meeting, the races and even the order of the races has remained remarkably stable. The pattern has been forming since the early nineteenth century, although some races long famous at the royal meeting, such as the Rous Memorial Stakes (run on the July Saturday), and the Fernhill Stakes (Saturday of Royal Ascot week), have been moved to other meetings. The Royal Ascot races are at present:

Tuesday

1. QUEEN ANNE STAKES (Group 3) for three-years-old and upwards over ONE MILE. Royal Hunt Cup (straight) course. £5,000 added in 1975.

Named after the founder of Ascot. First run in 1930 (replacing the Trial Stakes), over the then Royal Hunt Cup course of 7 furlongs 155 yds and was worth £1,260 to the winner.

Winners include Fair Trial (1935), Royal Charger (1946), Neron (1951), Blast (1960), Nereus (1962), Welsh Rake (1963), Showdown (1965), Virginia Gentleman (1968), Town Crier (1969), Welsh Pageant (1970), Roi Soleil (1971), Sun Prince (1973), Imperial March (USA) (1975).

2. PRINCE OF WALES STAKES (Group 2) for three-years-old and upwards ONE MILE AND A QUARTER. £10,000 added in 1975.

There was a Prince of Wales Plate run in three two-mile heats for four-years-old (named after the Prince Regent) as early as 1789. The direct predecessor to the present race (named after the Prince of Wales later Edward VII) was first run over 13 furlongs over a 'new' course in 1862, and was a twenty sovereign sweep with £500 added. There were penalties for winners of the Derby, Oaks and 2000 Guineas.

Winners include Vauban (1867), The Earl (1868), Silvio (1877), Iroquois (1881), Galtee More (1897), Jeddah (1898), Bayardo (1909), Sansovino (1924), Hyperion (1933), Royal Palace (1968), Connaught (1969 and 1970), Brigadier Gerard (1972), Record Run (1975).

3. ASCOT STAKES (Handicap, rated 50+) for three-years-old and upwards TWO MILES AND A HALF (to start at the Cup post and go once round) £4,000 added in 1975.

First run in 1839 over the same distance, £100 more added to the stakes if five horses were declared.

Winners include Vatican (1851), Brown Jack (1928), Zarathustra (1956), Trelawny (1962 and 1963), Shira (1967), Crash Course (1975).

4. COVENTRY STAKES (Group 2) for two-years-old. SIX FURLONGS (straight), £5,000 added in 1975.

Named after the 9th Earl of Coventry, Master of the Buckhounds 1886–1892 and 1895–1900. First run in 1890 as a race for two-years-old, colts and fillies over the Two-Years-Old Course, £1,000 added.

Winners include Persimmon (1895), Goletta (1896), Rock Sand (1902), St Amant (1903), The Tetrarch (1913), Tudor Minstrel (1946), Palestine (1949), King's Bench (1951), Whistler (1952), Typhoon (1960), Crocket (1962), Showdown (1963), Silly Season (1964), Bold Lad (Ireland) (1966), Murrayfield (1968), Prince Tenderfoot (1969), Mill Reef (1970), Galway Bay (1975).

5. RIBBLESDALE STAKES, (Group 2), for three-years-old fillies ONE MILE AND A HALF, Swinley course, with £10,000 added in 1975.

Named after the 4th Baron Ribblesdale, Master of the Buckhounds 1892–1895, £10,000 added in 1975.

First run in 1919 for three- and four-years-old over the Old Mile.

Winners include Rose en Soleil (1932), Almeria (1957), Cantelo (1959), Windmill Girl (1964), Bracey Bridge (1965), Park Top (1967), Sleeping Partner (1969), Galina (USA) (1975).

6. ST JAMES'S PALACE STAKES (Group 2), three-years-old entire colts and fillies, ONE MILE, over the Round course, £10,000 added.

First run in 1834 for three-years-old over the New Mile, as a 100 sovereigns sweep, with a 7 lb penalty for a Derby and a 5 lb penalty for an Oaks winner. Has produced more distinguished winners than any other Ascot race except the Gold Cup.

Winners include The Earl (1868), Bend Or (1880), Iroquois (1881), Ormonde (1886), Common (1891), Florizel II (1894), Sceptre (1902), Rock Sand (1903), Slieve Gallion (1907), Minoru (1909), Tracery (1912), Captain Cuttle (1922), Coronach (1926), Mr Jinks (1929), Cameronian (1931), Bahram (1935), Tudor Minstrel (1947), Black Tarquin (1948), Palestine (1950), King's Bench (1952), Nearula (1953), Tamerlane (1955), Pirate King (1956), Major Portion (1958), Above Suspicion (1959), Roan Rocket (1964), Silly Season (1965), Track Spare (1966), Reform (1967), Petingo (1968), Right Tack (1969), Brigadier Gerard (1971), Sun Prince (1972), Thatch (1973), Bolkonski (1975).

Wednesday

1. JERSEY STAKES (Group 3), for three-years-old which, at starting, have not won a Group 1 or Group 2 race. SEVEN FURLONGS. £4,000 added in 1975.

Named after the 4th Earl of Jersey, Master of the Buckhounds 1782–1783. First run in 1919, replacing the second (three-years-old) part of the Triennial Stakes. (The first part of the Triennial became the Chesham Stakes, and the third part the Churchill Stakes). In 1919 it was run over the then Royal Hunt Cup course of 7 furlongs 166 yards and was a £10 sweep, with £500 added for the owner, and £100 for the nominator.

Winners include Limelight (1932), Quorum (1957), The Creditor (1963), Casabianca (1965), St Chad (1967), Gay Fandango (1975).

2. QUEEN MARY STAKES (Group 2), two-years-old fillies FIVE FURLONGS. £5,000 added in 1975.

Named after the Consort of King George V, first run in 1921 with similar conditions and worth £2,680 to the winner.

Winners include Mumtaz Mahal (1923), Book Law (1926), Snowberry (1939), Bride Elect (1954), Abelia (1957), Farfalla (1969), Cawston's Pride (1970).

3. ROYAL HUNT CUP (Handicap) for three-years-old and upwards rated 55+. ONE MILE Royal Hunt Cup (straight) course. £8,000 added in 1975.

Named after the Royal Buckhounds, whose Master was in charge of Ascot racecourse from 1711 until the Accession of Edward VII, when the Buckhounds were abolished, the Royal Hunt Cup was an instant success, and has always been a big betting medium. First run in 1843, it has always been a handicap for three-years-old and upwards run over one mile, but was originally run over the Old Mile, with 200 sovereigns added to the stakes.

Winners include Conyngham (1848), Peter (1881), Knight of the Thistle (1897), The MacNab (1930), Choir Boy (1953), King's Troop (1961), Spaniard's Close (1963), Continuation (1966), Kamundu (1969), Ardoon (1975).

4. CORONATION STAKES (Group 2) for three-years-old fillies only. OLD MILE (round course), £10,000 added in 1975.

Named in honour of the Coronation of Queen Victoria, and first run in 1840, for three-years-old fillies over the New Mile, a sweep with 100 sovereigns subscription.

Winners include Marie Stuart (1873), Goletta (1897), Book Law (1927), Udaipur (1932), Belle of All (1951), Festoon (1954), Meld (1955), Aiming High (1961), Fleet (1967), Lucyrowe (1969), Humble Duty (1970), Magic Flute (1971), Jacinth (1973), Roussalka (1975).

5. THE QUEEN'S VASE (Group 3) for three-years-old and upwards TWO MILES. £5,000 added in 1975.

Named after Queen Victoria and first run in 1838, it was a gold vase added
to a 20 sovereign sweep for three-years-old, run over two miles. (In 1839 the
vase was silver but reverted to gold in 1840.) The race was named the King's
Vase in 1903, and returned to the Queen's Vase on the succession of Queen
Elizabeth II.

Winners include Alice Hawthorn (1844), The Hero (1847), Hermit (1854),
Fisherman (1856), Tim Whiffler (1862), Formosa (1870), Marie Stuart (1875),
Verneuil (1878), Isonomy (1879), St Gatien (1884), Florizel II (1895), The
White Knight (1906), Bally Russe (1966), Yellow River (1970), Parnell (1971).

6. BESSBOROUGH STAKES (Handicap) for three-years-old and upwards, rated
50+ ONE MILE AND A HALF. Swinley Course. £4,000 added in 1975.

Named after the 5th Earl of Bessborough, the Master of the Buckhounds
1848–1852, 1853–1858 and 1859–1866. The race was first run in 1914 on the
Tuesday as a five furlong race for two-years-old with £500 added.

Winners include Prince Hansel (1965), Fool's Mate (1975).

Thursday (Cup Day—Ladies' Day)

1. CORK AND ORRERY STAKES (Group 3) for three-years-old and upwards
SIX FURLONGS. £5,000 added in 1975.

Named after the 9th Earl of Cork and Orrery, Master of the Buckhounds
1866, 1868–1874, and 1880–1885. First run over the same distance in 1926,
when it replaced the former All-Aged Plate, and was worth £1,205 to the
winner.

Winners include Royal Minstrel (1929), Honeyway (1946), Matador (1957),
Right Boy (1958 and 1959), Compensation (1962), Majority Blue (1965),
Current Coin (1966), Mountain Call (1968), Tudor Music (1969), Welsh
Saint (1970), Swingtime (USA) 1975.

2. NORFOLK STAKES (Group 3) for two-years-old over FIVE FURLONGS. £5,000
added in 1975.

Named after the Duke of Norfolk, the sovereign's Representative at Ascot
from 1945 to the end of the 1972 season, and first run under that name in 1973.
It was formerly the New Stakes, first run in 1843, when it was run over the
slightly-under four-furlong Two-Years-Old Course for two-years-old, with
100 sovereigns added to the stakes.

Winners include Lady Elizabeth (1867), Marie Stuart (1872), Galopin (1874),
Isinglass (1892), Bayardo (1908), Lemberg (1909), Craganour (1912), Mr Jinks
(1928), Blenheim (1929), Hyperion (1932), Petition (1946), Tamerlane (1954),
Pall Mall (1957), Sound Track (1959), Floribunda (1960), Falcon (1966), Porto
Bello (1967), Song (1968), Tribal Chief (1969), Faliraki (1975).

3. THE GOLD CUP (Group 1) for three-years-old and upwards, entire horses and mares. TWO MILES AND A HALF, to start at the Cup Post and go once round. £25,000 added in 1975.

First run in 1807, and run as The Emperor's Plate, with a gift of plate presented by the Czar of Russia, Nicholas I, from 1845–1853, the Gold Cup was the central point of the Royal Meeting from its inception, although the interest in short-running horses has increased the importance of such races as the Hardwicke Stakes over a mile and a half and the five-furlong King's Stand Stakes. The original conditions were 'a Gold Cup of 100 guineas value, the remainder in specie, a subscription of ten guineas each, for three-years-old 6 st 12 lb, four-years-old 8 st 2 lb, five-years-old 8 st 12 lb, six-years-old and aged 9 st 4 lb, mares allowed 3 lb. The owner of the second horse to receive back his stake. Distance once round the course'. The weights today are three-years-old 7 st 7 lb, four-years-old 9 st, five-years-old and upwards 9 st 1 lb, fillies and mares allowed 3 lb.

Winners include Glaucus (1834), Touchstone (1836 and 1837), Grey Momus (1838), Beeswing (1842), Alarm (1846), The Hero (1847 and 1848), Van Tromp (1849), The Flying Dutchman (1850), West Australian (1854), Fisherman (1858 and 1859), Thormanby (1861), Ely (1865), Gladiateur (1866), Blue Gown (1868), Cremorne (1873), Verneuil (1878), Isonomy (1879 and 1880), St Simon (1884), St Gatien (1885), Isinglass (1895), Love Wisely (1896), Persimmon (1897), The White Knight (1907 and 1908), Bayardo (1910), Foxlaw (1927), Trimdon (1931 and 1932), Felicitation (1934), Quashed (1936), Precipitation (1937), Ocean Swell (1945), Alycidon (1949), Pan II (1951), Botticelli (1955), Zarathustra (1957), Gladness (1958), Sheshoon (1960), Pandofell (1961), Twilight Alley (1963), Fighting Charlie (1965 and 1966), Levmoss (1969), Precipice Wood (1970), Erimo Hawk (1972), Ragstone (1974), Sagaro (1975).

4. KING EDWARD VII STAKES (Group 2) for three-years-old, entire colts and fillies, ONE MILE AND A HALF, Swinley Course, £10,000 added in 1975.

First run as the KING EDWARD VII STAKES in 1926, it was formerly the Ascot Derby Stakes, first run in 1834, as a 50 sovereign sweep. There was a 5 lb penalty for the Derby or Oaks winner and a 3 lb allowance for fillies.

Winners include Coronation (1841), Conyngham (1848), Shotover (1882), Solario (1925), Sandwich (1931), Precipitation (1936), Foroughi (1938), Migoli (1947), Supreme Court (1951), Arctic Explorer (1957), Pindari (1959), Aurelius (1961), Only For Life (1963), Pretendre (1966), Connaught (1968), English Prince (1974), Sea Anchor (1975).

5. CHESHAM STAKES for two-years-old, sired by a winner of a race of a mile and a half or over. SIX FURLONGS. £4,000 added in 1975.

Named after the 3rd Baron Chesham, the last Master of the Buckhounds from 1900–1901. It was first run in 1919, and took the place of the first leg of the Triennial, which had been run over five furlongs for two-years-old.

Winners include Abernant (1948), Major Portion (1957), Tudor Melody (1958), Riboccare (1967), Ribofilio (1968), Smuggler (1975).

6. KING GEORGE V STAKES (Handicap), for three-years-old rated 50+. ONE MILE AND A HALF Swinley Course, £4,000 added in 1975.
First run in July 1946, under similar conditions.
Winners include Souepi (1952), French Beige (1956), Even Money (1958), Precipice Wood (1969), Zimbalon (1975).

Friday

1. WINDSOR CASTLE STAKES for two-years-old over FIVE FURLONGS, £4,000 added in 1975.
First run in 1839, it was originally a 100 sovereigns sweepstakes for three-years-old over the New Mile, winners of the Derby, Oaks or Two Thousand Guineas 5 lb extra. (The first horse past the post in the first running, Lord Lichfield's Corsair, did not carry the penalty and was disqualified.)
Winners include Volodyovski (1900), Goldhill (1963), Sky Gipsy (1965), On Your Mark (1966), Music Boy (1975).

2. HARDWICKE STAKES (Group 2), for four-years-old and upwards, entire horses and mares. ONE MILE AND A HALF, Swinley Course, £15,000 added in 1975.
Named after the 5th Earl of Hardwicke, Master of the Buckhounds 1874–1879, the race was first run in 1879 over the Swinley Course with 2,000 sovereigns added to a ten sovereigns sweepstakes.
Winners include Peter (1881), Tristan (1882, 1883 and 1884), Bendigo (1885), Ormonde (1886 and 1887), Sceptre (1903), Rock Sand (1904), Swynford (1910 and 1911), Coronach (1927), Limelight (1933), Mid-day Sun (1937), Sayajirao (1947), Guersant (1953), Aureole (1954), Elopement (1955), Hugh Lupus (1956), Aggressor (1960), St Paddy (1961), Aurelius (1962), Miralgo (1963), Salvo (1967), Hopeful Venture (1968), Park Top (1969), Rheingold (1973), Charlie Bubbles (1975).

3. WOKINGHAM STAKES (Handicap) for three-years-old and upwards, rated 55+. SIX FURLONGS (straight), £4,000 added in 1975.
Wokingham, from which it takes its name, is only seven miles from Ascot.
First run in 1813, and sometimes called the 'first handicap race', it has always been run over the last three-quarters of a mile of the Royal Hunt Cup course. It is Ascot's earliest surviving Ascot handicap (but was preceded by the Oatlands Stakes in 1791). It has always been very popular, and a betting medium, and in early days was often split into two divisions.
Winners include March Past (1954), Dionisio (1957), Charicles (1968), Sky Rocket (1969), Virginia Boy (1970), Boone's Cabin (USA) (1975).

4. THE KING'S STAND STAKES for three-years-old and upwards. FIVE FURLONGS.
£15,000 added in 1975.

A Stand Plate was run in 1837 'once round and a distance' with £100 added.
In 1858 the Royal Stand Plate was introduced over the same distance. In 1860
this race became a sprint under the name of The Queen's Stand Plate, run over
four furlongs on the Two-Years-Old course. It remains a sprint to this day.
In that year there was a Queen's Stand sprint on the Tuesday, a Royal Stand
Plate (distance and once round) on the Thursday and a Grand Stand Plate,
which was a claiming race, on the Friday. The Queen's Stand Plate became
the King's Stand Plate in 1901, but unlike the Queen's Vase, the name was left
unchanged when Queen Elizabeth II came to the Throne.

Winners include Ishmael (1881), Sundridge (1904), Tetratema (1921), Gold
Bridge (1933), Vilmorin (1946), Abernant (1949), Right Boy (1957), Sound
Track (1960), Goldhill (1965), Be Friendly (1967), Song (1969), Amber Rama
(1970), Swing Easy (1971), Flirting Around (1975).

5. BRITANNIA STAKES (Handicap) for three-years-old, colts and geldings only,
rated 50+. ONE MILE, Royal Hunt Cup course. £4,000 added in 1975.

First run in 1928 as a one mile handicap for three-years-old with £1,729
value to winner.

Winners include The MacNab (1929), Lord of Verona (1951), Chil the Kite
(1975).

6. QUEEN ALEXANDRA STAKES for four-years-old and upwards. TWO MILES,
SIX FURLONGS AND 34 YARDS, to start at the Hunt Cup Post and go once round.
£4,000 added in 1975.

The longest race under Jockey Club flat racing rules, it is named after Queen
Alexandra, consort of Edward VII, and was first run in 1864 as the Alexandra
Plate, over three miles, when it was the first race at Ascot to have £1,000 added
to the stakes. It will always be associated with Brown Jack, which won it in six
consecutive years.

Winners include Fille de l'Air (1865), Rosicrucian (1871), Cremorne (1873),
Verneuil (1878), Robert the Devil (1881), Finglas (1927 and 1928), Brown Jack
(1929, 1930, 1931, 1932, 1933 and 1934), Vulgan (1948), Bali Ha'i III (1959),
Trelawny (1962 and 1963), Hickleton (1971), Celtic Cone (1972), Cumbernauld
(1975).

For reasons of space it has not been practicable to give complete lists of the
winners of these races.

17

WINNERS OF THE KING GEORGE VI AND QUEEN ELIZABETH STAKES

Group 1, for three-years-old and upwards, entire horses and fillies, ONE MILE AND A HALF over the Swinley Course. £100,000 added to the Stakes in 1975, including a piece of plate presented by the Queen and a diamond award value £5,000, presented by De Beers Consolidated Mines Ltd. In 1975 De Beers Consolidated Mines Ltd gave £44,000, the Ascot Authority gave £29,000 and the Horserace Betting Levy Board allocated £27,000 towards the added money.

Year	Horse	Age	Owner	Trainer	Jockey	Value to winner	Odds	Time
KING GEORGE VI AND QUEEN ELIZABETH FESTIVAL OF BRITAIN STAKES								
1951	Supreme Court	3 br c	Mrs T. Lilley	E. Williams	E. C. Elliott	£25,322	100/9	2' 29 2/5"
KING GEORGE VI AND QUEEN ELIZABETH STAKES								
1952	Tulyar	3 br c	Aga Khan	M. Marsh	C. Smirke	£23,302	3/1 F	2' 33 1/2"
1953	Pinza	3 b c	Sir Victor Sassoon	N. Bertie	G. Richards	£23,175	2/1 F	2' 33 3/5"
1954	Aureole	4 ch c	The Queen	C. Boyd-Rochfort	E. Smith	£23,302	9/2 F	2' 44"
1955	Vimy	3 b c	Pierre Wertheimer	A. Head (France)	R. Poincelet	£23,430	10/1	2' 33 3/5"
1956	Ribot	4 b c	Marchese Incisa della Rocchetta	U. Penco (Italy)	E. Camici	£23,727	2/5 F	2' 40·24"
1957	Montaval	4 b c	R. B. Strassburger	G. Bridgland (France)	F. Palmer	£23,090	20/1	2' 41·02"
1958	Ballymoss	4 ch c	J. McShain	M. O'Brien (Ireland)	A. Breasley	£23,642	7/4 F	2' 36·33"
1959	Alcide	4 b c	Sir H. de Trafford	C. Boyd-Rochfort	W. H. Carr	£23,642	2/1 F	2' 31·39"
1960	Aggressor	5 b h	Sir H. Wernher	J. Gosden	J. Lindley	£23,345	100/8	2' 35·21"
1961	Right Royal V	3 br c	Mme J. Couturie	E. Pollet (France)	R. Poincelet	£23,090	6/4	2' 40·34"
1962	Match III	4 br c	F. Dupré	F. Mathet (France)	Y. Saint-Martin	£23,515	9/2 F	2' 32·02"
1963	Ragusa	3 b c	J. R. Mullion	P. Prendergast (Ireland)	G. Bougoure	£28,742	4/1	2' 33·80"
1964	Nasram II	4 b c	Mrs H. E. Jackson	E. Fellows (France)	W. Pyers	£30,740	100/7	2' 33·15"
1965	Meadow Court	3 ch c	G. M. Bell	P. Prendergast (Ireland)	L. Piggott	£31,207	6/5 F	2' 32·27"
1966	Aunt Edith	4 ch f	Lt Col J. Hornung	N. Murless	L. Piggott	£29,167	7/2	2' 35·06"
1967	Busted	4 b c	S. Joel	N. Murless	G. Moore	£24,389	4/1	2' 33·64"
1968	Royal Palace	4 b c	H. J. Joel	N. Murless	A. Barclay	£24,020	4/7 F	2' 33·22"
1969	Park Top	5 b m	Duke of Devonshire	B. van Cutsem	L. Piggott	£31,122	9/4 F	2' 32·46"
1970	Nijinsky	3 b c	C. W. Engelhard	M. V. O'Brien (Ireland)	L. Piggott	£31,993	40/85 F	2' 36·16"
1971	Mill Reef	3 b c	Paul Mellon	I. Balding	G. Lewis	£31,558	8/13 F	2' 32·56"
1972	Brigadier Gerard	4 b c	Mrs J. Hislop	W. Hern	J. Mercer	£60,202	8/13 F	2' 32·91"
1973	Dahlia	3 ch f	N. B. Hunt	M. Zilber (France)	W. Pyers	£79,230	10/1	2' 30·43"
1974	Dahlia	4 ch f	N. B. Hunt	M. Zilber (France)	L. Piggott	£81,240	15/8 F	2' 33·03"
THE KING GEORGE VI AND QUEEN ELIZABETH DIAMOND STAKES								
1975	Grundy	3 ch c	Dr C. Vittadini	P. Walwyn	P. Eddery	£81,910	4/5 F	2' 26·98"

RECORD TIMES AT ASCOT
(electric timing)

All these times were achieved on firm ground, with the exception of the ten furlong record (Brigadier Gerard) when the ground was officially described as good.

Distance	Time	Horse	Age	Weight	Owner	Trainer	Jockey	Date
5F	0' 59·27"	Amber Rama	3y	8 st 6 lb	A. Plesch	F. Mathet	Y. St-Martin	19.6.70
5F (2yo)	1' 0·78"	Raffindale		8 st 11 lb	C. Olley	Ryan Price	A. Murray	22.6.74
6F	1' 13·70"	Virginia Boy	4y	7 st 4 lb	B. Schmidt-Bodner	Doug Smith	D. McKay	19.6.70
6F (2yo)	1' 15·09"	Fabled Diplomat		8 st 4 lb	Mrs L. Schwitzer Jnr	F. Armstrong	F. Durr	23.9.72
7F	1' 27·05"	Jan Ekels	3y	8 st 9 lb	A. Bodie	G. Harwood	J. Lindley	23.9.72
7F (2yo)	1' 28·87"	Midsummer Star		8 st 7 lb	B. Walsh	M. Masson	P. Eddery	6.10.72
8F (rnd)	1' 39·96"	Brigadier Gerard	4y	9 st 7 lb	Mrs J. Hislop	W. Hern	J. Mercer	23.6.72
8F (2yo rnd)	1' 42·62"	Adios		8 st 11 lb	G. Weston	N. Murless	G. Lewis	23.9.72
8F	1' 39·53"	{ Richboy	3y	7 st 13 lb	Lady Beaverbrook	Sir G. Richards	E. Hide	19.6.70
		{ Final Chord	3y	8 st 10 lb	T. Egerton	W. Hern	J. Mercer	21.6.74
10F	2' 6·32"	Brigadier Gerard	4y	9 st 8 lb	Mrs J. Hislop	W. Hern	J. Mercer	23.9.72
12F	2' 26·98"	Grundy	3y	8 st 7 lb	Dr. C. Vittadini	P. Walwyn	P. Eddery	26.7.75
16F	3' 24·76"	Bally Russe	4y	9 st 4 lb	F. R. Hue-Williams	N. Murless	A. Breasley	14.6.66
20F	4' 21·86"	Tubalcain	5y	8 st 0 lb	H. Fellowes	E. Goddard	G. Lewis	14.6.66
22F 34 yds	4' 53·69"	Gurkha	5y	7 st 3 lb	J. J. Astor	W. Hern	Brian Lee	17.7.64

Ascot Specialists — Horses

Date	Race	Owner	Trainer	Jockey
The Bishop of Romford's Cob				
1844	Royal Hunt Cup	Sir R. W. Bulkeley		Marlow
1847	Sweepstakes	Mr Rolt		E. Edwards
1847	Wokingham	Lord Exeter		W. Abdale
1848	Wokingham	Lord Exeter		W. Abdale
Fisherman				
1856	Queen's Gold Vase	T. Parr		Quindon
1858	Gold Cup	J. B. Starkey		Wells
1858	Queen's Plate	J. B. Starkey		Wells
1859	Gold Cup	F. Higgins		Cresswell
1859	Queen's Plate	F. Higgins		Cresswell

Tristan 1882–4 won five races including three Hardwicke Stakes

Date	Race	Owner	Trainer	Jockey
Eager				
1896	1st Triennial	'Mr Fairie'		F. Pratt
1897	Rous Memorial	'Mr Fairie'		Calder
1898	Rous Memorial	'Mr Fairie'	Ryan	Allsopp
1899	Wokingham	'Mr Fairie'	Ryan	M. Cannon
1900	Queen's Stand Stakes	L. Neumann	Gilpin	M. Cannon
Bachelor's Button				
1904	Gold Vase	S. B. Joel	C. Peck	Halsey
1905	Gold Vase	S. B. Joel	C. Peck	D. Maher
1905	Hardwicke Stakes	S. B. Joel	C. Peck	D. Maher
1906	Gold Cup	S. B. Joel	C. Peck	D. Maher
Hornet's Beauty				
1911	Trial Stakes	Sir W. Cooke	Captain Dewhurst	J. H. Martin
1911	Fern Hill	Sir W. Cooke	Peebles (Upavon)	H. Jones
1911	King's Stand	Sir W. Cooke	Peebles (Upavon)	J. H. Martin
1913	All-Aged	Sir W. Cooke	Leach (Newmarket)	J. H. Martin
1913	King's Stand	Sir W. Cooke	Leach (Newmarket)	J. H. Martin
1914	All-Aged	Sir W. Cooke	Elsey (Baumber)	F. Fox
Diadem				
1919	Rous Memorial and King's Stand	Lord D'Abernon	Hon G. Lambton	S. Donoghue
1920	Rous Memorial, All-Aged and King's Stand—the same owner, trainer and jockey.			

Finglas
1926 King Edward VII Stakes M. E. de St Alary   Gilpin (Newmarket)   G. Archibald
1927 Churchill Stakes and
        Queen Alexandra Stakes M. E. de St Alary   Gilpin (Newmarket)   C. Elliott
1928 Queen Alexandra Stakes M. E. de St Alary   Gilpin (Newmarket)   C. Elliott

Brown Jack
1928 Ascot Stakes   Major H. A.   A. Hastings   S. Donoghue
                              Wernher   (Wroughton)

      1929, 1930, 1931, 1932, 1933, 1934
              Queen Alexandra   Major H. A.   I. Anthony
              Stakes   Wernher   (Wroughton)   S. Donoghue

Elysium
1944 (wartime racing) Six Furlong race for two-years-old, maidens, Woodley Stakes, Division 1, Knowle Hill Stakes and Reading Stakes. Owned J. Hylton, trained V. Smyth, ridden M. Beary, in each of the four races.

Trelawny
1961 Brown Jack Stakes   Mrs L. Carter   R. J. Colling   J. Mercer
1962 Ascot Stakes   Mrs L. Carter   Todd   A. Breasley
1962 Queen Alexandra Stakes Mrs L. Carter   Todd   A. Breasley
1963 Ascot Stakes   Mrs L. Carter   Todd   A. Breasley
1963 Queen Alexandra Stakes Mrs L. Carter   Todd   A. Breasley

Brigadier Gerard   all races:
1971 St James's Palace Stakes Mrs J. L. Hislop   W. Hern   J. Mercer
1971 Queen Elizabeth II Stakes
1972 Prince of Wales's Stakes
1972 King George VI and Queen Elizabeth Stakes
1972 Queen Elizabeth II Stakes

Jumping
Roman Holiday (foaled 1964) (to end 1975)
1970 John Commons Opportunity
        Steeple Chase   Lord Chelsea   C. Bewicke   P. Blacker
1971 Manicou Steeple Chase   Lord Chelsea   C. Bewicke   J. King
1972 Bagshot Steeple Chase   Lord Chelsea   C. Bewicke   J. King
1973 Kirk and Kirk
        Steeple Chase   Lord Chelsea   C. Bewicke   J. King
1974 Bagshot Steeple Chase   Lord Chelsea   C. Bewicke   J. King
1975 Kirk and Kirk
        Steeple Chase   Lord Chelsea   C. Bewicke   J. King

Aurelius (foaled 1958)
had a remarkable record at Ascot, where a race is named after him. Winner of the 1961 St Leger and two valuable Ascot Flat races, and of £42,308 in stakes, after proving infertile at stud, he returned to the racecourse, and won, among other jumping races, a hurdle race and a steeplechase at Ascot.
1960 (fourth in the Royal Lodge Stakes)
1961 King Edward VII Stakes Mrs V. Lilley   N. Murless   L. Piggott
1962 Hardwicke Stakes   Mrs V. Lilley   N. Murless   A. Breasley
        (2nd King George VI and Queen Elizabeth Stakes)
1965 Bingley Novice Hurdle, Mrs V.
        Div II   Hue-Williams   K. Cundell   W. Rees
1968 Grange Steeple Chase   Mrs V. Hue-Williams K. Cundell   S. Mellor

Ascot Specialists — Jockeys

Elnathan Flatman ('Nat') b. 1810

Rode 104 Ascot winners from 1834 to 1859.

His first Ascot winner was Charles Greville's Pickle in the Albany Stakes in 1834. Won nine races Royal Ascot 1845, including both classes of the divided Ascot Stakes, the Coronation Stakes, the Great Ascot Produce Stakes, the Albany Stakes, the St James's Palace Stakes and the Emperor's Plate.

Won eleven of the twenty-nine races and matches at Royal Ascot 1847 including the Trial Stakes, the Welcome Stakes, the Queen's Plate, the Visitors Plate, the first class of the Wokingham Handicap, the Great Western Railway Race and the Borough Members Plate.

He won the Ascot Derby seven times, the Ascot Stakes six times, and the St James's Palace Stakes, the Coronation Stakes and the Wokingham Stakes each five times.

Nat's last win at Ascot was on Rechab in a sweep, for the Duke of Bedford, on Cup Day, 1859.

Jem Robinson

Figures for Jem Robinson are necessarily incomplete, as the jockey was not always recorded in the early part of his riding career. His first recorded win at Ascot was in 1840, and in all we know of over fifty wins during a long career.

Jem Robinson won the Gold Cup at least six times in 1830 on Lucetta, 1831 on Cetus, 1832 on Camarine, 1835 on Glencoe, 1839 on Caravan and 1843 on Ralph. His last win was on Strongbow in a division of the Wokingham Handicap in 1851.

George Fordham

won ninety-nine races at Ascot from his first win in the Trial Stakes on Mr T. Parr's Coroner in 1855 until his last, in the New Stakes on Wild Thyme in 1883. He won the Gold Cup four times (1866 on Lecturer, 1871 on Mortemer, 1872 on Henry and 1883 on Tristan), the New Stakes seven times, the Queen's Gold Vase six times, the Ascot Derby five times, the Royal Hunt Cup three times and the Wokingham twice.

Fred Archer

won eighty races at Ascot in a span of only fourteen years. His first Ascot win was in 1873, and many of his wins were in the sprints he rode so well. He never won the Ascot Gold Cup, but won the Royal Hunt Cup in 1878 and 1881, the Fern Hill Stakes five times, and had four wins apiece in the Wokingham Stakes, the High Weight Stakes and the Queen's Gold Vase. In 1878, he won twelve races at the royal meeting and in both 1881 and in 1883 he won ten races.

John Osborne

principally a northern jockey, won twenty-three races at Ascot, including the Gold Cup on Apology in 1876, the Coronation Stakes, and the Jubilee Cup of 1887 on Minting.

Steve Donoghue

rode fifty-three winners at Ascot, including seven on Brown Jack.

Tommy Carey

packed thirty winners at Ascot into the three year period between 1943 and 1945. He has the best record of any jockey at Ascot, with five consecutive Ascot winners on Saturday, August 28th, 1943, with a sixth win in the first race at Ascot's next meeting on Saturday, September 11th, 1943. In all he had eighteen Ascot winners that year, and finished second in the overall table to Gordon Richards.

Gordon Richards

rode 178 winners at Ascot between 1925 and 1954, most of them during a period when there were only four days' racing a year at Ascot. His first winning ride at Ascot was on Tuesday, June 16th, 1925 (the Trial Stakes), and he had ridden forty-two winners at Ascot up to the outbreak of war in 1939. During the war, when Ascot was a southern-zone racecourse, Gordon Richards rode forty winners there and after the war he added a further ninety-six winners at the same course, culminating with a win on the Queen's Landau in the Rous Memorial Stakes in 1954. Gordon Richards won the Gold Cup in 1934 on Felicitation, beating Hyperion and in 1952 on Aquino II, as well as the King George VI and Queen Elizabeth Stakes on Pinza.

Lester Piggott

has been an outstanding rider at Ascot. From his first Ascot win on Tancred, trained by Ken Cundell on September 21st, 1950 until the end of the 1975 June meeting he had ridden 206 winners at Ascot, seventy-four of them at the royal meeting, besides the winners of eleven more Ascot races which had been moved to Newmarket, Newbury or Kempton Park. His first Royal Ascot win was on the 100 to 6 shot Malka's Boy, trained by Walter Nightingall, on Friday 1952. He has ridden the winners of six Gold Cups, five each of the King Edward VII Stakes and the New (now Norfolk) Stakes, four apiece of the Hardwicke and the King's Stand, and three times the winner of the Hunt Cup. His most successful Royal Ascot race is the Cork and Orrery Stakes, which he has won seven times. Piggott's best Royal Ascot meetings were in 1965 and 1975, in each of which he rode eight winners, and his best year was in 1966, when he had twenty-three winners at Ascot. Lester Piggott has won the King George VI and Queen Elizabeth Stakes five times.

Master of the Buckhounds

Ascot was under the control of the Master of the Buckhounds, irrespective of his interest in racing, from the time the racecourse was built by Queen Anne in 1711 until the death of Queen Victoria in 1901. King Edward VII abolished the Royal Buckhounds, and thereafter the Sovereign has appointed a Representative to look after the racecourse.

Masters of the Buckhounds
Sir William Wyndham, Bart, 1711–1712
George, 3rd Earl of Cardigan, 1712–1715
No Master of Buckhounds appointed, 1715–1727
Colonel Francis Negus, 1727–1732
Charles Bennett, 2nd Earl of Tankerville, 1733–1737
Ralph Jennison, 1737–1744 and 1746–1757
George Montague Dunk, 5th Earl of Halifax, 1744–1746
John, 2nd Viscount Bateman, 1757–1782
George Bussey, 4th Earl of Jersey, 1782–1783
John, 5th Earl of Sandwich, 1783–1806
William Charles, 4th Earl of Albermarle, 1806–1807
The Marquess of Cornwallis, 1807–1823
William Wellesley-Pole, Lord Maryborough (afterwards 3rd Earl of
    Mornington), 1823–1830
Thomas William, 2nd Viscount Anson and 1st Earl of Lichfield, 1830–1834
George, 6th Earl of Chesterfield, 1834–1835
William George, 16th Earl of Erroll, 1835–1839
George William Fox Kinnaird, 9th Baron Kinnaird, 1839–1841
The Earl of Rosslyn, 1841–1846 and 1852–1853
Granville George Leveson-Gower, 2nd Earl Granville, 1846–1848
John George Brabazon Ponsonby, 5th Earl of Bessborough, 1848–1852 and
    1853–1858, 1859–1866.
John William Montagu, 7th Earl of Sandwich, 1858–1859
Richard Edmund St Lawrence Boyle, 9th Earl of Cork and Orrery, 1866,
1868–1874 and 1880–1885

Charles Philip Yorke, 5th Earl of Hardwicke, 1874–1879
Lord Colville of Culross, 10th Baron, 1866–1868
John Henry De La Poer-Beresford, 5th Marquess of Waterford, 1885–1886
Charles Harbord, 5th Baron Suffield, 1886
George William Coventry, 9th Earl of Coventry, 1886–1892 and 1895–1900
Thomas Lister, 4th Baron Ribblesdale, 1892–1895
Charles Crompton William Cavendish, 3rd Baron Chesham, 1900–1901

The King' Representative at Ascot
Victor Albert Francis Charles Spencer, Viscount Churchill, 1901–1934
Lord Hamilton of Dalzell, 1934–1945
Bernard, 16th Duke of Norfolk, 1945–1952

The Queen's Representative at Ascot
Bernard, 16th Duke of Norfolk, 1952–1972
John, 5th Marquess of Abergavenny, 1972–

Index

The names of horses are printed in capitals.

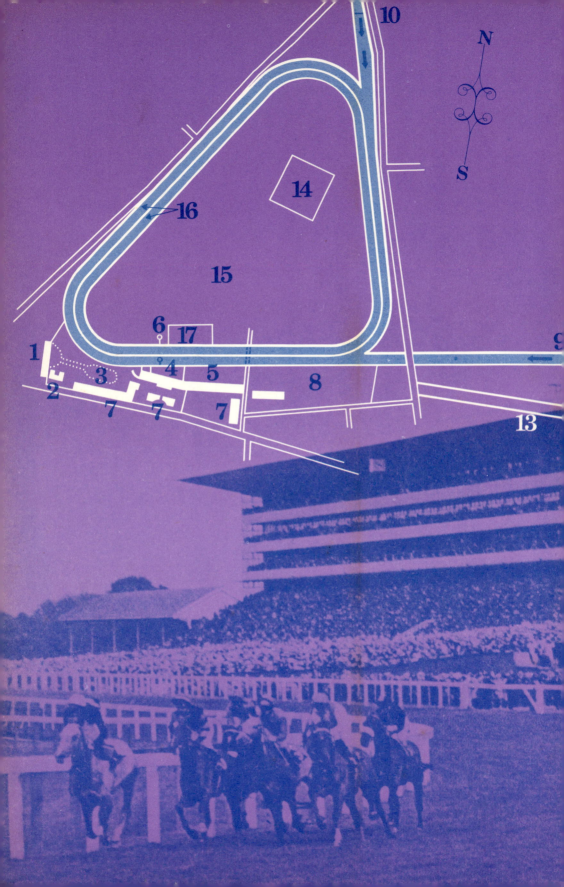